Shakespeare Valued

Shakespeare Valued
Education Policy and Pedagogy 1989-2009

Sarah Olive

intellect Bristol, UK / Chicago, USA

First published in the UK in 2015 by
Intellect, The Mill, Parnall Road, Fishponds, Bristol, BS16 3JG, UK

First published in the USA in 2015 by
Intellect, The University of Chicago Press, 1427 E. 60th Street,
Chicago, IL 60637, USA

A catalogue record for this book is available from the
British Library.

Copy-editor: MPS Technologies
Cover designer: Shine Chuah
Production manager: Jessica Mitchell
Typesetting: Contentra Technologies

Print ISBN: 978-1-78320-438-0
ePDF ISBN: 978-1-78320-439-7
ePub ISBN: 978-1-78320-440-3

Printed and bound by TJ International.

For my family

Contents

Acknowledgements

In writing this book, I have been enabled by the help and support of many people. First and foremost, my thanks go to my family old and new. Elaine, Michael, John, Lisa, Amelia and Ruth Olive must be writ large, along with grandparents, aunts, uncles, cousins and in-laws. My husband, John, and step-children, David and Hannah, came into my life as this research started. This item seems too small a return for their enduring love.

Kate McLuskie led the AHRC 'Interrogating Cultural Value project' at The Shakespeare Institute, University of Birmingham, to which my work belongs, and through which I was supported financially. Kate Rumbold and Emily Linnemann, also members of the project, offered unstinting encouragement. I welcomed the input of the project's advisory board members, especially Diana Owen, Sharon O'Dair and Paul Yachnin.

I have been fortunate to gain feedback on some of this work through conferences, publication and subsequent discussion. A version of the section 'The Royal Shakespeare Company as "cultural chemist"' appeared in *Shakespeare Survey* (64).

Eleanor Collins, Cait Fannin Peel, Lisa Houghton-Reed, the Rev'd Stuart Langshaw, Jami Rogers, James Stredder and Alison Stewart all contributed ideas or items specifically towards this book. Catherine Alexander, Karen Ashton, Chelsea Avard, Cat Clifford, Christine Knight, Heather Kerr, Lizz Ketterer, Michelle Morton, Beccy Roberts, Elizabeth Sharrett, Erin Sullivan, Vanita Sundaram and Yolana Wassersug are among those who frequently asked after my writing and never got a short answer. Jessica Mitchell and Megan Jones at Intellect are models of approachable, efficient publishers.

This work could not have been sustained without the friendships and collegiality that abound at the Shakespeare Institute and Department of Education, University of York.

Introduction

S hakespeare has inhabited an unrivalled position as the only compulsory author in English education since the subject's National Curriculum was introduced in 1989. Reading his works aloud had been required for the minority of the population sitting the very highest levels of the Victorian Standards (and similar subsequent leavers' qualifications) and study of Shakespeare had been recommended for extension to all pupils in publications such as the *Newbolt Report*. The National Curriculum, however, finally guaranteed an experience of Shakespeare to all children before leaving school: 'all' excluding students for whom the curriculum could be disapplied, such as those with learning difficulties, and independent schools (though in practice many chose to follow it). Its statutes are prime examples of the immense value that was formally assigned to Shakespeare by policy-makers, in English education, in the late 1980s: specifically, for a universal Shakespeare that could be taught, examined and legislated. That examination of his value was witnessed further by the amount of pedagogic literature on Shakespeare produced in the immediate aftermath of – and much of it in opposition to – the introduction of the National Curriculum. Beyond education in the classroom, Shakespeare's long-standing value in theatre, heritage and tourism has, for decades, been attested to by organisations such as the Royal Shakespeare Company, the Shakespeare Birthplace Trust and Shakespeare's Globe – each of which also acknowledges his place in the curriculum through their substantial education departments.

Commonplace statements that declare Shakespeare to be 'the greatest writer in the English language' and 'the greatest playwright of all time' both draw on and reinforce values for Shakespeare in education. Such clichés usefully highlight Shakespeare's unique position and widely-constructed, high cultural value. As conclusions in themselves they are, however, reductive: they unhelpfully elide the processes of negotiation and contestation that have gone in to creating his value; the tensions that exist around it; as well as the multiple definitions and everyday practices that help to construct it. Yet expressions such as 'that's not Shakespeare' or 'that's not really Shakespeare', heard in the theatre, the living room or on the streets of Stratford-upon-Avon, are reminders of the fraught and contested nature of his value. Extending over the twenty years following the inception of National Curriculum Shakespeare, this book goes beyond asking what the value of Shakespeare is in England; it explores *how* it is constructed in the documents created by governments as well as educators, writing for and working in schools, theatre education departments and heritage organisations.

Some of the constructions of Shakespeare's value herein are deliberate and explicit, such as those resulting from a particular political persuasion or a need to get punters to attend

Shakespeare-related events. For instance, policy and reality-television cast knowledge of and facility with Shakespeare's works as a solution to crises in education, social mobility, aspiration, youth unemployment and immigration (Olive 2013). Other assumptions about value, however, appear more unwitting, organic or incidental, although they may be taken up to support particular agendas. These include Shakespeare as human, icon and icon-maker. The range of stakeholders engaged in these constructions includes politicians and policy-makers; educators, scholars and students in schools, universities and arts organisations; as well as scriptwriters and programme-makers (Olive 2013). Using diverse, often everyday, sources from teacher training manuals to marketing material, this book explores the way in which the existing, multi-faceted and pervasive value of Shakespeare is generated, modified and sustained by key individuals and organisations (governments and theatre companies, for example) in formal and informal educational settings. In doing so, it counteracts assertions, still too readily made and received, of his inherent value in terms of the universality or the greatness of his works. It also problematises generalised, essentialist explanations by attributing individual agency for the origins and proliferation of such constructions where possible. It does not attempt to duplicate teachers' accounts of their practice with Shakespeare in the classroom as articulated in collections such as Martin Blocksidge's *Shakespeare in Education*.

Despite formal education being the most common way in which the population encounters his work, and hence formative of attitudes towards it, education has been historically under-examined in scholarly Shakespearean publications and at international conferences. This is especially conspicuous in comparison to the volume of titles and seminars on performance history, literary criticism and the textual study of Shakespeare. With almost every child nationally, and fifty per cent of children globally, experiencing Shakespeare in the classroom, there is a need for much more detailed research and publication in this area (Royal Shakespeare Company 2008). The impetus for such work has been largely demonstrated by individual, cross-sector organisations leading to the development of saleable products. For example, the University of Warwick and Royal Shakespeare Company's CAPITAL Centre, designed to demonstrate the mutually beneficial relationship between classroom and rehearsal room techniques, has evolved into 'Teaching Shakespeare'. Teaching Shakespeare is a centre run in collaboration with Warwick's Business School, which provides professional development for teachers worldwide using online resources.

In terms of publications on Shakespeare in education, *Teaching Shakespeare* is also the name of a magazine published and made freely available online by the British Shakespeare Association to disseminate research and resources to Shakespeare educators across the sectors (a magazine which I edit). The journals of teaching organisations such as the National Association for Teachers of English and English Association also demonstrate an ongoing concern with Shakespeare in policy and practice. However, the limited scope and word lengths of articles in such publications, combined with an intention to shape and guide teaching practice, means that research tends to be ungeneralisable and under-theorised. This may, in turn, perpetuate the editorial policy of academic journals, such as

Shakespeare, of declining to publish education-related articles. From individual researchers, there are publications (rather than series) on Shakespeare in education and culture that go beyond describing and recommending classroom practice or close-reading individual manifestations of his presence in popular culture; examples include Andrew Murphy's *Shakespeare for the People* and Denise Albanese's *Extramural Shakespeare.* Yet, the scope of these two recent publications is centred on nineteenth-century Britain and present-day North America respectively, offering space for this book's attention to Shakespeare in twentieth- and twenty-first-century England.

Meaning by Shakespeares

Before going further in demonstrating the enmeshed relationship of education and culture in regards to Shakespeare, it is crucial to outline what this book means when it invokes the terms 'Shakespeare', 'culture', 'education' and 'value'. Since he is a 'public object' – 'his name [...] as familiar in bars and restaurants as it is in classrooms and lecture-halls' – 'Shakespeare' invokes a plethora of meanings in a variety of contexts (Albanese 2010: 3; Hawkes 1996: 1). A non-exhaustive list might include: 'Shakespeare' the person; 'Shakespeare' the body of works; 'Shakespeare studies' the academic field; and 'Shakespeare' the theatrical, heritage or tourist phenomenon. Each of these propagates sub-categories. 'Shakespeare' the person, for instance, could be broken down into the child, the grammar school student, lover, husband, father, actor, writer, businessman, Londoner and Stratfordian. Douglas Lanier summarises these Shakespeares succinctly and poetically as: 'The Shakespeare of the London stage, The Shakespeare of the printed page, The rural Shakespeare of Stratford' (2010: 147). Michael Bristol, demonstrating the 'complex semantics and patterns of usage' associated with the name 'Shakespeare', adds further categories still, broadening out from the more objective definitions to include the negative connotations that the word might carry for some users: Shakespeare is 'a system of cultural institutions, and, by extension, a set of attitudes and dispositions. It defines taste communities and cultural positioning [...] it may also signify privilege, exclusion and cultural pretension' (1996: ix). Where Bristol shows Shakespeare to be a loaded term for a certain audience, Lanier ends his list with a definition that illustrates how the term is deliberately invested with meaning by certain groups: 'The increasingly mythic "Shakespeare" praised by critics and nationalists – and the specific interests they serve' (2010: 147). Unless otherwise specified or evident from the context of its usage, it is these multiple and messy meanings that I want to evoke when the word 'Shakespeare' appears in this book.

Tracing a Cultural Politics of Shakespeare

This book is overwhelmingly concerned with constructions of Shakespeare's value in England's educational culture. Raymond Williams describes 'culture' as one of the most complicated words in the English language (1983: 87). Culture, for instance, is variously conceived of as an end *and* a means of education. In the former sense, the word has been used for several centuries to refer to exclusively 'high' or 'elite' culture: art forms such as theatre, literature, painting and music. It has been described as 'the work and practices of intellectual and especially artistic activity' (1983: 90). Such a definition of culture all too frequently excludes entertainment, 'mass' pursuits or 'popular' pastimes, as already illustrated by then culture secretary Tessa Jowell's use of the term, which is discussed in detail later in this chapter. This continuity suggests that the critique of the New Left (activists and educators seeking wide-ranging social reform in the United States and the United Kingdom during the 1960s and 1970s) has not been wholly successful in realising its aim of rethinking and reconstructing definitions of 'culture'.

Culture, when defined as elite art forms, is connected directly to the purpose of education: it is objectified as a group of items, or experiences, exposure to and familiarity with which will lead to the concrete outcomes of being (perceived as) educated and cultured. Pierre Bourdieu has explicated the way in which this learning about culture is unarticulated, indirect, passed between generations of the bourgeois, through his work on cultural capital theory. Others, including Paul DiMaggio, have demonstrated the positive relationship between possessing cultural capital and social mobility. Despite Bourdieu's emphasis on its untaught and unstudied nature and because of DiMaggio's insistence on its relationship to social mobility, culture continues to be something that schools are expected to bolster in their students.

Yet, 'culture', in its more egalitarian, anthropological sense of 'the society we live in', can also be figured as a *means* of education. For progressive educationalists such as Ivan Illich and A.S. Neill, as well as the psychologist Jerome Bruner, education is culturally saturated: not only do we learn informally from our everyday existence and participation in society but our education systems operate within those of our wider culture (Bruner 1996: ix). Bruner, for example, points to the way in which cultural expectations of what children should achieve drive educational provision: 'How one conceives of education, we have finally come to recognize, is a function of how one conceives of the culture and its aims, professed and otherwise' (x). Where I use the term 'culture', as opposed to citing or analysing others' usage, it is this anthropological meaning of 'a particular way of life' for a nation or a tribe, the objects and activities of a people, group or time, that I wish to invoke, largely England between 1989 and 2009 (Williams 1983: 92). While such usage has a homogenising tendency, it has the merit of treating even the most mundane objects and activities as important – in contrast to the evaluative and hierarchical idea of culture.

This book adds to cultural histories of the development of English as a subject, by looking specifically at Shakespeare's place in English education in the late twentieth and early twenty-first centuries. Francis Mulhern's *The Moment of Scrutiny* contextualises the particular influence of Leavis, and the journal that he edited, within the growth of English as a subject, English culture and 'taste' more generally. Others such as Chris Baldick's *The Social Mission of English Criticism: 1848–1932*, and William St. Clair's *The Reading Nation in the Romantic Period*, reach back to the eighteenth and nineteenth centuries. They detail the way in which mass literacy and access to literature was won, largely against the wishes of the cultural elites, and on what terms. Baldick highlights, for example, paternalistic rationales for the widespread teaching of English: literature as a civilising influence and as a source of moral fortitude, especially against the allegedly corrupting influence of mass culture. Cultural histories of reading and literature with a greater focus on Shakespeare include those by Michael Bristol and Gary Taylor. In *Big-time Shakespeare*, Bristol traces the role of Thatcherite policy in commercialising the playwright; he also conveys the way in which the 'phenomenon' of Shakespeare is collectively 'generated out of the innumerable small-time accomplishments of actors and directors, advertising copy-writers, public relations specialists, as well as scholars, editors, and educators' (1996: 6). Using models from economics – such as 'supply' and 'demand' – he delineates how and why Shakespeare continues to have cultural currency in British society with reference to examples from modern popular culture throughout. In this way, his book is emblematic of another genre of work on the value of Shakespeare, which is concerned not with old ruling elites, or recent politics, but with his worth as constructed by present mundane, cultural and commercial practices. In doing so, it draws on the growth of cultural studies in academia during the second half of the twentieth century.

In addition, other interdisciplinarities (or multidisciplinarities) are evidenced in such work by the influence of cultural economics, media studies, anthropology and sociology. Gary Taylor, for example, in *Cultural Selection*, explores how and why certain cultural objects or memories survive and prevail while others perish. Where Bristol confines himself to Britain, Taylor employs a global frame of reference. To further compare Bristol's and Taylor's approaches, Bristol's discourse is predominantly that of cultural economics, deploying vocabulary such as 'the Shakespeare industry', cultural 'product' and 'market', where literary critics have traditionally written of Shakespeare and his audiences. In contrast, Taylor uses the mechanisms of individual memory and psychology to illustrate his discussion. Meanwhile, two of Taylor's other works, *Reinventing Shakespeare* and 'The incredible shrinking Bard', deal more specifically with Shakespeare's fate in print, in theatre, higher education and popular culture, with the latter title suggesting, quite uniquely among the criticism, that Shakespeare's cultural lifespan – and thus perhaps his value – is finite.

These books are overwhelmingly characterised by a concern with cultural history. They are not energetically engaged in an activist struggle, for example, to liberate the present and future from the still-felt implications of these values for literature generally, and Shakespeare in particular. Peter Widdowson's edited collection of essays, *Re-reading English,* stands out among other cultural histories of the discipline in its explicit sense of activism – since it was written in response to the Cambridge crisis in English of 1981. Its context and contents render it part of the tradition of heavily politicised (left-wing), English literary and cultural criticism from the period, reacting against the Thatcher government and its Conservative values for the arts, humanities, education and society. It combines the description of what English has been in the past, both ideally and in actuality, with impassioned, yet well-reasoned, suggestions of directions in which the subject might develop – what we now identify as new historicism, cultural materialism and interdisciplinarity. Widdowson is adamant that 'English is necessarily a site on which social meanings are constructed' (1982: 14), and a tool with which they must be deconstructed. Moreover, he asserts that these social meanings (or cultural values) represent legitimate material for study in the discipline.

Widdowson's overtly politicised account of the growth of English as a subject is indicative of a burgeoning body of literature, predominant in the late eighties and mid-nineties, that relates the condition of culture, literature and education to the then prevailing political conditions: those of the Thatcher, and later Major, governments (1979–1990 and 1990–1997 respectively). For instance, an anthology of essays edited by John J. Joughin, *Shakespeare and National Culture*, illustrates the grounding of Shakespeare's cultural value in concepts of nationalism, exploring the 'powerful collusion of Shakespeare and education to shape a national culture' (1997: 4). It depicts, with concern, the cultivation of these forces, towards the satisfaction of various social agendas, by these two successive Conservative governments. As such, it is part of the body of work in British cultural criticism from 1970s onwards, including Jonathan Dollimore and Alan Sinfield's *Political Shakespeare*, which combines explicit criticism of specific governments with Marxist and other left-wing critical theory in order to examine the value of Shakespeare in education. Other works in this vein include, in the year the National Curriculum came into force, Isobel Armstrong's 'Thatcher's Shakespeare?' and Ann Thompson's article for a dedicated education issue of *Shakespeare Quarterly*, '*King Lear* and the politics of teaching Shakespeare'. These articles correlate the proliferation of radical strains of Shakespeare performance and criticism with historical periods where Britain has been governed by parties on the political right.

Such works represent a peak in politically-radical, literary critique in English that has since abated. Despite thirteen years in power before its demise at the general election in May 2010, few accounts exist of the impact of New Labour's meta-education policies on English or Shakespeare specifically. However, some analyses of meta-education policy under New Labour are available: see Richard Pring's 'Labour Government Policy 14–19' and Geoff Whitty's 'Twenty Years of Progress?' which are discussed in chapter one. The recognition by such authors of the construction and delivery of subject English as a political activity sets a helpful precedent for sustaining a discussion of government policy on the value of Shakespeare as part of a broader concern with his value in the English culture of education.

Contextualising Shakespeare in Education

Having outlined the way that culture figures in this book, I turn now to defining 'education'. Education, as used throughout, refers not to (perceptions of) a condition of being (educatedness), but practically, to a state-run activity in schools: specifically, secondary school education. However, the following chapters recognise that it is an activity sometimes undertaken by other agents, state-funded or commercial. These include, but are not limited to, the education departments of the Royal Shakespeare Company (RSC), Shakespeare's Globe and the Shakespeare Birthplace Trust (SBT). State-conceived notions of education inflect popular culture too, through the public service remit of the BBC and other English broadcasters, that is to entertain, inform and educate. 'Real' experience of education is also actively drawn on by programme-makers as a resource with which to engage audiences in television viewing (Olive 2013).

Writing on education, from literature on the curriculum at large to the state school system as a whole, has enabled me to locate Shakespeare as a figure on which to hinge larger debates about the value of education. The existence of a national narrative or myth of perpetual decline regarding a wide range of English preoccupations, from the national economy to families eating together, has been noted by Hewison (1995: 305) and by Jackson, Olive and Smith (2009). This sense of a growing and unbridgeable gap between real and ideal experience, represented as a collective feeling of failure, also applies to education in general and Shakespeare specifically. It is evidenced by television programmes, such as *Jamie's Dream School*, that frame their content within the context of missed government targets for employment, training and literacy (Olive 2013). A narrative of decline in education is also testified by the wealth of literature that ostensibly tackles public perceptions of flaws in the education system, but can also be seen to devalue the experience of education. Such texts include C.B. Cox and A.E. Dyson's *Black Papers*, Peter Abbs' *Living Powers: The Arts in Education* and Frank Furedi's *Wasted*; these attack the negative influence of progressivism and the lack of arts education and authority in schools respectively. They seek to impress onto the reader that the failings of education are both produced and further jeopardised by culture in England.

The publication of these books – which aim for a readership among the general public and teaching profession, perhaps to a greater extent than aspiring to an academic audience – is part of a trend that Stephen Ball identifies as the overall growth of education as a major political issue since the mid-twentieth century – and in particular to a hyperactivism in education policy over the last three decades. His argument, that change is visible at a surface level without resulting in radical alterations to education, aligns with the research of Pring and Whitty. Hyperactivism, their research suggests, is evident in successive governments' ineffectually (but noisily) targeting similar resources and policies, differentiated not in substance but spin, at the same stubborn 'problems'. The implications of this for Shakespeare in education, including his construction as a problem area within English, will be reflected on throughout the book.

While debates about the nature and value of education generally provide a useful context for thinking about constructions of Shakespeare in the curriculum, educational research on Shakespeare specifically is characterised by the local, anecdotal, under-theorised and un-reflexive. Much of the literature reports research undertaken with a single group of students – for instance, Jane Coles's 'Testing Shakespeare to the limit' and Susan Leach's 'Student teachers and the experience of English'. Potentially worthwhile because of the depth and focus such a project allows, this kind of research becomes problematic when used (as it often is) to generalise about the value of Shakespeare on students' education and welfare; or to boast of students' engagement in lessons on the Bard, without taking into consideration the effect of the enthusiastic researcher's presence or the novelty of the activities that differ from the mundane, average classroom. Such research adds value to Shakespeare: it rarely asks *why* Shakespeare is valuable.

Problematising *Shakespeare Valued*

In terms of 'value', this book is not concerned to quantify the worth of objects (the value of a 1623 folio) or experiences (a trip to the Globe's production of *Titus*). The verb 'to value' is an act defined by the *Oxford English Dictionary* as 'that amount of some commodity, medium of exchange, etc., which is considered to be an equivalent for something else'. In this way, the book rejects the now deeply-unfashionable, Leavisite, evaluative function of cultural criticism, an activity that involved determining, studying and recommending 'good' literature, art and music. F.R. Leavis is one of the figures of the first half of the twentieth century who attracts a weight of criticism for his apparently elitist attitudes towards literature, arguably shared by the modernist authors T.S. Eliot, H.G. Wells and Virginia Woolf (Carey 1992). Shakespeare is rarely the centre of attention in his writing, although he wrote three Shakespearean essays included in the collection *The Common Pursuit* and used speeches from *Macbeth* to evolve his close-reading methods (Storer 182). In works such as *Mass Civilization and Minority Culture,* he appoints a select group as the guardians of 'culture' – a term that he defined, in opposition to the mass-produced, the commercial and the popular, as involving, morality, tradition and literature. These guardians' task is to protect the valuable, high culture from the diluting or corrupting effects of low, popular culture. Titles such as *The Great Tradition* and 'Valuation in criticism' further testify to his controversial attempt to delineate the value of specific literary genres and authors generally. Despite this constant work on 'value', and use of related discourse, Leavis resisted defining such terms. In part, he explains, this results from his desire to avoid what he considers as unjust criticism: 'the only way to escape misrepresentation is never to commit oneself to any critical judgment that makes an impact – that is, never to *say* anything' (Leavis 1993: 1). In *The Great Tradition*, for example, Leavis forgoes any positive definition of 'value' instead relying on its relative meanings. He reels off names of novelists and traces their lineage or situation within a tradition relative to each other: so, for Leavis, Henry Fielding feeds into the work of Fanny Burney, who feeds into Jane Austen. Jane Austen herself inspires a tradition that can be seen in George Eliot and passes from Eliot to Henry James. In terms of outlining any criteria that make them valuable, these writers, he judges, 'belong to the realm of significant creative achievement' (Leavis 1993: 2). He describes them as distinguished, major, important and 'classically' distinct (Leavis 1993: 3). Some recurrent traits he identifies among them include their reputations and influence, aesthetic 'value' and moral significance and formal and technical originality. These are part of their undefined value – never the sum of it. A criterion that comes closest to being definitive, used to evaluate Joseph Conrad's worth, is the 'achievement of work addressed to the adult mind, and capable as such of engaging again and again its full critical attention' (Leavis 1993: 226). The sentiment is almost repeated in summing up his discussion of James' 'fiction as a completely serious art addressed to the adult mind' (Leavis 1993: 172). However, what constitutes an 'adult mind' remains resolutely obscure. In refusing to outline 'value' definitively or precisely, he excludes from understanding those readers who lack the appropriate, and specifically Leavisite, cultural and intellectual capital or literary critical education.

The volume of criticism of Leavis sits uneasily with the extent to which his views of the value of literature, education and culture are still prevalent in schools today. These include strongly held but poorly-evidenced and under-interrogated beliefs that 'Shakespeare *is* better than Super-Nintendo' or that 'school bus trips to the local [Shakespeare] festival might save [...] children from the seductions of rock videos' (Bristol 1996: 109). The criteria for Shakespeare's superiority in these statements draw on, and prioritise, a hidden moral and educational agenda that is imposed on these children, whose primary objective in undertaking these pastimes is probably entertainment. This prejudice exists in spite of the clear conviction, demonstrated in left-wing academic movements such as cultural studies, that these prejudices are outdated and unacceptable. A comparable elitism is, however, still discernible in other academic disciplines. Jerome de Groot, for example, elucidates ways in which academic historians have consistently neglected popular forms of history, which they view as a debasement of the subject. He also argues that, like Leavis, 'academic history sees its mission as to protect the public from "the threats of consumer society"' (2009: 5). In returning to Leavis' influence in chapters one and two, I will demonstrate the way in which cultural criticism – particularly discussion of texts' or authors' value – from past eras continues to have an enduring impact on the subject of English and the construction of its value, which consequently affects students' experience of Shakespeare. Rather than seeking to evaluate Shakespeare's worth – relative or inherent, this book explores the dynamic sociocultural and educational discourses by which the value of Shakespeare (high or low, positive or negative) is continually reproduced (and sometimes more dramatically modified) by individuals and organisations. These mechanisms include requiring children to study his works, developing materials and methods for classroom practice, courses for teachers' Continuing Professional Development, and quoting his works in a script for television.

A recent context for this book is provided by the vigorous debates of 'public value' that dominated discussions of culture from the 1990s onwards. In the majority of literature from this period, value is not explicitly conceived of as an *evaluative* task of establishing a 'great tradition' by tracing the inherent value of a work or object. However, terms such as 'quality' of provision and comparisons of the arts with popular culture activities (which imply the superiority of the former) demonstrate that this Leavisite lineage is not altogether lost. Nor is the definition confined to a monetary sense of value – although successive governments' judgements as to whether an organisation could be seen to offer value have been used to determine its funding allocation. In terms of definitions of good value, the buzzwords of government policy-making in recent decades have included 'public access', 'participation', 'accountability' and 'affordability'.

Exploration of value and its implementation in relation to cultural policy was actively encouraged by the New Labour government. The Secretary of State for Culture, Media and Sport, Tessa Jowell published the essay *Government and the Value of Culture* in 2004. The document opens with the assertion that engagement with culture has a key role to play in alleviating the 'poverty of aspiration' the Labour government then perceived as contributing to a social and economic malaise (2004: 4). Defining culture against passive entertainment (a questionable concept if we accept theories that posit all meaning as resulting from the relationship between product and consumer, text and reader) as art that 'makes demands not only on the maker or performers but on those to whom the work of art or performance is directed', Jowell simultaneously claimed that the government would overcome perceptions of the arts' elitism (2004: 4). She argued that culture is at the centre of a happy and healthy society and that, as such, governments must subsidise the arts and offer support through an increased emphasis on the arts in school education. In turn, arts providers must widen participation and provide 'quality' products. The essay concluded with Jowell insisting that the cultural sector is duty-bound to take up the debate (2004: 39).

Her challenge was taken up by individuals and organisations. Critics, such as John Holden (working with the think-tank DEMOS), did so by urging the government towards 'a wholesale reshaping of the way in which public funding of culture is undertaken' (2004: 9) and arguing that cultural policy needs a democratic mandate (2006). Holden additionally suggested a 'value triangle' model that classifies constructions of value as inherent (or intrinsic: residing *in* an object or art work), instrumental (the use of culture to accomplish a certain outcome) or institutional (culture as created by the actions of cultural organisation) (2006: 15). The government-funded Arts Council – whose 'arts debate' constituted 'their first ever public value enquiry' (Bunting 2006: 4) – also rose to Jowell's challenge; they have contributed significantly to the debate in recent years, leading publications on the value of the arts, with documents such as *Call It a Tenner: The Role of Pricing in the Arts*. Similarly, the Arts and Humanities Research Council funded the Interrogating Cultural Value project, led by Kate McLuskie at the Shakespeare Institute, out of which this research emerged (see also Linnemann 2010; McLuskie and Rumbold 2014). The project's focus emerged as a concern with cultural value as a process of ascription, whereby individuals, institutions and sectors (public, private, educational, political) play various roles in managing competing claims for the value of particular content. Its emphasis on process inflects the thinking of this book, with value described variously throughout as 'flowing', 'saturating' and 'constructed'. It is also manifested in this book's concern with agency. The project asked, 'Who is constructing what value, for whom?' The value of Shakespeare, and the discourse used to express it, it argued, must also be considered in relation to its audience and producers, including parents, students, teachers, schools, policy-makers, theatres, heritage organisations, politicians, theatregoers and tourists. The media – notably the publicly funded British Broadcasting Corporation with its public service remit – has also been active in engaging the public imagination with issues of cultural value; for example the Radio 4 series *National Treasures*, described on its BBC website as 'the programme that attempts to put a price on culture', and the BBC 2 series *Restoration*, where viewers vote to choose from a selection of buildings needing to be saved. It is with these various and plural senses of value as socially- and interactively-determined, inherent, instrumental and institutional that this book proceeds.

Previewing *Shakespeare Valued*

Each chapter in this book focuses on the discourses of value in a different domain relating to Shakespeare and education from 1989–2009. These include education policy, pedagogy, heritage and theatre education departments. This structure enables me to discuss the interplay of the value of Shakespeare inside and outside the formal classroom. It is also central to demonstrating the importance of individual people and organisations in British education and culture in establishing value. Chapter one locates Shakespeare within the meta-narratives of wider government policy over the last twenty years, dominated first by the Conservative government, and, later, by New Labour and the Conservative-Liberal Democrat coalition. The chapter argues that National Curriculum Shakespeare is affected by these governments' broader agendas for raising skills, standards and social inclusion and that the objectives of these parties are perennial and demonstrate considerable overlap in spite of their different ideological backgrounds. Analysis of policy documents reaching back over a century demonstrates the way in which the first two of these agendas are rooted in historically-enduring, non-partisan values that represent Shakespeare as contributing to economic, moral and personal growth. In this way, they represent an English consensus on his value, which has outlasted the disintegration of the post-war political consensus on other matters during the late twentieth-century. Such documents do not necessarily detail how that value should translate into the details of pedagogy or assessment.

Chapter two again takes up the concern of over-prescribed Shakespeare, this time relating it to pedagogy rather than policy. It elucidates whether the 1999 National Curriculum endorses any particular pedagogy for teaching Shakespeare over others, for instance, drama, personal response or creative writing approaches. The chapter then explores literary critical active methods and contextual pedagogies for teaching Shakespeare in policy documents, such as the non-statutory National Strategy entitled *Shakespeare for All Ages and Stages* (DCSF 2008), as well as a range of pedagogic literature; reports of classroom practice; and school editions of the plays. Manifestations of the three pedagogies in contemporary educational resources are read through their use of discourse. The way in which these pedagogies are located within wider ideologies, including progressivism and humanism, is explored, as are criticisms and limitations. Particular attention is focused on pedagogic advice given to trainee teachers in manuals and guides to delivering the subject. The final section of the chapter contextualises developments in teaching Shakespeare in England with evidence of global pedagogies.

Looking at the language and content of websites, pamphlets and education events (such as the RSC Regional Festival, Young People's Shakespeare and Youth Ensemble), chapter three analyses the provision of educational Shakespeare experiences to students outside the classroom. It begins by demonstrating a strong relationship between theatres, schools and young people before the advent of theatre education departments. The chapter then looks at the education programmes of key theatres today – including the RSC and the Globe – and heritage sites, such as the SBT. The chapter demonstrates that not only do these organisations share constructions of Shakespeare as inherently valuable they also manifest common ideas about the instrumental value of education departments in cultural institutions. These include making Shakespeare accessible and inclusive as well as rendering their educational provision accountable to the public and of a good quality. These commonalities, however, can be seen to present the organisations with the challenge of differentiating their products from each other. Having examined some of the strategies and discourses that achieve this, the chapter closes by arguing that, in the attempt to brand their organisations, the value of Shakespeare is sometimes occluded by the value of their own institutional ethos.

The topicality of this research is, on the one hand, its strength, and on the other a weakness: its vulnerability to change – the ephemeral nature of its sources (including websites), the hyperactivism in education policy that it seeks to describe, and personnel changes in government and theatre alike – means that its content may be rapidly outdated. However, this negative aspect must be balanced with the strength that such data and foci lend the research in terms of the opportunity to examine, critically, a particular moment in Shakespeare's cultural and educational afterlife. The conclusion, which posits the overwhelming continuity of Shakespeare in education from 1989 to 2009 – valued instrumentally and as a universal experience for English students in policy and pedagogy, also serves as an afterword in which to consider Shakespeare's newly precarious place in England's education system.

Chapter 1

Shakespeare in Policy: Agendas for Standards, Skills and Inclusion

Shakespeare's value as a gold standard of English education had already been established, before he was made the only compulsory author in the National Curriculum for English in 1989, to some extent, by early state interventions in education. The following overview of education policy concerning Shakespeare in the century prior to this will demonstrate that this valuation of Shakespeare was dramatically *reinforced* as he was made uniquely mandatory. Furthermore, this chapter will explore the way in which Conservative (embodied by the Thatcher and Major governments) and Labour (unless otherwise evident, the 'New Labour' governments of Tony Blair and Gordon Brown, 1997–2010) governments' macro-policy variously threatened and shored up his position, during the twenty years following the introduction of National Curriculum Shakespeare. Particular attention will be given to continuity and change in their treatment of skills, standards and inclusion. Although policy in the English education system is the focus here, the importance of these agendas in countries such as the United States and Australia has been similarly identified by scholars such as Timothy Duggan and Liam Semler.

The Victorian Standards

Shakespeare featured increasingly in British school education from the early eighteenth-century onwards. That period, for example, established the tradition of staging Shakespeare plays in schools, a tradition which continues today. The evolution of a system of state schooling in England from the late nineteenth-century on, however, saw Shakespeare increasingly identified not only as a necessary component of schoolchildren's education, rather than an extra-curricular, dramatic activity, but as representing a gold standard of education. However, as the following account suggests, Shakespeare as an object of the academic study of literature on school syllabi is a yet more recent phenomenon.

In the early nineteenth-century, church societies' education programmes and schools played an important role in raising the literacy rate among working-class children. They were run by organisations such as the Sunday School Society, the British and Foreign School Society and the National Society for the Education of the Poor in the Principles of the Established Church. Around the same time, working men's and philanthropic organisations, such as the Mechanics Institute, Working Men's College and the Society for the Diffusion of Useful Knowledge, provided forerunners of adult and university-extension education (Murphy 2008: 111; St. Clair 2004: 260). While the main texts read by children at these schools were biblical, Andrew Murphy argues that many working-class readers applied their literacy skills to the enthusiastic pursuit of other literary diets, including Shakespeare, outside the classroom (2008: 51). Similarly, Richard Halpern describes the reading of literature, such as Shakespeare's plays, as constituting 'a broadly popular form of entertainment' during the period (1997: 65). Evidencing such claims can be problematic: Murphy, for example, uses the autobiographies of Victorian working-class readers – a group that is somewhat self-selecting in its literacy capabilities and literary interests. However, the engagement in reading Shakespeare among the working-class population suggested by these autobiographies is triangulated with Murphy's incontrovertible evidence that multiple, affordable editions of Shakespeare, aimed at such a market, were published during the nineteenth century.

Also clearly demonstrable, through reference to early education policy documents, is the expansion of teaching Shakespeare in British schools alongside the development of a state education system through legislation such as the Revised Code (1862) and the Education Act (1870). The state became more involved in issues of educational rigour, standards and accountability as its responsibilities for the funding and regulation of education increased. The Revised Code, of 1862, introduced a payment-per-results system as a supposedly efficient way to fund schools. The system – a recommendation of the 1861 Newcastle Commission – rewarded schools whose pupils obtained good marks. It also led to the development of national Standards for each skill (reading, writing, arithmetic) or, later, subject, against which pupils could be measured. These set out the requirements across six levels of achievement – later amended to seven in 1882. The revision of the Standards in this year saw Shakespeare named alongside other authors and genres in the requirements for the first time. Thus, as the state rather than the church assumed primary responsibility for the school sector, increasingly 'English literature entered the educational and imaginative space which had traditionally been occupied by the Bible' (St. Clair 2004: 11). Early versions of the Standards focused on students' ability to read aloud from books specially designed for learners as well as 'modern narratives' from everyday resources such as newspapers. In the revised version, however, Shakespeare became associated, very literally, with a gold standard of literacy: that is to say the best or highest standard; something that, like a gold card, gains its owner an uncommon and preferential range of benefits. The penultimate standard, Standard VI, demanded that students 'read a passage from one of Shakespeare's historical plays or from some other standard author, or from a history of England'. Standard VII, slightly broader in scope, asked that they 'read a passage from Shakespeare or Milton, or from some other standard author, or from a history of England' (Ellis 1985: 177).

Shakespeare in the Standards was, however, far from a universal experience for children since only a minority of pupils stayed in school long enough to attain the highest levels. Nonetheless, the Gladstone government's endorsement of Shakespeare's place in the education system would initiate a century of attempts to make the provision of his study as universal to pupils as education itself, regardless of class, wealth or merit. Moreover, the acceptance of Shakespeare as a necessary element of education *for all* itself marked a huge degree of progress from the disputes of the eighteenth century over whether the mass population should be educated, whether they should have access to literature, and whether that access would appease or provoke revolution (St. Clair 2004; Baldick 1983; Murphy 2010). Shakespeare had, by the latter half of the nineteenth century, been incorporated into a curriculum of sorts and used to demarcate the highest performing students from their peers.

Shakespeare's function in sorting students by narrow reading ability means that these early attempts at education policy cannot be regarded as unreservedly positive advances for the value of Shakespeare in education. Placing Shakespeare at the pinnacle of attainment also constituted an early message reinforcing views about his difficulty and unsuitability for younger readers. Another limitation of Shakespeare as a feature of schooling at this time was his use as a narrow measure of students' literacy – their ability to read off a page of text was deemed more important than demonstrating understanding of that text or using it as a springboard for creative or critical writing, functions of Shakespeare which are prominent in schools' work with him today. Thus in these Victorian policy documents, major ideas about the value and nature of Shakespeare in education were established, ideas which still dominate discussion, and invite contestation, over a century later.

Twentieth-Century English Education Policy

In the last century, the place of Shakespeare in school was cemented by the *Newbolt Report*. Its author, Henry Newbolt, fought against media accusations of elitism in the content of state education declaring that,

> Writers in the press are apt to assume that school lessons in literature are confined to the study of elaborately annotated texts of Shakespeare, and that school essays chiefly revolve upon vague and abstract themes like Patriotism and Moral Courage, with occasional but doubtful relief in the form of an essay on Football.
>
> (1921: 103)

However, in the report, the Bible and Shakespeare compete for the highest amount of type space given to a single text or author. Discussion of teaching the Bible occupies five pages, to Shakespeare's three. This is evidence not only of successive policy documents constructing Shakespeare in a premier position to other authors but also testifies to policy-makers' continued commitment to expanding *access* to this gold standard of English literature.

Rather more ambiguously, Shakespeare was simultaneously acknowledged by Newbolt as *in*accessible to schoolchildren, as becoming increasingly 'an unfamiliar tongue'. The obstacle of Shakespeare's difficulty was assuaged, wrote Newbolt, only 'by his wonderful power of re-telling a story in dramatic form, and his equally wonderful power of characterization, and, we may add, his incomparable mastery of word-music' (1921: 313). As this quotation from Newbolt illustrates, the value of Shakespeare in education per se was widely agreed on at this time, as were some of the elements that jeopardised his value. Yet the report also engages with values for methods of teaching Shakespeare, which were then, and remain even now, less securely established. It explores to a greater degree than its Victorian predecessors, the seven Standards: the importance of pedagogy in adding value to (or detracting value from) a particular subject or, in this case, author. Newbolt foreshadows later exponents of active methods in his recommendations to treat Shakespeare as drama, as a script and as enhanced by performance and other dramatic methods.

Rising standards in education generally; long-running campaigns for the universal right to a *liberal*, rather than purely vocational, education; and the evolution of English as a discipline in the universities of the early twentieth-century created further changes to the expectations of teachers' provision and students' experience of Shakespeare. For example, I.A. Richards' and Leavis' work on the interpretation of texts through close-reading exercises at the University of Cambridge, after the First World War, resulted in this technique's naturalisation as part of the teaching of literature at school, replacing the mere ability to declaim Shakespeare as a marker of skill and knowledge. Instead of declaiming or acting Shakespeare's texts, students were increasingly required to synthesise from their teachers and the play texts (or anthologised excerpts from the texts) an understanding of character, theme, plot and the craftsmanship of Shakespearean language. This would then be demonstrated in and assessed by their production of essays and other written work. Although they dominated the last century, such approaches were increasingly subject to criticism for fostering passivity in students. As early as 1917, Henry Caldwell Cook had argued, in *The Play Way*, that 'effective learning comes not from reading and listening but from action and experience' (Cunningham 2011). Students' action and experience were also valued in the *Newbolt Report*, which argued that English teachers should 'allow adolescents to write out of themselves what they are not always prepared or able to talk about' (Monaghan and Mayor 2007: 159, 168). Another widespread criticism asserted that such pedagogy reinforced the treatment of Shakespeare within schools as literature over drama (Gibson 1998).

It is noticeable in the examples above, explored more fully in chapter two, that pedagogy is one site where the value of Shakespeare has been consistently complicated by stakeholders. With the possible exception of the most strident exponents of technical or vocational education – a pathway defined by George Sampson in *English for the English* as involving fitting students narrowly with the skills for a particular and pre-determined place in the workforce – most teachers and most policy-makers in the nineteenth- and early twentieth-centuries agreed that it was important for schoolchildren to have some experience of Shakespeare. What they found difficult to agree on was the relative value of various methods for experiencing his texts. Early education reports, such as the one by Newbolt, exemplified this. They made very little statutory, except for the minimum leaving age and some components of religious education. Reports otherwise offered advice, moderation and plurality rather than prescription. This policy trend persisted for several decades with major education legislation, such as the 1944 Education Act (based on the *Butler Report*), being overwhelmingly concerned with centralising the structure rather than prescribing teachers' pedagogic delivery or minutely detailing the content of the state education system.

The 1989 National Curriculum

In contrast to earlier reports on the teaching of English, the National Curriculum of 1989 set out, in a very specific way, the substance of what children would be taught – although Michael Gove (the Coalition's Secretary for Education 2010–2014) has since argued that it was never meant to represent the sum of what would be covered in any given subject (Gove 2013). The document can be seen as the conscious creation, by the Thatcher government, of a state-wide repository of all that had, and should continue to have, educational and cultural value. Dwelling on questions of educational value as it undertook to build a National Curriculum, the Thatcher government made the teaching of English the focus of previously unprecedented concern in the late 1980s. It commissioned two reports on the subject in as many years. Long-held preoccupations with the value of education as making a positive impact on individuals' personal growth, cohesive national identity and even economic prosperity – values which I will discuss further in chapter two – clearly motivated the government's attempts to fix a set of prescriptions for the subject in the forthcoming National Curriculum. This involved obtaining testimony, preferably in support of their right-wing preconceptions on the subject, from the reporting committees, as the experience of the two committee chairs demonstrates.

The first committee, led by Sir John Kingman (a mathematician and the then vice chancellor of Bristol University), was appointed by the Secretary of State for Education Kenneth Baker in 1987. Its remit was to propose a model of English language training for students and teaching professionals in response to popular alarm, among parents, lecturers and employers, about young adults' ability to use grammar (Times 1989b). The *Report of the Committee of Inquiry into the Teaching of English Language* (known as the *Kingman Report*), submitted the following year, eschewed an emphasis on Latinate grammar to the dismay of the government. Its proposals failed to find favour with the Prime Minister, Margaret Thatcher (Cox 1991: 3). In reaction to her disapproval, Baker swiftly convened another committee with a very similar responsibility to prepare a model of English to be implemented in the National Curriculum. The scope of this was broadened slightly, in that its work was to take account of both language and literature, as well as the influence of drama, media studies and information technology. The recommendations were to arrive in two stages, with attainment targets for primary schools due by the end of September 1988 and those for secondary schools due in late April 1989.

The second committee was led by C.B. Cox, a Professor of English at the University of Manchester and a member of the previous Kingman Committee, who appealed to the right-wing leadership of the Conservative government because of his editorship of *The Black Papers on Education* in the 1960s and 1970s. These publications had decried a perceived decline in education and educational standards, which the authors identified as due to the influence of progressivism. Cox and Dyson had criticised this educational movement, especially its extreme implementation, as characterised by an unchecked emphasis on self-expression and the harbouring of anti-authoritarian attitudes. Cox was invited to chair the committee because his views were seen as 'sympathetic' to Thatcherite education policy by the politicians and civil servants in charge of curriculum reform. However, unknown to, or ignored by, those in power, Cox's beliefs about education had never easily fit a partisan mould.

Rather than evidence of a linear progression from conservative to radical, articulated in claims by his seniors that Cox had 'gone native' during the curriculum consultation process, this uneasy combination of interests and beliefs testifies to the way in which Cox had balanced elements, in his life and work, from both ends of the political spectrum since his student days (Graham 1985: 176). Taught by Leavis at Cambridge, he was part of a then-widespread culturally conservative tradition, founding the journal *Critical Quarterly* with Dyson, as a successor to his mentor's *Scrutiny*. Cox inherited an interest in Henry James and Joseph Conrad from Leavis, completing a dissertation and publishing several monographs on their writing. Like Leavis, he also positioned himself, after the inception of the National Curriculum, as caught in a fight for education against the establishment. Yet, a striking difference was that Cox's battle was always more explicitly political than Leavis', involving various, specific governments. Alongside indications of a culturally conservative bent, Cox also voted Labour and demonstrated a consistent concern for liberal issues such as equality of sexual orientation (Hewison 1995: 168). Moreover, unlike some cultural conservatives discussed in the introduction, he was committed, in an Arnoldian way, to making the best writing available to all and to creative writing, publishing his own poetry and, in later life, chairing the Arvon Foundation that fosters writing talent (Cox 1992: 150).

The naivety of the government's appointment of Cox to the position on the basis of decades-old writing which they took as evidence of fixed ideological and political views, was not an isolated example. Like Cox, his fellow committee members were chosen on the basis of work that supposedly gelled with a right-wing, traditionalist education agenda. Yet, many of them held radical ideas on the teaching of language or were concerned to promote multi-cultural attitudes towards language and literature that were in opposition to the government's stance on these matters. Cox offers a fuller, if adversarial, account of this process and his committee – including the circumstances that led to Roald Dahl's resigning his position – in his monograph *Cox on Cox* (1991: 5).

In developing attainment targets, the group had to follow a framework common to all National Curriculum subjects that stipulated that targets should be set for knowledge, skills and understanding, to be tested and reported on at the end of four key stages (ages seven, eleven, fourteen and sixteen); that each target should be divided into seven levels of attainment; that assessment would be conducted through a combination of national Standard Attainment Tests and tasks set by individual teachers; and finally, that assessment would be used both formatively, to improve teaching and children's progress, and summatively to inform parents of their child's and school's progress (for instance, through the publication of league tables). The Cox Committee made the further decision to organise the English curriculum into three basic components: speaking and listening, reading, and writing. These divisions had been identified decades earlier by the Dartmouth Conference of 1967 on the teaching of English, and were published in an account of proceedings, *Growth Through English* (Dixon 1967).

In spite of following these rigid frameworks and structures, the committee's radical and progressive elements did find expression in the content of their recommendations to upset leading Conservative politicians. The committee's submissions on English in primary schools were criticised by the government and much of the media alike for a perceived lack of attention to grammar and standard English (Times 1989a) and for being originally 'too woolly' (Baker quoted in Tytler 1989). Paradoxically, left-leaning educators decried an over-emphasis on the same areas. Nonetheless, the National Curriculum English Working Group presented the government with its slightly-delayed final report for English in secondary schools in May 1989. Like its primary counterpart, the report did not find favour with senior Conservative politicians, who criticised the lack of emphasis on spelling, grammar, punctuation and traditional pedagogies such as rote-learning. Thatcher also objected to its failure to prescribe the use of standard English, although a compromise was reached whereby the curriculum required its use except 'where non-standard forms are needed for literary purposes' (Cox 1991: 12). Nonetheless, the programmes of study were implemented in English and Welsh classrooms by 1990 with minimal changes. Perhaps because the report was not warmly embraced by the government, free copies were provided only to schools, rather than being made available to parents and the wider public. Even then, Baker insisted that the final chapters of the report, containing the attainment targets and programmes of study (fifteen to seventeen), be printed at the front on yellow paper. The originally preceding chapters, one to fourteen, containing the committee's rationale for the curriculum, were relegated almost to the status of appendices. Since Cox's initial National Curriculum for English, reviews and revisions designed to boost standard English and reduce prescribed content were undertaken in 1993 and 1995, 1999, and 2008 respectively. All of which, however, left Shakespeare's place as sole compulsory author intact, while adjusting the quantity of his texts to be studied.

Why Shakespeare?

Much of the debate around the teaching of English in the late 1980s was concerned with the teaching of the English language: spelling, grammar and standard English, rather than Shakespeare. This is evidenced in the dedication of three whole chapters of the *Cox Report* to language, in comparison to one on literature in which Shakespeare features. However, the elevation of Shakespeare to an unparalleled position of prominence in schools was also a prominent and popular feature of narratives around the curriculum decision-making process, especially in the media. Lists of essential literary texts for schoolchildren were debated in newspapers, although the largest share of attention was reserved for measures concerning grammar, correct usage and dialect (Wilby 1989; Bissell 1990). The volume and nature of this discussion influenced Cox's decision to omit a list of authors from the final report (1991: 68). The committee instead opted to prescribe only Shakespeare and to include a paragraph on the importance of English cultural heritage that named a few more optional, exemplar authors to inform teachers' own choices: these included Dickens, Wordsworth and the Authorised Bible. The passage requiring Shakespeare in the 1990 curriculum publication, evolved from Cox, stipulates that 'pupils should be introduced to […] some of the works of Shakespeare' (DfE/Welsh Office 1995: 30). Over the years, it has evolved to incorporate slightly more detail and quantification: the 1995 and 1999 versions require 'two plays by Shakespeare' be studied during key stages three and four (DfE/Welsh Office 1995: 20; DfEE/QCA 1999: 35).

Cox saw the brevity of his list of authors as a strength that would allow teachers freedom to choose texts (as long as they included Shakespeare and some pre-twentieth-century authors). He also argued that a shorter list would prevent the curriculum rapidly outdating as new authors emerged and others fell out of fashion. However, others criticised its exclusive masculinity and emphasis on the past (1991: 69). In response to the first criticism, Jane Austen and the Brontës were added to the list of recommended authors in the programmes after the *Cox Report* was submitted, in preparation for the government's publication of the curriculum. In *Cox on Cox*, Cox responded to allegations that the National Curriculum was too nationalistic and too pluralist, as well as too focused on Leavisite ideas about developing moral sensitivity and 'great literature' (1991: 70–83). He also reveals here the direct influence of the *Kingman Report* on his committee, a report which had made these authors (besides more of the same ilk) a priority. His autobiography, meanwhile, is explicit about the influence of Arnoldian thought on his own belief that 'great books possessed an absolute and inalienable value, and […] that any culture or class of society to which they were irrelevant must be miserably impoverished' (Cox 1992: 150). It is interesting that Cox does not dwell on an alternative route he could have taken to naming select authors: he could have produced a list of criteria that suitable texts for the classroom should meet. This path may have seemed equally fraught to Cox, given criticism of Leavis' attempts to delineate the value of various authors in works like *The Great Tradition*. The time constraints placed on the committee may also have eliminated such a route. Despite feeling the need to explain, even justify, the decisions reached by his committee about literature in the curriculum to a wide audience – to the extent that Cox produced three books on the subject in five years – the final recommendations pertaining to the range of literature were, in contrast to much of the report, well received by the government.

One reason suggested for the untroubled reception of Cox's literary recommendations is Thatcher's lack of interest in such particularities – along with the arts in general – at least in comparison to her preoccupation with language and 'skills' and to the interests of her successor as party leader and Prime Minister, John Major (Cox 1991: 12; Hewison 1995: 171, 213). Thatcher's interest in the value of literature in the curriculum was apparently limited, unless it could be demonstrated that it would help achieve the government's agendas of, and methods for attaining, economic growth and social cohesion. The way in which the value of Shakespeare has become inextricably linked with such instrumental values in more recent education policy decisions will be further discussed in this chapter. However, it should be emphasised here that Shakespeare came to be mandated in the curriculum somewhat against the odds: despite Cox's declared reluctance to prescribe authors and texts, despite literature being a lesser priority of the Thatcher government and despite heated public debates.

Why Still Shakespeare?

Although Shakespeare is present in an overarching way – as the only compulsory author for English students from key stages one to four – he is also absent from much of the curriculum, existing only in the statement that the range of literature at key stages three and four should include 'two plays by Shakespeare, one of which should be studied in key stage 3' (DfEE/ QCA 1999: 35). Other stipulations in the Curriculum document that elliptically reinforce Shakespeare's place, by both enabling his works to be chosen and by not always naming 'rivals', include those to teach 'drama by major playwrights'; a certain number of works of fiction and poetry before and after 1914 (lists of authors to select from are included in the document); and 'drama, fiction and poetry by major writers from different cultures and traditions' (examples of suitable writers are given but not prescribed) (DfEE/QCA 1999: 36).

In spite of this network of requirements that lend themselves to the study of Shakespearean texts, Shakespeare's presence in the National Curriculum is undercut by a series of gaps. The curriculum is silent about what should be achieved through the study of Shakespeare in particular. Standards to which students should aspire in their work are defined across English rather than in relation to Shakespeare: the skills, and increasing quality with which they are to be performed, are articulated over four key stages through phrases such as students should 'listen, understand and respond to others' at key stage one (DfEE/QCA 1999: 16), 'listen, understand and respond *appropriately* to others' at key stage two (22, my emphasis) and 'listen, understand and respond *critically* to others' at key stages three and four (31, my emphasis). Furthermore, reasons why Shakespeare might be the most fitting author to make compulsory go unwritten in the document. Yet several explanations could have been integrated into the document: if not inserted into the body itself, which details *what* should be taught but does not reason *why*, at least into an introduction. Some such preface could, for instance, have argued that Shakespeare's large corpus offers students and teachers the chance for variety in terms of texts and genres studied from year to year. It could have highlighted that the material prepared and learnt on the theatrical context of the plays, Shakespeare's biography, his use of language and craftsmanship (themes, imagery, stylistics etc.) can remain reasonably stable, even while the choice of plays is varied. It could have delineated the way in which Shakespeare is also potentially useful to teachers (although not alone among playwrights) in rendering the plays in both prose and poetry. Additionally, it could have pointed to the fact that one legacy of Shakespeare's use over several centuries is the existence of an industry of editions and teaching resources, a reality that is unparalleled for other authors, and therefore facilitates and perpetuates his status. Shakespeare's eminence in education policy has proliferated editions for schools that pay close attention to the requirements of examination and coursework. Furthermore, importantly for schools, which are perpetually represented as operating on tight budgets for teaching resources, Shakespeare also exists largely as a free resource: plenty of out-of-copyright or free-for-educational-purposes material exists that can be duplicated or downloaded from the Internet, and there is no fee to be paid to an estate for permission to stage productions (as with work by most modern playwrights). The study of his works speaks to, but is not spoken of, as meeting multiple requirements of the curriculum. The rationale for his presence is instead diffused through discussion of the statutes in the writings of Cox and in supporting strategies, such as *Shakespeare for All Ages and Stages* (DCSF 2008). The latter, for example, proposes that Shakespeare should be studied on the grounds that his work 'has lasted', is universal in appeal, challenging and extending (in terms of developing our own linguistic and creative competencies) (DCSF 2008: 6).

In addition to omitting the rationale for compulsory Shakespeare, there is a marked lack of detail regarding pedagogies and outcomes for teaching Shakespeare's plays in the legislation itself. This paucity of explanation is partly explained by the functional nature of the document, which is to state requirements for the content of teaching clearly – with assessments prescribed by awarding bodies and teachers left to negotiate the style of their teaching with those assessments in mind. However, since the statement requiring Shakespeare to be taught falls under the programme of study for reading, it could be inferred that textual pedagogies are to be preferred over performance approaches. The implications of this ellipsis will be teased out further in chapter two. Nor does the legislation itself give any indication of why those implementing the National Curriculum believed that Shakespeare would be particularly fitting to growing national and individual wealth; to preparing students for their contribution to the economy; to imbuing them with functional skills; or to encouraging the values of enterprise, entrepreneurship and creativity – despite these being pressing macro-educational agendas (derided decades earlier by Sampson). One critical strain has cast Shakespeare himself in the figure of canny businessman – the biographical criticism of Edward Dowden, for example (Murphy 2010) – but this is nowhere referred to explicitly in the statutes. Similarly, Shakespeare's own creativity is affirmed by almost every publication on the subject – whether honouring his originality or skill in adapting old plots (Bate 1997; Bloom 1973) – but not mentioned in the National Curriculum.

Apart from media coverage of the emerging curriculum, there was a marked time lag between the document's publication and the process of decision-making becoming publicly available. Cox published his committee's rationale in a separate volume because he felt it had been sidelined by the Thatcher government (1991). Furthermore, although Labour added its own foreword to the revised National Curriculum in 1999, it addressed its general policy agendas for raising social inclusion, standards and skills. The foreword is not subject specific nor does it mention Shakespeare's unusual place in English (DfEE/QCA 1999: 3–4).

For someone whose works attained a unique position in the National Curriculum for English in 1989, against the odds, in a climate otherwise characterised by hyperactivism in relation to policy, and with minimal justification of his place in education department legislation, Shakespeare has had a perhaps surprising longevity in education legislation. In seeking to explain Shakespeare's tenacious hold on the singular role of compulsory author, the remainder of the chapter explores the way that the value of Shakespeare is underpinned by agendas for macro-education, particularly instrumental values including skills, standards – educational and moral – and inclusion. That Shakespeare has remained in the curriculum, it will be argued, is symptomatic of a high degree of continuity in the core agendas of the Conservative Thatcher/Major governments and those of Labour, led by Tony Blair and Gordon Brown. There is a demonstrable circularity to policy-making between the parties, in spite of their origins in distinct, even opposing, political ideologies. This suggests that deep-seated changes in educational values do not actually happen at the pace of other changes, such as technology, and certainly rarely through revisions to existing documents. Recycled policies were, during this period, made palatable to a left-leaning electorate and compatible with left-wing ideology (defined by the *Oxford English Dictionary* as a systematic set of political ideas or beliefs) through the manipulation of discourse, popularly termed 'spin'. An account centred on successive governments of the two main political parties highlights the way in which attention to policy matters has been concentrated on a relatively small number of issues. Working within a time frame limited from 1989 to 2009 is inherently rewarding as the National Curriculum (and subsequent revisions to it) marked a heightening of education as a major political issue, subject to 'policy overload' or 'hyperactivism'. Stephen Ball demonstrates this with reference to the number of education policy documents produced. For instance, he alerts readers to the fact that in July 2000 the then Department for Education and Employment's (DfEE) list of publications totalled 106 items, 39 of which were statutory instruments (2008: 3). Moreover, the past twenty years are distinct from other periods of education policy-making because of an explicit concern with, even micro-management of, the content of the curriculum, through, for example, documents such as the DCSF National Strategy *Shakespeare for All Ages and Stages*, discussed further in chapter two.

Comparing these governments' education policies necessarily involves the problematisation of notions such as past and present as well as regression, stability and progress. It also involves probing the difference between ideological discourse and what is being enacted through the legislation. Education policy is marketed to the voting population as educational reform, as being 'about doing things differently, about change and improvement' (Ball 2008: 7). This view of policy as a salvation, elaborates the sociologist Zygmunt Bauman, is dependent on the use of a political rhetoric that devalues the present, rendering it 'ugly, abhorrent and unendurable' (1991: 11). Bauman's writing, in books such as *Modernity and Ambivalence* and *Liquid Modernity*, is concerned with the age we live in, as one defined by constant change, fragmentation, uncertainty and the questioning of the conventional. Society, he argues, has been persuaded to believe that change is positive and that citizens are primed to be ready and willing to accept constant alteration. Thus the hyperactivism outlined above, however superficial or meaningless, will be largely accepted as progress.

Further contradicting this ideal of policy as 'an enlightenment concept', which is about progress in the sense of 'moving from the inadequacies of the present to some future perfection', Ball points to the ironic reality of policy (2008: 7). Concerned with the sociology of education, he explains how policy actually works 'by accretion and sedimentation, new policies add to and overlay old ones, with the effect that new principles and innovations are merged and conflated with older rationales and previous practices' (2008: 55). This process leaves practitioners, in this case teachers, with a legacy of 'inconsistencies and contradictions that they must solve' (2008: 55). Moreover, the sheer volume of policy initiatives addressing issues such as skilling the workforce for a successful economy, raising standards and social inclusion suggests the failure, perhaps impossibility, of legislating education to achieve the desired outcomes expected by politicians and the public.

Shakespeare for Skills

Although Shakespeare is not specifically linked in the curriculum to any skill other than the ability to read a broad range of texts, policy-makers often represent the study of his works as lending itself to helping students achieve the gamut of skills set down in the document. These include pupils demonstrating their capacity 'to imagine, explore and entertain' by drawing 'on their experience of good fiction, of different poetic forms and of reading, watching and performing in plays' (DfEE/QCA 1999: 37). Moreover, understanding 'how language varies', specifically 'the development of English, including changes over time, borrowings from other languages, origins of words' (1999: 32), might well draw on Shakespeare – given his contribution to the evolution of our vocabulary. It is arguable, however, that these requirements could be met through the use of other playwrights and authors. The few points above represent the extent to which Shakespeare can be seen to directly contribute to successive governments' agendas for raising the skills of the workforce – even then, it is debatable whether it is an essential skill for the entire workforce to know how the English language has evolved historically or to be able to write imaginative and entertaining pieces. Yet skills were as much a priority for the Labour governments of 1997–2009 as other political leaderships, from the beginnings of state education to Thatcher. Using education to skill a workforce has been termed an internationally-recognised 'prerequisite of economic modernization' (Whitty 1992: 270). The importance of education in producing a skilled workforce that meets the demands of employers and industry (whether heavy, manufacturing or services) has been further articulated in economics as 'human capital theory' (Becker 1964). In sociology, 'correspondence theory' contends that education replicates the structures and relationships of the workplace, constituting a 'hidden curriculum', to prepare students for their future role in the national economy (Bowles and Gintis 1977). The work of these researchers and theorists both reflects and further fosters governments' obsession with skills. The following section will explore ways in which governments' macro-agendas for skills provided a context that helped to secure and maintain Shakespeare's unique place in the curriculum.

The criticism that governments have developed a narrow utilitarian set of values for education has been continually expressed over the last century. Educators have petitioned for policy to institute a wider valuing of education as empowering life rather than just work. In the early-twentieth-century, George Sampson insisted that 'elementary education must not be vocational, it is the purpose of education not to prepare children for their occupations, but to prepare children against their occupations' (1921: viii). Leavis was horrified by the pressure put on education, in the era of Newbolt, to cater to the needs of mass production by producing factory workers with a standardised but limited skill set. Other dissenting voices include *Scrutiny* collaborator Denys Thompson, who declared that English 'is not really a subject at all. It is a condition of existence' (1934: 380). Moreover, the educator A.S. Neill took action to claw back the decision about what subjects to study from the demands of industry and the influence of parents anxious about their children's employability, because he wanted to empower the child. Founding Summerhill School in the same year as Newbolt's Report and Sampson's *English for the English*, he ensured that individual children chose what to learn and when – by and large, driving their own individual agendas. These educators perceived an inability, even unwillingness, of governments across the political spectrum to implement a system of education less strongly tied to the instrumental values that industry holds for it. Their conclusion has been that the value of education as 'a preparation for successful "life" in material terms' proves intractable in a state-run education system (Leach 2000: 153), especially in capitalist countries where the value of education will always be coupled to the imperative of a healthy, preferably growing, economy. Those opposed to such pressures have had to campaign for policy change to protect liberal education or to operate, like Summerhill, outside the state school system. Even then, Summerhill has had to weather attempts from organisations such as Ofsted, in 2000, to close it down because of (misunderstandings of) its lack of conformity to the vision of education espoused by the government of the day.

The importance of skills to Labour's immediate predecessors, the Conservative governments of Thatcher and Major, is inscribed in the National Curriculum for English. That skills-based education rivals (if not outstrips) a traditional liberal-humanist orientation is evidenced in the sub-section headings that set out objectives for 'knowledge, skills and understanding', under the key areas of speaking and listening, reading and writing at each level. Skills, along with processes and matters, also constitute the definition of a programme of study in the 1996 Education Act (Great Britain 353b). This emphasis in the curriculum is not only evidence of the work of the Cox committee, but also of the Thatcher government's commitment to stemming a perceived decline in skills. Cox writes of the pressure that ministers and civil servants put on the committee to focus the teaching of English around the use of language: grammar, spelling, punctuation and standard English (1991: 12). Along with Major's later agenda of going 'Back to Basics' – that is to say, concentrating teaching on the 'three Rs', upheld in nineteenth-century classrooms: reading, writing and arithmetic – Thatcher's education policy indicates the generally nostalgic or retrogressive value system of past Conservative parties. It is characterised by a New Victorianism. It also represents a backlash against left-wing educational theories, which they consistently dismissed as mere (even passing) trends. For these Conservatives, skills were valued as 'real knowledge' as opposed to the supposedly ephemeral stuff of the 'ideological curriculum' (Ball 2008: 2), a term for progressivism that denies the existence of ideology in their party's own preferred methods. That these attitudes still exist in the party is evident in the use of the phrase 'faddy ideologies' in public speeches on education (Gove 2009). I discuss the Coalition government's macro-agendas for education and their implications for Shakespeare in detail at the end of the chapter.

Despite the emphasis on skills in the National Curriculum, it is noticeable that not all skills were equally valued or equally present. In terms of the National Curriculum for English, critical literacy was not foregrounded, although it had been embraced by Commonwealth countries including Canada and Australia (Monaghan and Mayer 2007: 155–171). Critical literacy enables students to deconstruct the political nature of texts, to understand how they are positioned by texts (their subjectivity) and to participate and intervene in society through critical engagement with texts and their meaning. However, the version of the curriculum produced from Cox's report, against his own wishes, instead shored up a literary canon, including Shakespeare, designed to be received by teachers and students as enduringly and unquestionably great.

Labour consistently emphasised the value of education as key to economic success during its time in office. Tony Blair declared that education is 'our best economic policy' while Gordon Brown 'signalled […] the increasingly close-knit relationship between the processes of education and requirements of the economy' (Ball 2008: 3). Such a pronouncement, whether or not it has proven effective, encapsulates the way in which educating the nation's workforce to produce an internationally competitive economy has been a major driving force (or, viewed cynically, a desirable rhetorical justification) for successive governments, regardless of ideological difference. The Labour governments of Blair and Brown pursued, to some extent, their Conservative predecessors' practice of emphasising a narrow set of skills. Their strong emphasis on literacy was realised materially in the implementation of a National Literacy Strategy, which included prescriptive advice on how to teach reading (through phonetics) and for how long (one hour a day, the 'Literacy Hour'). In addition to focusing on improving basic skills from an early age, Labour built on Conservative gestures towards extending education to a higher age group. In 1988 the Youth Training Guarantee stated the aim for all sixteen- and seventeen-year-olds to be in education, training or employment, while Labour envisaged, from 2007 onwards, raising this to seventeen by 2013, then eighteen by 2015.

Nonetheless, some change from Conservative to Labour policy was evident in the skills and attributes through which economic growth was to be attained. Although the Blair government maintained the strong place of skills in the curriculum, 'New' Labour realised early on during its term in office that a narrow set of skills alone was not sufficient to boost economic growth. This led to an emphasis on nurturing various values in education derived from the world of business. Failure to embed 'appropriate' values such as 'enterprise', 'entrepreneurship' and 'creativity' from the corporate world into the nation's wider culture has often been identified as a cause of stagnation in English industry (Whitty 1992: 282). In the education policy devised under Blair, 'creativity' was not limited to the production of artistic works but extended to include new and original ways of thinking in all arenas – something akin to creative problem-solving. Drawing on advice from economists and educationalists, such as Ball, creativity was championed by Labour and treated as the vanguard of economic competitiveness:

[W]ith increased mobility of information through information technology (IT) systems and a global workforce, knowledge and expertise can be transported instantaneously around the world, and any advantage gained by one company can be eliminated by competitive improvements overnight. The only comparative advantage a company or more generally a nation can attain will be its processes of innovation – combining market and technology know-how with the creative talents of knowledge workers to solve a constant stream of competitive problems – and its ability to derive value from information.

(Ball 2008: 19)

In this extract, Ball makes explicit the need to foster 'the creative talents of knowledge workers' as essential to growing the nation's role and success in the world economy, transformed by globalisation and the continuous advent of new information and communications technology. 'Creativity' here is narrowly redefined in a way that ties it to economic, instrumental values: the ability to think and innovate in a way that is beneficial to industry. Creativity was also frequently cast in the education policy of the Labour government as beneficial for the individual and the amorphously-imagined wider community. Thus 'enterprise', in its new guise as 'creativity', was superficially dissociated from notions of corporate greed and was presented to party members and the wider electorate as 'the new educational virtue' (Pring 2005: 74).

In addition to rebranding culture as central to increased economic performance, rather than a distraction from it, Labour attempted to improve the status of vocational education. Labour recognised the inflexibility of Tory policy, expressed in legislation such as the National Curriculum, which reified teaching a homogenous content based on the anticipation of a fixed set of skills required for economic growth. To counter it, the Blair and Brown governments instigated changes to education policy to diversify the skills students were being trained in. They sought to offer a range of diverse educational pathways, which, they argued, would be equally valued by employers and higher education institutions. This included enhancing the range and status of qualifications that skill students for specific careers – through policy documents such as the 1997 National Traineeships scheme, the 2002 *14–19: Extending Opportunities, Raising Standards* Green

Paper, and the 2005 *14–19: Skills and Education* White Paper (both DfES). All of these, however, built on existing policy initiatives of the previous Conservative government, such as the 1995 Modern Apprenticeships scheme. Beyond this, they made concerted efforts to remove the stigma from vocational education by establishing equivalence in, for example, the quality of provision: to have vocational qualifications recognised as rigorous and comparable to other forms of qualification at the same level, and thereby to enable students to move between advanced-level qualifications (whether vocation or academic) (Pring 2005: 73–81). Media suggestions that the Russell Group of universities use a secret list of banned 'soft' A-level subjects in their admissions procedures, if true, are but one example that attempts at parity have not been universally successful (Shepherd 2010).

Labour also inaugurated diploma qualifications for secondary school students, such as the 14–19 Diploma in Humanities and Social Sciences, which were designed to offer traditional academic content via a more modular structure with the potential for 'integrated codes'. This involves the weakening of traditional strong subject boundaries, which have occasionally been identified as contributing to the poor performance of the English education system. It was also designed to appeal to students by delivering greater flexibility in terms of what they could study as well as giving the content of education a more 'real world' focus, by potentially uniting diverse subject knowledges (e.g. science, geography and citizenship) under themes such as 'climate change'. In terms of a role for Shakespeare in the qualification, the Royal Shakespeare Company – who advised Labour on its development of the humanities diploma – suggested that the playwright's works could be used to teach concepts such as 'democracy, dictatorship and humanity' (Higgs 2009). In line with this applied-knowledge focus, the diplomas contain a requirement for students to pass in functional skills. Tens of thousands of students opted for this educational pathway, although in 2010 the Coalition government was accused of leaving the qualification to 'wither on the vine' and concern about the negative impact of a possible withdrawal of funding to support the diplomas was expressed (Baker 2010). Rather than diversifying qualifications to allow for a blend of academic and vocational education, the Coalition has focused on nurturing diversity of school types.

The rationale behind the vision for the increasingly pluralised provision of education articulated by Labour was that students have diverse interests and aspirations that can be channelled into diverse learning outcomes: an academic qualification, a technical qualification or something in between. These heterogeneously qualified students will, it has been proposed, benefit diverse sectors of the economy (industry, services and so on). However, such educational provision assumes that state education's failings, and ultimately those of the economy, stem from a lack of choice of educational pathways. It does not recognise or address external impacts on the economy, the complexity of reasons for non-participation or lack of social mobility. That these limitations are acknowledged by governments is suggested by simultaneous attempts to target improvements in education through standards and social inclusion, discussed further into this chapter.

It is evident that under Labour there was a shift in value away from the desirability of students having uniform, basic skills mandated by the National Curriculum, as articulated by Thatcher's and Major's education policy, towards them choosing from a wider skills base. Continuity in value between the Labour government and its Conservative predecessors, however, included the belief in education as key to economic success and an emphasis on skills – rather than knowledge-based education – especially in political rhetoric. In terms of the implications of these macro-educational agendas on Shakespeare, the study of his works, particularly as outlined in the National Curriculum, provides a few specific skills. They include reading, writing, performing and understanding the evolution of language – required for further study of English or drama at university, or for careers involving a knowledge of etymology or the ability to write creatively. However, Shakespeare could be constructed as having been placed on (and survived in) the National Curriculum *in spite* of a heavy emphasis, from both the Conservatives and Labour, on skills. It is arguable that Shakespeare-derived skills were 'spun' initially to secure, and later to justify, Shakespeare's continued status in the curriculum in the face of pressure for items within the curriculum to conform to this macro-agenda. The following sections will explore the way in which Shakespeare's unparalleled position in the curriculum may owe more to his potential to contribute to other government agendas, such as standards and social inclusion, than skills.

Shakespeare for Standards

Shakespeare's role in the Victorian Standards, discussed at the start of this chapter, was to identify students performing at the very top of their class in terms of reading ability. However, since the introduction of compulsory Shakespeare for all students in England, working with Shakespeare's texts in itself no longer represents students' attainment of an elite level. Rather it should constitute a common experience and a shared knowledge base. The concept of Shakespeare for all in the National Curriculum was supposed to raise educational standards through his incarnation as part of every child's learning, regardless of ability or background. Not only should universal access to Shakespeare enhance the individual's standard of education, but, ran successive governments' thinking, it should have a positive effect on the workforce collectively and the nation's economic competitiveness. The following pages will show that a macro-political agenda for raising standards in education, with the aim of benefitting the economy, is evident in the main parties' use of discourse and models from business and finance. Furthermore, I will argue that Shakespeare's perceived contribution to such an agenda has secured his continued privileged place in the curriculum.

Rather than providing an explicit rationale for Shakespeare's place in the curriculum, both its authors under Conservative governments and its revisers under Labour have invoked existing narratives of Shakespeare as a 'gold standard' author: the best playwright, the best poet, a genius (Bate 1997). He continues to be co-opted into the curriculum as an Arnoldian example of 'the best' that has been written in order to encourage equally skilled thinking and writing in students and as a 'cultural catalyst' (the theme of the 2010 International Shakespeare Conference) who inspires those who experience his works to generate further greatness. The Blair and Brown governments were understandably reluctant to alter such inclusive-looking policy substantially when social justice was one of their core agendas, a situation examined in detail in the closing section of this chapter. The apparent egalitarianism of Shakespeare for all in the National Curriculum was somewhat undercut by the fact that, while students' access to Shakespeare was no longer determined by their performance, Shakespeare was used to measure students' performance in English as part of the Standard Attainment Tests first implemented by Major in 1991 and only abolished by Labour in 2008.

The Conservatives' establishment of Shakespeare at the centre of a National Curriculum for English – designed to boost standards by stipulating and facilitating regular and standardised target-setting and assessment – can be seen as in tension with more liberal humanist values around the delivery of arts and humanities subjects. Pring, writing of the teaching of history, notes a mismatch between traditional pedagogies for these subjects and performance targets: 'Highly disciplined discussion was at the centre of the learning experience, lacking therefore precise targets to be attained. For who can set precise targets to a well informed and vigorous conversation?' (2005: 84). The question could similarly be articulated in relation to Shakespeare as: 'for who can set precise targets to a lively role play? An innovative performance of some scenes? A poem inspired by one of his characters?' The problem of assessing students on their experience of Shakespeare through a severely limited and delineated set of questions may have contributed to Labour's decision to end the testing of Shakespeare through key stage three Standard Assessment Tests (SATs), discussed in detail below. This move enabled Labour to maintain an emphasis on improving standards through allowing access for all to knowledge, texts and authors deemed critical for raising individual and national standards, while arguing that standards are less crucially linked to students' ability to perform set tasks on an examination paper.

Tested or not, compulsory Shakespeare represents only a fraction of governments' concern with the quality of the English education system and its products. Successive governments have identified low standards in schools' performance as a problem to be tackled with educational policy reform. Related to fitting young people to make a future contribution to the national economy, standards are another abiding point for concern and policy action. Anxiety that England is performing poorly against competitor nations is perennially expressed by the media, apparently evidenced by international research from large-scale quantitative datasets such as that of the Programme for International Student Assessment (PISA) and Progress in International Reading Literacy Study (PIRLS). This research is in turn cited by opposition politicians to articulate their disparagement of the government. Michael Gove, as Shadow Education Secretary, used such statistics at the Conservative party conference in 2009 to criticise Labour's (alleged lack of) achievement in this area: 'We have dropped from fourth in the world for science standards to fourteenth. From seventh in the world for literacy to seventeenth. And from eighth in the world for mathematics to twenty-fourth' (Gove 2009). The wielding of such comparisons by the media and politicians exploits the public's sense of national identity and national pride, particularly, a fear among the electorate of being outstripped by economic and cultural rivals. For political parties, to be seen to be committed to or, better still, working at improving standards in the performance of the education system is identified as a certain way of gaining votes. Moreover, for those assuming or maintaining power, targeting standards is a way of gaining a mandate that might allow for the exploration of other, more contentious, agendas. The response from governments, on both side of the political spectrum, over the past twenty years has included attempts to reform the whole school system. In particular, as the following paragraphs will demonstrate, both Conservative and Labour governments have targeted standards through provision of uniform content (curriculum); testing; teacher recruitment; use of models from business, marketisation, decentralisation and partnerships between education and other sectors.

The 1988 Education Reform Act prepared the way for a National Curriculum that aimed to improve students' performance by delivering an education with a uniform content (Great Britain). Other Conservative reforms, including the formation, by Kenneth Baker, of a Task Group on Assessment and Testing (TGAT) in 1988, the 1992 Education (Schools) Act and the rolling out of SATs during the early nineties, focused on testing, inspection and the subsequent publication of results and reports (Great Britain). Introduced from 1993 onwards by the Major government, the latter involved examining students on Shakespeare at key stage three as part of a wider scheme of nationally standardised testing. SATs aimed to improve performance by increasing the points at which schools would be assessed, their performance quantified and the results published. That is to say, these measures proliferated the opportunities at which the government could hold schools accountable for their performances.

Consequentially, these tests were, at their inception, heavily resisted by schools and teaching unions, who argued that their rapid implementation put undue pressure on students, teachers and the education system more widely. In addition, the measures were opposed on the grounds that league tables, based on schools' performance in SATs and published in the media, would adversely affect teachers' morale and student enrolments (especially at 'under-performing' schools). Other fears surrounding SATs, more specific to Shakespeare than to the system itself, were that the plays would be taught to the test; that teaching of the plays would be limited to desk-bound, literary critical methods; and that the choice of plays was limited (teachers had to choose one of three set plays prescribed by the state each year). These trepidations and criticisms were openly discussed in teaching journals. They were also addressed by Rex Gibson's Cambridge Shakespeare and Schools project, and a glut of monographs on the political, pedagogical and social implications of the new system. Having never gained widespread popularity, key stage three SATs were finally abandoned by the Labour government in October 2008 after a fiasco with the marking of key stages two and three papers, that made national headlines (Mansell 2009; Brocklehurst 2008): practicality, rather than ideology, was the ultimate reason given for their downfall.

Teachers were a key target of the Conservative government's bid to raise standards. The Thatcher government's attitude towards teachers has already been discussed in relation to *The Black Papers on Education.* It is sufficient to recapitulate here that they criticised the *un*professionalism of teachers, especially in adopting progressive pedagogies. The invocation of notions of 'professionalism' is crucial to the construction of the business paradigm I have proposed as dominating policy reform. Other examples of past Conservative education policy constructed the education system as benefitting from the application of market-like forces, such as competition and choice. This was despite the fact that the majority of schools continued (and continue today) to be overwhelmingly funded by the state and centrally controlled by the state through the National Curriculum and other such legislation.

The responses to students' and schools' alleged poor performance by both parties described above, utilising target-setting, accountability and motivation through pay incentives, only hint at the embrace of ideas from the corporate world within state education by successive governments during the last twenty years. In fact, it can be demonstrated that efforts to raise performance in education were characterised by governments' urgings to be more business-like. Such a model, which takes big business as an exemplar of effectiveness and efficiency, is typically associated with Conservative policy. Its adoption by the Labour government marks a break with traditional socialist-inflected party ideology. Throughout the discussion below it is worth monitoring the language of education policy for jargon from the world of business: it resounds with terms such as 'partnerships', 'sponsors', even 'behaviour contracts'. The latter is a formal written agreement between students, parents and schools, that delineates acceptable behaviour agreed between the parties as well as the consequences of breaking the agreement. Labour proposed that the contracts would become compulsory in the 2008 *Youth Crime Action Plan* (HM Government). Such discourse alone suggests, if only on a surface level, that the values of education are contiguous with those of business. At the least, it demonstrates the way in which business has become, for Labour, a prominent paradigm for education. The implicit discontinuity with old Labour policy was, however, reconciled to traditional Labour ideology (and its supporters) through a tactic of stressing that modelling education on business could achieve the party's agenda for a strong state system of education and, through that, social justice (e.g. equality of opportunity) more widely. To trace how Labour has continued Conservative values for business as a model for education, and where they have diverged from it, the following paragraphs offer a resume of the latter party's previous policy directions.

Adopting market-style competition was also viewed by these Conservative governments as a route to improving standards. Competition between state schools was encouraged through the much-criticised voucher scheme, which would have allowed parents to take the funding the state gives their child to a school of their choosing. Furthermore, parents were increasingly presented with a choice of school for their child as the Conservatives shifted priorities away from the comprehensive model of education encouraged by Labour during the mid-twentieth century. Instead, their education policy signalled a desire to return, if not quite to the tripartite system (grammar schools, secondary moderns and technical schools), to a system of diversified schools. Within this system, parents would be able to choose from schools differentiated by faith or by their emphasis on particular curriculum areas such as languages (specialist schools). Meanwhile, increased competition between the state and independent school sectors – and in some sense a move towards the privatisation of schooling (for certain types of students, for example the academically 'gifted') – was indicated through policy such as the Assisted Places Scheme. Established in the 1980 Education Act, and later abolished by the Labour government, the scheme made government funding available for pupils excelling in the state system to attend independent schools (in addition to long-running scholarship schemes offered and administrated by independent schools themselves).

Another element of encouraging competition to raise standards, 'the decentralisation of government control of education' was implemented by measures that shifted power from the local educational authorities to individual schools. However, education markets, quasi-markets, 'are not in any simple sense free markets', and the stripping of powers from certain bodies coincided with an increase in the centralised control of the outcomes that schools were expected to achieve (Ball 2008: 45) with schools' funding made increasingly conditional on their performance against government targets (Pring 2005: 84; Whitty 2008: 174). Thus decentralisation offers an example of Conservative inability to render the education sector truly marketised. That these represent enduring Conservative strategies, up to twenty years later (and despite thirteen years in opposition), was confirmed by Gove's 2009 party conference speech. He promised that, should the Conservative party gain office, it would 'drastically reduce the intrusive regulation which holds back good teachers', give parents 'control over the money which is spent on their children's education' and the power to 'demand the precise, personalised, education your children need' through the creation of new schools including academies, and by rendering schools and teachers accountable to parents rather than 'central [...] bureaucracy' or local authorities. This last policy is built on constructions of parents and students as consumers and of their consumer sovereignty – again, a concept borrowed from free-market economics. Whether these policies have come to fruition, and their impact on Shakespeare, will be considered at the end of this book.

Labour energetically pursued these Tory policies for boosting standards from 1997 to 2010, isolating certain areas of performance in succession. Attempts at large-scale overhauls of the system were left until later in their term of office, coinciding with apparently increasing economic health and further election victories. Teachers' performance, and the recruitment of high-quality graduates to the profession, was targeted with financial incentives such as better remuneration. By 2009, the then Secretary of State for Education Ed Balls felt able to claim at the party conference that Labour measures had made teachers 'the best paid in our history', with the implication that it was becoming a highly desirable, and therefore selective, profession. To add another example, illiteracy was tackled through the implementation of the National Literacy Strategy (DfEE 1997) and the document *A Fresh Start – improving literacy and numeracy*, endorsed the idea of a long-term national strategy (DfEE 1999). Attempts to alter the system holistically, which I will discuss below, were left until later in Labour's term of office.

The party developed further the quasi-privatisation of the education sector initiated by the Conservatives: the school system was to be 'more like business' while the private sector was 'to have an increasing role in the management and delivery of public services' (Ball 2008: 18). This included the government incentivising schools to form partnerships with 'employers, the Regional Development Agencies, the (occupational) Sector Skills Councils and the local Learning and Skills Councils' (Pring 2005: 74) – even other local schools, with whom they were in competition for pupil enrolments, and hence, funding. In part, these partnerships were to be economic, with schools involved in the academies programme asked to obtain financial 'sponsors': individuals, businesses, charities, universities and religious groups. The implausibility of such unions being strictly monetary, without any influence on the ethos or ideology of the schools, was widely observed. However, funding for schools from all sectors has dried up in the recent economic climate, meaning that successive governments have intervened to fund a scheme that was originally conceived to be largely privately financed.

Apart from encouraging input from beyond the state into funding schools, Labour sought to remove some pressure on education budgets while improving standards by effectively outsourcing certain areas of responsibility. Other schemes, such as the Co-op Trusts and National Challenge Trusts, focused on raising standards through the sharing of good practice between organisations; for example, between co-operative businesses and schools or between strongly performing schools and those demonstrating low levels of achievement. The 2005 document, *Children, Young People and the Arts*, for instance, demonstrates the way in which arts provision has been largely devolved to organisations such as the Arts' Council and the arts providers it funds, using notions of 'collective responsibility' (a notion that has manifested its recent popularity in business as 'corporate social responsibility'). Through schemes such as Creative Partnerships schools were encouraged to connect with theatres, museums and other creative workers so that every child would gain experience of the arts. Hence, the pursuit of these Conservative-style policies was made palatable to Labour voters by framing them 'explicitly in terms of furthering social justice through a modernised public sector' (Whitty 2008: 166).

It is evident from the above that Labour sought to solve the problem of standards by encouraging schools, on the one hand, to be more business-like and on the other hand for businesses to be more publicly-minded. Simultaneously, their policy-makers and politicians adopted Conservative strategies in encouraging parents and students to see themselves as valued customers or consumers with a role to play in determining provision. Labour placed an unusually strong value on personalisation (given that a rhetoric of individualism has long been associated with Conservativism): addressing issues at a personal level such as students' (and parents') aspirations, and barriers to achievement for individuals such as poverty, learning and behavioural difficulties. Exemplifying this approach, the 2005 White Paper, *Higher Standards, Better Schools for All,* 'emphasized the tailoring of education around the needs of each child, including catch-up provision for those who need it' (Whitty 2008: 174).

With regards to arts education, the tailoring of arts provision for individual students was central to the Arts Council's strategy (Arts Council England 2005). Furthermore, Ed Ball's speech at the 2009 Labour Party conference promised one-to-one tuition for students who 'fall behind'. These promises are directly comparable with those of the Conservatives' electioneering in the recent past. Gove's party conference speech, for example, invited parents to imagine 'a small school – where the headteacher knows every child's name with smaller class sizes – and personal support for your child'. Such policies are redolent of the economic theory of consumer sovereignty even as they are part of Labour's more socialist agenda to 'tackle disadvantage by focusing additional resources on pupils who need greater support' (Whitty 2008: 166–167).

While I have suggested above that Labour overwhelmingly continued to target perceived problems with standards in education by using or building on old Conservative policies, it appears that an inversion of rhetoric (rather than values), in the area of standards at least, between the Conservatives and Labour has occurred. It could be argued that in adopting Conservative discourse the Labour party unintentionally prepared the ground for its own defeat, by lessening the gap between itself and the opposition, making the Conservative party appear a less radical alternative for disgruntled Labour voters. For the Conservative party, their adoption of a more Labourite discourse may have been partly responsible for their last election performance and coalition formation with the Liberal Democrats.

Shakespeare fitted well into Labour's emphasis on improving standards in education through partnerships, part of their larger paradigm of education as business. Although not explicitly a provision for the teaching of Shakespeare, the statement that the National Curriculum for English 'provides a framework within which all partners in education can support young people on the road to further learning' (DfEE/QCA 1999: 3) is an invitation to collaborate with schools, and has been taken up by the education departments of organisations such as the Globe, RSC and SBT. These organisations have pledged to support young people in their learning of Shakespeare through writing education programmes for teachers and students that explicitly refer to the National Curriculum programmes of study, attainment targets and assessment objectives. As I will demonstrate further in chapter three, they have also proved to be a spur to policy change and to improving the experience of Shakespeare for all children – and, in turn, they claim, children's academic performance – lobbying the government through campaigns such as 'Stand Up for Shakespeare'.

Shakespeare's place in the curriculum can be understood through another pseudo-market concept: protectionism. It is ironic but representative of Conservative policy that the party should espouse free-market economics yet arrive at a culturally protectionist policy that insulates Shakespeare from change and challenge. The National Curriculum had the effect of protecting Shakespeare, 'our national poet', from competition with international authors and modern literature: other authors are only recommended to be selected from lists of major playwrights, major writers of fiction, major poets and so on. Much of this extension of the canon was added by the Labour government as non-statutory annotations to the revised curriculum (DfEE/QCA 1999: 12). These authors are not insulated to the same extent as Shakespeare against trends in consumption: that is to say, from fluctuating demand for knowledge of them from students, parents, teachers and employers.

Indeed, the very act of making Shakespeare uniquely compulsory suggests the possibility that, if left to consumers (students, parents) and producers (teachers, schools), Shakespeare might not be taught. Putting Shakespeare on the curriculum represents one of the ways in which

> at the end of the twentieth century Shakespeare enthusiasts assume, for perhaps the first time since the end of the eighteenth century, that Shakespeare needs defending, that his genius is not universally appreciated, that his supremacy is contested.
>
> (Taylor 1999: 199)

Elaborating his contention, Taylor argues that such education policy is only one of the proofs that Shakespeare is not inherently universal but heavily 'marketed'. To exemplify this Taylor cites the example of the film industry and blockbuster productions such as Baz Luhrmann's *Romeo + Juliet*, which attracted teenage viewers by relocating the story in 1990s America, used a pop soundtrack and cast 'heartthrob' actors in the lead roles (1999: 202).

Returning to protectionism in the curriculum, from Taylor's evidence of its necessity, it is arguable that not only is Shakespeare placed under threat by the calibre of other authors' work but also from his own quality. What makes Shakespeare 'great' and special can also make him less attractive. Many other authors' works are easier to teach because they are shorter in length, written in modern English, and therefore consume less time in class. Taylor forces us to ask,

> If Shakespeare were not so massively supported by corporate capital and government subsidy, if he were not forced upon schoolchildren, would he still loom so large in our culture? Or would he collapse to the status of Chaucer? A great writer admired by specialists, but paid little attention by the larger world.
>
> (1999: 205)

While Taylor is predominantly concerned with the corporate culture of America, instances of corporate sponsored Shakespeare in the United Kingdom – many of which have developed since he was writing – range from the financial backing of Globe projects by Deutsche Bank to, on a smaller scale, the sale of advertising space in programmes for community and regional theatre. Taylor's critique thus articulates the fears of the Conservative/conservationist authors of the National Curriculum, and those who have upheld it in subsequent years, about Shakespeare's threatened status. He himself professes indifference to this fate in this publication, although such a position is somewhat undercut by his reprisal of the role of general editor for the forthcoming edition of the *Oxford Complete Works*.

In terms of successive governments' policies for raising standards, Shakespeare has been made to gel with macro-policies that urge the education sector to embrace the language and concepts of business. However, his continuing protected status in the National Curriculum contrasts with both main parties' experimentation with the marketisation of education. Since both the Thatcher and Labour governments encouraged elements of market forces within the education system, such as competition, elements of privatisation and consumer sovereignty, Shakespeare's sheltered place on the curriculum is here demonstrably at odds with education policy more widely. The Labour governments of 1997–2009 could be seen to have challenged Shakespeare's protected status by increasing competition to traditional academic routes through extending vocational and diploma qualifications. However, these reforms remain concentrated on the post-sixteen sector, where English is not compulsory – lessening their impact on Shakespeare. Hence, the legislation that enshrines the playwright as the only compulsory author in students' experience of English at school is an example of successive governments' inability to be fully marketised, to relinquish regulation of the education market and to trust the interaction of market forces to produce education of a high standard.

Shakespeare for Inclusion

Arguably, the implementation of social values in policy is the area in which the two parties are most discernibly differentiated in accordance with their traditional ideologies. However, Labour's minimal changes to policy concerning Shakespeare in the National Curriculum made them vulnerable to the criticism that they perpetuated Tory values for literary education in the curriculum. The holding up of Shakespeare as a figure through which to assimilate children from diverse backgrounds to one great, English tradition, for example, can be seen as at odds with their desire elsewhere to figure inclusion as embracing diverse cultures rather than a single, unified national culture, espousing cultural pluralism rather than a common cultural heritage. The following paragraphs examine relationships between Shakespeare and macro-political agendas for achieving social inclusion in education in both parties' policies. In particular, it will elucidate the way in which both the Conservatives and Labour have been able to maintain Shakespeare in a site of peculiar privilege in the National Curriculum on the basis of their agendas for inclusion, despite having almost antithetical conceptions of inclusivity.

For Conservative education policy in the late 1980s, the *Cox Report*'s suggestion that Shakespeare become the only required author in the National Curriculum for English offered a solution to the perception that education was failing to preserve a British tradition. The committee's decision was built on three much older beliefs, extremely palatable to Thatcher's government. Firstly, the committee's decision represented a conviction in the power of literary studies to promulgate a 'common culture'. Secondly, it reconfirmed established ideas about the value of Shakespeare specifically as father of the modern English language

(Kingman 1988). Thirdly, it alluded to Shakespeare as universal – in the sense of speaking to all – rendering Shakespeare a key entity around which to build a common curriculum, even a common culture. Such a view of the social mission of Shakespeare, and other canonical writers, meshed neatly with the Conservative conception of inclusion, derived from thinkers such as Arnold, as a matter of 'raising up' or assimilating people into 'the best that has been thought and said' by the nation's authors.

While the Cox committee had aimed to broaden the range of children's reading to include non-fiction, children's fiction and writing from other cultures in the curriculum, the attention to canonical, English authors in the first National Curriculum document is inescapable. For instance, it stipulated that key stage two pupils' 'taste in reading' should be developed 'with guidance from the teacher' and that by key stages three and four

> Pupils should be introduced to:
> - the richness of contemporary writing;
> - pre-twentieth-century literature;
> - some of the works which have been most influential in shaping and refining the English language and its literature, e.g. *the Authorised Version of the Bible, Wordsworth's poems, or the novels of Austen, the Brontës or Dickens*;
> - some of the works of Shakespeare.
>
> (DfE/Welsh Office 1995: 30; Cox 1991: 193)

The authors italicised here are non-statutory. They are, however, part of an elite canon of English (both nation and language) literature recognised as such by, among others, the Kingman Committee on which Cox had served, only a year previously, and Leavis (Cox's tutor), four decades earlier. Leavis had included Austen, and later Dickens, in his canon-building work *The Great Tradition*.

In the curriculum document, the status of these authors is reinforced by the physical space they occupy on the page. Contemporary writing, for example, is quickly passed over – it merits the label 'rich' but not 'influential' (a later version of the curriculum felt it necessary to specify that contemporary authors should have 'well-established critical reputations', presumably to ensure the quality of literature taught) (DfE/Welsh Office 1995: 20). Additionally, the 1995 revisions state that 'within a broad programme of reading' pupils 'should be given opportunities to' 'appreciate the significance of texts whose language and ideas have been influential e.g. *Greek myths, the Authorised Version of the Bible, Arthurian legends*' (DfE/Welsh Office 1995: 21). Again, the italics indicate non-statutory material. In the 1999 revisions, under the Labour government, the requirement was reiterated as part of the 'knowledge, skills and understanding' subheading for reading at key stages three and four:

> 2. Pupils should be taught:
> a   how and why texts have been influential and significant [for example, the influence of Greek myths, the Authorised Version of the Bible, the Arthurian legends]

b the characteristics of texts that are considered to be of high quality

c the appeal and importance of these texts over time.

(DfEE/QCA 1999: 34)

It is important to note that, again, the bracketed material is non-statutory and, as such appears in grey font in this edition. The examples given of Greek myths and the Bible – the text of a Judeo-Christian tradition, translated from Hebrew and Greek – as primary literatures in an English literary tradition obviously draw on a (nostalgic) model of premium education from the independent and grammar schools which those revising the *Cox Report* may themselves have attended in the mid-twentieth century. In setting these examples, they may have recalled the strong bent towards the classics, Middle English (partially from French sources, in the case of Malory's *Le Morte D'Arthur*) and early modern and religious studies in their own formative educational experiences. However, the foreign provenance of at least two of the texts listed also offers some curious and ironic potential for deconstructing the blatant and latent nationalism in the curriculum. Such a curriculum had the potential to empower students to question actively rather than passively receive the canon, by teaching them how texts are constructed as canonical and about the assumptions that underlie distinctions between English works and those from other cultures, literary and non-literary texts, 'high-quality' works and 'pulp fiction'. This opportunity was not seized by either the Conservative or Labour governments.

Labour's first, minimally-altered version, of the curriculum was published in 1999, overrun with hangovers from the older prescriptions and their elitist assumptions about the nature of English, assumptions that conceive the subject as being about introducing students to '*the* English literary heritage', the 'best' texts, and teaching them to 'appreciate' those texts as, it is supposed, their forbears have done (DfEE/QCA 1999: 8, my emphasis). Their revisions to the document also left the clause that makes Shakespeare the only compulsory author untouched. However, there was some evidence of discontinuity between the parties, particularly in Labour's commitment to give voice, through dedicated time, space and money, to a plethora of literary traditions, voices and cultures. Half a page of the revised Curriculum is filled with (mostly non-statutory) suggestions of post-1914 poets, recent and contemporary drama and fiction, and writing by authors from 'different cultures and traditions' (DfEE/QCA 1999: 36). Hence, the revised curriculum offers evidence that during their time in power, Labour developed a catholic literary tradition in English education that nevertheless maintained Shakespeare at its head.

As noted previously, the testing of all students on Shakespeare at key stage three was removed in 2009, touted by commentators as belatedly marking Labour's different attitude to assessment. Explanations for this move could include a change in Labour's attitude to Shakespeare in the curriculum more widely; different pedagogic values; the unpopularity of tests with teachers; and, more practically, the difficulty of administering a massive examination system. The axing of SATs at stage three alone does not, however, suggest an attempt on Labour's behalf to differentiate their own position on social inclusion from that of the Conservatives, particularly when Shakespeare in the curriculum was unchanged. The handful of changes to English instead suggest that Labour was prepared to accommodate Shakespeare's status as the only compulsory author into an agenda for equality that could be defined by access for all, and to all elements of culture and education – almost indistinguishable, in terms of outcome, from traditional Conservative notions of assimilation. The adoption of a more radically left-wing position of treating all culture, and all knowledges, as equal through abolishing existing hierarchies within the curriculum was incontrovertibly eschewed.

A context through which to understand Shakespeare's default place as a key part of a diverse, literary education that extends inclusion can be gained by considering the way in which the Labour government of 1997–2010 attended reflexively to the 'role of education in positioning human subjects in relation to the prevailing social order' (Whitty 1992: 269). It will be argued that although Labour's rhetoric expressed the value it places on equality, deployed in a swathe of policy documents, their commitment to social justice was underscored by the similarity of some of their policies to those of the two preceding Conservative governments. Meanwhile, the Conservatives' failure to separate themselves from a nationalist vision of cultural cohesion, which pre-dates even the Thatcher government, undercut that party's conscious cultivation of a new, Labour-like social ideology under Cameron's leadership.

Labour's emphasis on education's 'role in building a new social order, via notions of progress, perfectibility, and empowerment' (Whitty 1992: 269) can be interpreted as an attempt to refute the negative connotations of writers who have criticised the way in which education is always driven by other agendas of the state. These include the sociologist Emile Durkheim, who argues that 'far from having as its unique or principal object the individual and his interest, [education] is above all the means by which society perpetually recreates the conditions of its very existence' (1956: 123). Louis Althusser reiterates, in an overtly left-wing way, that education is centrally concerned with the 'reproduction of submission to the ruling ideology for workers, and a reproduction of the ability to manipulate the ruling ideology correctly for the agents of exploitation and repression' (1971: 133). With varying degrees of politicisation, the corresponding theory of Bowles and Gintis, Raymond Williams' notion of a 'selective tradition' and Pierre Bourdieu's 'cultural capital' all make contentions about the way in which children are educated into social traditions and economic models, inside and away from the classroom. Not denying that these mechanisms exist, but challenging the sinister aspect cast on them by the writers above, Labour instead attempted to harness as a positive force for change the social traditions and economic models with which its education system would imbue children. It advertised its traditions and models as based on the equality (of opportunity, participation and access) of all ethnicities, genders, sexualities, abilities and economic statuses.

Labour's desire to use this normative and conformational power of education to advance social inclusion, rather than for economic gain or to perpetuate a society based on unequal social, racial and other hierarchies, can be seen throughout the policy directives they produced while in office. Their equalising intentions are expressed in their use of the word 'entitlement' to promise 'a clear, full and statutory entitlement to learning for all pupils' in the foreword added to the revised *National Curriculum* by the then Secretary of State, David Blunkett, and the QCA chairman, Sir William Stubbs (DfEE/QCA 1999: 3). Labour explicitly acknowledged that 'equality of opportunity is one of a broad set of common values and purposes which underpin the school curriculum' (1999: 4) and, as such, is a precursor to gaining one's entitlement. Other preconditions for achieving inclusiveness in education included raising aspiration towards an entitlement, and the quality of products or experience that constitute those rights.

As the party's Culture Secretary, Tessa Jowell, argued, as well as increasing chances for material wealth and fulfilment, addressing the 'poverty of aspiration' was 'also necessary to build a society of fairness and opportunity' (2004: 14–15). Additionally, she emphasised the need for 'excellence' in terms of the 'quality' of provision, criteria applied beyond arts education by Labour in their pursuit to raise standards across various endeavours (2004: 10). Schools were advised to make provision for an arts entitlement for all through government recommendations on prospectuses for primary and secondary schools (DfEE 1998a, 1998b). These documents offer proof of Labour's policy for inclusion being put into action, or, at least, communicated to schools. Throughout such documents, organisations were warned that this should not equate to elitism of content or provision, as this would jeopardise accessibility (another government target for education).

The ability to demonstrate adherence to government-endorsed values became a requirement for many publicly funded organisations early in the new millennium, with a particular focus on the arts and arts education. Thus, in *From Policy to Partnership: Developing the Arts in Schools*, the QCA and the Arts Council England include a section on 'ensuring entitlement'; and profess the 'right' to 'high-quality arts experience for every pupil, whatever their background or ability' and the role of the community in strengthening and broadening arts provision in school (2000: 4). This led to heated debate in the arts sector about whether culture should 'become a tool of government policy', as a quotation on the front of John Holden's *Capturing Cultural Value* attests. Moreover, he questioned the 'degree to which cultural organisations should be obliged to use instrumental arguments to justify their public funding' (2004: 9). In doing so, he raises the possibility that the government's values for arts education and culture were only superficially shared by some organisations in order to access the financial incentives on offer. The government's counter-argument to this accusation, that it was ensuring the public value of these bodies' use of tax-payers' funds, sparked further debate about cultural value and public funding in these areas.

Looking beyond the discourse and measures wielded by Labour's policy-makers in attempting to reform arts education, it is evident that the party's reign produced a glut of legislation to promote equality. On gaining office in 1997, one of their first education initiatives was the inclusion of children with special needs, where possible, into mainstream schooling, through the *Excellence for All Children* Green Paper (DfEE 1997). Other initiatives that year, countering the perceived lack of careers guidance, information and advice, are outlined in the documents *The Learning Age* (DfEE 1998) and *Learning to Succeed* (DfEE 1999) as well as in the establishment of the nationwide Connexions employment service. Exclusion stemming from poverty and a lack of resources for urban working-class youth was acknowledged by the 1998 *Disaffected Children* report (Education and Employment Committee 1998); the creation of Education Action Zones and the Excellence in Cities schemes; as well as the Educational Maintenance Allowance, a scheme first piloted in 1999, then implemented more fully in 2004, following the publication of the *14–19: Opportunity and Excellence* document (DfES). These policy interventions aimed to keep children at the highest risk of dropping out in education or training for longer using economic incentives (such as the Allowance) and by strategically channelling more resources into urban areas. Further into their time in power, Labour vigorously pursued policies designed to appeal to the range of students' educational interests and aspirations. The Curriculum 2000 reforms to study beyond the age of sixteen stressed the benefits of modular rather than linear course structure for secondary education. Through promoting modularisation it aimed to encourage a wider range of subjects to be taken post-sixteen (including those seen to be previously unappealing to university admissions bodies) by facilitating greater choice, flexibility and parity between subjects. It established, on paper, the parity of vocational education with academic routes through the 2002 Green Paper *14–19: Extending Opportunities, Raising Standards* (DfES 2002). In this way, the party approached the reform of education policy with a broad range of policies to extend inclusivity.

A critical perspective on Labour's achievements and failures in implementing its values is available in articles by Pring and Whitty. Labour has been criticised for treating social justice issues as peripheral (Ball 2008: 150), for multiplying different and unequal outcomes for students through proliferating different qualification pathways and school types, and for taking too long to focus additional resources on disadvantaged pupils and therefore failing to reduce significantly the gap between them and children from advantaged backgrounds (Whitty 2008: 166–167). These criticisms are obviously inflected with the belief that Labour has not pursued the party's traditional and distinctive social justice agenda with enough force. This concern is fanned by analysis that suggests that one gap certainly closed during this period was between Labour values and rhetoric and that of David Cameron's 'compassionate Conservatism', with both parties moving towards a political centre ground. Whether this narrowing rhetorical gap has been mirrored by a corresponding alignment in terms of practice will be discussed in the conclusion.

In undertaking a weighty comparison of Conservative and Labour education policy during the past twenty years, Whitty, however, also acknowledges the limitations to his criticism of Labour. He asserts that a new admissions code, plans for free school transport and 'choice advisers' to open up the choice of schools to less advantaged families 'is a welcome, if belated, recognition of the impact of structural and cultural factors on the capacity of different groups to exercise choice meaningfully in a diverse system of schooling' (Whitty 2008: 178). As part of Labour's campaign for the social good, these policies represent moves to ameliorate those structural and cultural factors. They suggest at least some degree of synergy between their values for education (especially social inclusion) and the likely impact of the policy designed to realise them.

While social inclusion was a central concern for both parties, they each envision distinct ways of achieving it (which, in turn, affect its definition): Labour by promoting equality, pluralism and parity within all facets of education policy and the Conservatives by assimilating those excluded into dominant values, structures and practices as, for example, part of an English cultural heritage. Such an agenda was evident in their development of the National Curriculum as a vehicle for delivering this British 'national culture' to all students, which, protected from market forces, would also elide the previous varied content and delivery of 'trendy teachers' who were perceived to be 'subverting traditional moral values and selling the nation short' (Whitty 1992: 301; also Ball 2008: 110). The influence of such ideas, espousing the assimilation of the British population into a common cultural heritage and thereby supposedly contributing to the nation's stability, is traceable in the National Curriculum for English, which states that 'cultural development can be achieved by introducing pupils to *the* English literary heritage' (DfEE/QCA 1999: 8, my emphasis). The use of the definite article is significant in indicating the underlying assumption of a fixed and unified literary heritage, based arguably on nostalgia for the past and a belief in the fantasy of a homogenous British culture. This is in spite of the increasing diversity of the population and accelerating pace of globalisation. The above clause demonstrates an immediate continuity of thought with the *Kingman Report*'s declaration that:

> Our modern language and our modern writing have grown out of the language and literature of the past. The rhythms of our daily speech and writing are haunted not only by the rhythms of our nursery rhymes, but also by the rhythms of Shakespeare, Blake, Edward Lear, Lewis Carroll, the Authorised Version of the Bible. We do not completely know what modern writing is unless we know what lies behind it
>
> (Kingman 1988: 2:21)

Delving deeper into history, such sentiments are comparable with Leavis' desire for a 'national conscience' founded on literature and literary language to 'breach the continuity' between the past and present caused by rapid social and technological changes (1986: 279); the place of English in the *Newbolt Report* as 'the only possible basis for a national education', since national self-understanding is to be gained through the (re)discovery of England's literary past (1921: 14); and the Romantics' belief that literary works caught 'the essence, or some of the historical essence, of the historical context from which they emanated' (St. Clair 2004: 2). Ball articulates the way in which this ancient 'restorationist agenda' was particularly pronounced in the National Curriculum documents for history, geography, English and music, 'as part of a curriculum seeking to eschew relevance and the present, concentrating on "heritage" and "the canon"' (2008: 83). He also identifies the neo-victorianism and nationalism identified elsewhere in this chapter as characterising Conservative education policy: 'It is a fantasy curriculum founded on Victorian myths about, and inventions of, ethnic Englishness and an assertion of tradition, of morality and literary history in the face of "declining standards", cultural heterogeneity and a fragmented modernity' (2008: 83). This persistent longing for the past, as a way of securing the future, remains a hallmark of both culturally Conservative and politically Conservative attitudes to national identity.

Given his continued associations with elite 'ruling' culture, made prominent in literary criticism over the past few decades (including that which sort to challenge this positioning), Shakespeare never offered a solution to Labour's agenda for social inclusion, as he did for the Conservative's social project for assimilation. Nevertheless, the party was presumably disinclined to depose Shakespeare lest it be accused of depriving those disadvantaged citizens it is supposed to represent the chance to experience the literary 'greats'. Having diversified the profile of its voters, Labour was particularly sensitive to 'the dual and contradictory policy imperatives that derive from the aspirations and fears of the middle classes, on the one hand and the limited participation and underachievement of various sections of the working class, on the other' (Ball 2008: 97). On a practical level, a further imperative to retain the Conservative's curriculum in a reasonably intact form (with piecemeal revisions in 1999 and 2008) was motivated by a reluctance to engage in years of upheaval within the school system, upsetting teachers and trade unions. Constant tinkering with the National Curriculum, including an unpopular review and rewriting of it to strengthen standard English between 1993 and 1995 by the chemical engineer David Pascall, had poisoned Conservative educational reform, as depicted in Cox's later titles *Cox on the Battle for the English Curriculum* and *The Great Betrayal*. Labour's equivocation over how best to implement inclusion, as well as a desire not to be derided for narrowing access to key figures resulted in Shakespeare being sustained as the only compulsory author in English education policy.

Naturalising Shakespeare's Curriculum Presence

Whether in spite or because of successive governments' maintenance of Shakespeare's position in the curriculum, Shakespeare's continuing presence on the National Curriculum demonstrates the way in which he now exists as part of a 'dominant ideology' for education policy that largely transcends party politics (Hawkes 1996: 43). The naturalness of his unique place in education will be shored up as long as vast swathes of the English population experience Shakespeare as a part of the National Curriculum, enter the voting population, fill roles as policy-makers, civil servants, politicians and educators, and in turn play their part in shaping policy for schools. Shakespeare's supreme position does not mean that his role is always unquestioned – although, as I will suggest in the following chapter, the value of various pedagogies is more often at the centre of debate, rather than the value of Shakespeare per se – rather, such questions constitute exceptions to the rule and are often treated as scandalous, radical or deluded – see Taylor on the treatment of Shakespeare's critics (1989: 399–400).

In twenty years, the focus of education policy arguably changed from one concerned primarily with what is taught – with outlining a National Curriculum – to one interested in the overall operation of the state school system – with the proliferation of qualifications for example. However, relating the main parties' policy agendas and overall ideological values to Shakespeare has served to highlight the circularities in education policy; the way in which policy overwhelmingly continues across changes of government, with little absolute rupture or revolution – despite variations between and within party agendas; and the persisting legacy of early policy-makers and cultural critics. In seeking to explain this, it is worth returning to Ball's assertion that policy 'works by accretion and sedimentation, new policies add to and overlay old ones, with the effect that new principles and innovations are merged and conflated with older rationales and previous practices' (2008: 255). True reform of education is hampered by the accreted weight of education policy and legislation, which, although intended to offer a solution to perceived problems, may be experienced as constraint. The implications of this for the take-up and endurance of three pedagogies for Shakespeare will be examined in chapter two.

Chapter 2

Shakespeare in English Pedagogy: Values, Influence and Criticism

This chapter considers how three pedagogical approaches – literary critical, active methods and contextual – are underpinned by various conceptions of the value of Shakespeare, relating to the influences that are evident in their discourses. These conceptions include progressivism, humanism and critical theory. It also traces the extent to which these 'Shakespearean' pedagogies are concerned with features inherent in (or specific to) his works or represent the influence of larger trends and organisations in education, especially in English academia. The contested value of the pedagogies themselves will be indicated through overviews of the key criticisms of each. Evidence for the existence and implementation of these pedagogies is taken from current literature on Shakespeare in the classroom, where teachers are the writers, or report their teaching to the writer, or are observed by them. This attempts to recognise that this body of work offers a large, broad, nationwide sample intended to resist the anecdotal nature of many studies where the researcher enters the classroom. It does, however, mean that representations of practice, rather than actualities, experienced first-hand, are being discussed.

The National Curriculum for English ignited vigorous debate not only about *what* Shakespeare should be taught (Which works? Whole plays or excerpts?) and to *whom*. It also raised the question of *how* he should be taught – partly because this question is answered only elliptically in the curriculum document itself. Relatively unchanged by three successive governments and their party politics, the 1999 version of the Curriculum legislated that each student should encounter, in the English classroom, 'two plays by Shakespeare, one of which should be studied in key stage three' (DfEE/QCA 1999: 35). The prescription of the quantity of Shakespeare to be studied is well-defined as are the stipulations for assessing and reporting students' academic performance in the subject. Assessment included, in the past, being examined on one of three set Shakespeare plays at key stage three for SATs. While these tests were abandoned after 2008, Shakespeare coursework continued to be a component of GCSE English at the end of key stage four. Shakespeare also currently forms part of the requirements for English at A-level. Content at this level has historically been determined by a group of awarding bodies, formerly known as examination boards, rather than the education department. What Shakespeare should be taught and how he should be assessed are consequently reasonably well-defined in publicly available documents.

Less determined within the statutes is the pedagogy with which to teach and prepare students for testing on the plays. Under New Labour, the existing legislation was supplemented with a non-statutory National Strategy entitled *Shakespeare for All Ages and Stages*, which guides teachers towards, rather than mandating, preferred pedagogies. The government thereby attempted to display inclusive attitudes towards teachers' methods. The document was first archived by the Coalition government that came to power in 2010, but in 2012 it was reinstated on the Department for Education's website. This move adds to the sense of circularity in policy and highlights the contradictions within Gove's actions (as embracing the product of a New Labour national strategy conflicts with his denouncement of New Labour education policy elsewhere). It may also suggest that the need to ensure quality of provision of Shakespeare transcends party politics.

At a glance, the curriculum neither prescribes nor proscribes particular pedagogies as long as students can display a range of skills, knowledges and understandings, outlined by the curriculum, when they come to be assessed. So, study of a Shakespeare play might equally involve 'watching [...] recordings' or 'working in role' (DfEE/QCA 1999: 33) or both. The following sections will argue, however, that, reading through the 1999 curriculum document itself, it is possible to discern pedagogies for teaching the subject that are either necessitated by the content of the programme of study or implicitly recommended to teachers. These include drama, ICT, media studies and creative writing approaches. In addition, three pedagogies in particular deserve detailed discussion: literary critical, active and contextual approaches.

Drama in the Curriculum

Long advocated by innovative, but isolated, teachers, such as Henry Caldwell Cook in his 1917 book *The Play Way,* and arts practitioners including the RSC's Cicely Berry, the growth in the popularity of drama methods for teaching Shakespeare is attested to by the coverage of the subject in leading academic journals and monograph publications during the 1980s and 1990s. In 1984 the editor of the international journal *Shakespeare Quarterly* wrote, in an issue dedicated to teaching Shakespeare, that 'performance consciousness' has transformed the teaching of the plays, so that 'virtually everybody acknowledges the need to approach Shakespeare's plays as dramatic rather than literary works' (Andrews 1984: 515–516). While his statement reflected the focus of that particular edition of *Shakespeare Quarterly*, I will suggest, in this chapter, that he may have overstated the case, especially in terms of English secondary schooling during the period (rather than American higher education to which he primarily referred). Six years later, in another issue dedicated to teaching Shakespeare, Ann Thompson argues that 'performance consciousness' has not 'been forgotten or entirely superseded' by new historicist and other critical theory approaches. Rather, it has been politicised and has broadened out to include video technology (1990: 141). Other articles in the same issue explore revisions to performance-centred criticism (Rocklin 1990), ask how we can learn from the staging and theatricality of the plays (Freedman 1990), consider the way in which the plays dramatise paradox (Hirsch 1990), juxtapose performance-oriented pedagogy with 'older' methods of lecture and discussion (Ozark Holmer 1990) and posit that performance should become as naturalised a classroom practice as communication or interpretation (Beehler 1990). Braham Murray, writing in the 2009 essay collection *Teaching Shakespeare*, explains how he tries to bring 'the theatre into his classroom and his classroom to the theatre' (1985: 56) – as does Peter Reynolds, who addresses the issues of casting, silent characters and stage properties in school productions (1985). In the same volume, Neil King considers how younger students might be introduced to Shakespeare through playing out cut-down versions or isolated scenes (1985: 57–76). This catalogue of publications on drama methods in the Shakespeare classroom offers a reminder that the two elements were united in some English classrooms long before the National Curriculum's requirements.

Dramatic approaches to texts generally (if not Shakespeare specifically) were made mandatory, however, in the National Curriculum for English in 1989. The document features 'drama' as a subheading under the requirements for 'speaking and listening' at each of the key stages, along with 'group discussion and interaction', 'standard English', and 'language variation'. In addition, drama as a pedagogy is represented through a set of discrete activities featured in the curriculum's programme of study. They include improvising, role-playing, script-writing, performing and reviewing. Table 1 allows easy comparison of the way in which drama is expected to be employed and developed over the various key stages in English teaching.

Table 1: National Curriculum requirements for drama across the key stages.

Key stage	Requirements for drama
Key stage one	To participate in a range of drama activities, pupils should be taught to: a use language and actions to explore and convey situations, characters and emotions b create and sustain roles individually and when working with others c comment constructively on drama they have watched or in which they have taken part (DfEE/QCA 1999: 16)
Key stage two	To participate in a **wide** range of drama activities **and to evaluate their own and other's contributions**, pupils should be taught to: a create, **adapt** and sustain different roles, individually and in groups b use **character, action and narrative** to convey **story, themes, emotions, ideas in plays they devise and script** c **use dramatic techniques to explore characters and issues** d **evaluate how they and others have contributed to the overall effectiveness of performances** (DfEE/QCA 1999: 23)
Key stages three and four	To participate in a range of drama activities and to evaluate their own and other's contributions, pupils should be taught to: a use a **variety** of dramatic techniques to explore ideas, **issues, texts and meanings** b use **different ways** to convey action, character, **atmosphere and tension** when they are scripting and **performing** in plays c **appreciate how the structure and organisation of scenes and plays contribute to dramatic effect** d evaluate **critically** performances of dramas that they have watched or in which they have taken part (DfEE/QCA 1999: 32)

Bold font indicates new and additional requirements or different phrasing from one key stage to another. Key stages three and four are grouped together by the curriculum.

From this collation of the curriculum requirements, it is evident that drama pedagogies have been implemented by the curriculum authors as a means towards ensuring that students develop a certain set of skills, for example, to evaluate, communicate, convey, appreciate, use, create, sustain, participate, comment and adapt. Furthermore, these skills are evidently to be practised in relation to a set of techniques and concepts from drama and literary studies: language, action, situation, character, narrative, story, theme, emotion, meaning, text, atmosphere, tension, structure and organisation. Development between the key stages is indicated by the increasingly wide range of activities to be undertaken or the higher standard of performance expected to be attained. For example, the requirement for 'constructive comment' on performances becomes 'evaluation' at the intermediate level and finally 'critical evaluation' for the most advanced level.

The curriculum instructs teachers on the range of drama activities that should be included in English lessons under the heading 'breadth of study'. From Table 2, which compares requirements for drama activities across the key stages, it is evident that drama as a pedagogy is represented in the National Curriculum through a set of activities (improvising, role-playing, script-writing, performing and reviewing), which are designed to impart a set of skills. These skills are only part of the requirements for speaking and listening, which, along with reading and writing, constitute the programme of study for English. Thus, the structure of the curriculum, as well as its language, does little to communicate a sense of drama as a holistic, self-contained and self-sufficient pedagogy, relating to a set of dramatic techniques, texts and performances. Rather, it appears as a pedagogy from which elements can be borrowed to enrich the study of language and literature, which dominated (and continues to be at the core of) the subject of English for much of the twentieth century.

Moreover, Jonothan Neelands argues, drama in the National Curriculum reflects the Thatcher government's reductive focus on drama as a set of skills 'that will prepare young people for their economic roles after schooling' rather than as a means of fostering

Table 2: National Curriculum requirements for drama activities across the key stages.

Key stage	Requirements for drama activities
Key stage one	a working in role b presenting drama and stories to others c responding to performances (DfEE/QCA 1999: 17)
Key stage two	a **improvisation** and working in role b **scripting and performing in plays** c responding to performances (DfEE/QCA 1999: 24)
Key stages three and four	a improvisation and working in role b **devising**, scripting and performing in plays c **discussing and reviewing their own and others'** performances (DfEE/QCA 1999: 33)

imagination or as a 'shared cultural activity' (1992: 4–7). His complaint noticeably echoes George Sampson's much older warning against the vocational bent of education, in *English for the English*: 'elementary education must not be vocational, it is the purpose of education, not to prepare children *for* their occupations, but to prepare children *against* their occupations' (1921: viii). By invoking this classic piece of liberal humanist literature, Neelands casts the Conservative government of the early 1990s as denying all schoolchildren the equal right to a liberal education; that is to say, the right to a broad range of knowledges and experiences, for their own sake and for personal enrichment. In this way, he identifies the government as implementing a retrogressive educational policy. This old-fashioned English curriculum, Neelands maintains, also offers a (mis)representation of drama as an instrument for teaching and learning English rather than as a subject in its own right. Yet, in spite of his protests, it is a representation of drama that is *as* enshrined by the curriculum as the teaching of Shakespeare itself.

Although nowhere in the curriculum document is the requirement to teach Shakespeare explicitly linked to the requirements for drama, the National Strategy *Shakespeare for All Ages and Stages,* which is designed to engage primary students onwards in the study of his plays, champions drama activities in its 'suggested teaching approaches'. In addition, the fitness for purpose of the pedagogy – with its emphasis on predominantly assessed aspects such as character and plot – as well as the pressure on teachers to forge cross-curricular links with relevant subjects has resulted in the two becoming inseparable in much reported classroom practice. Yandell (1997) as well as Thomas (1994), for example, offer articles on teaching Shakespeare through drama, but these represent a fraction of the overwhelming presence of the pedagogy in English teaching journals.

ICT, Media and Creative Writing

ICT and media studies approaches to literary and non-literary texts are also required by the legislation. At key stages three and four, the requirements for reading state that teaching should develop students' 'reading of print and ICT-based information texts' as well as demanding the analysis of 'media and moving image texts' (DfEE/QCA 1999: 35). Throughout the curriculum teachers are encouraged to use film, radio, television and computer technology 'to support [classroom] study of literary texts' (DfEE/QCA 1999: 8). 'ICT opportunity' annotations, which are non-statutory, also appear in the margins of the main curriculum text (DfEE/QCA 1999: 26, 33). Evidence that these prescriptions have been taken up in teaching occupies the pages of teaching journals, including Gibson's *Shakespeare and Schools* magazine (see, for example, issues 9 and 23), while Aers and Wheale's *Shakespeare in the Curriculum* includes two chapters with suggestions for using film versions in the classroom and 'video-teaching' the bard through making films. Four out of seven chapters in the anthology *Shakespeare in Education* refer to the use of film in teaching Shakespeare; two discuss the use of the Internet as a classroom resource.

Teachers in three contrastingly achieving Cambridgeshire schools, observed for a project on school editions, demonstrated their use of the computer programme Car2ouche, as well as audio-visual and Smart Board technology in their Shakespeare lessons (Olive 2006). The DCSF document *Shakespeare for All Ages and Stages* includes suggestions for using film and PowerPoint in the classroom (2008: 32, 34). This suggests that although policy directives concerning ICT and media studies pedagogies have been embraced in Shakespeare lessons nationwide for some time now, the government still perceives the need to reinforce teachers' awareness of such methods and technologies through supplementary strategy documents.

In terms of personal response techniques and creative writing, John Saunders' 1985 article on creative writing responses to the plays in O-level exams again provides evidence that methods endorsed by the National Curriculum mark a continuity with, rather than revolution of, the teaching of Shakespeare in schools (97–117). Although these approaches to Shakespeare were evident in innovative classroom practice prior to the legislation, under the National Curriculum teachers are required by the Curriculum to give students opportunities to 'respond imaginatively in different ways to what they read' (DfEE/QCA 1999: 19). Even the youngest students are obliged to 'express preferences, giving reasons' for the fiction, poetry and drama they have encountered (19). Moreover, the curriculum document reproduces sample images of students' poems and short stories as inspirational examples for teachers' own work (14–15).

The take-up of these activities in classrooms is attested to by an increase in features dedicated to personal response and creative writing in *Shakespeare and Schools* newsletters after the curriculum's introduction. Issue 12 deals with how to meet examiners' expectations for high-quality personal responses, while issues 15 and 22 report classroom teaching of Shakespeare involving creative responses to the plays: writing poems on *King Lear*, scripting a play about 'Living with Lady Macbeth' and creating storyboards. A decade later, in *Shakespeare in Education*, Sue Gregory suggests getting students to keep a *Romeo and Juliet* scrapbook containing personal responses, creative writing and love songs (2003: 28). None of the approaches above – drama, personal response, creative writing, ICT or media studies – is explicitly linked to Shakespeare in the National Curriculum document itself. Yet, the publications and resources cited above show that there is concern within and beyond the teaching profession about how these requirements may be fulfilled through studying Shakespeare. They are evidence that pedagogies for teaching Shakespeare are an evolving but continuously insistent concern.

Literary Critical Approaches

From the early twentieth-century, literary critical approaches to Shakespeare have dominated English pedagogy in schools. At its most limited and old-fashioned, the literary critical approach in schools is characterised, almost caricatured, by Richard Adams as 'reading round, explaining obscure textual references or preparing potted character-sketches' (1985: 14). In this approach, Shakespeare is valued principally as literature: that is to say, as a text to be read rather than as a script for performance. Moreover, at school level, the texts are generally treated as 'literary *objects*' (Adams 1985: 1); that is to say, in the main, single, fixed representations of plays on pages – 'almost no reference is made to the diverse forms which the play has taken and may take' (Sinfield 1985: 138–139). The processes involved in 'making' a play, beyond the playwright's individual craftsmanship, are also largely ignored: consideration of printing, publishing, revising and editing is left for study at the university level, where textual studies will also explore the unstable, plural and fragmented nature of Shakespeare's works. Hence, literary criticism of Shakespeare for school students, at least, remains an altogether more positivist task, one which constructs value in students 'discovering' inherent 'truths' hidden in Shakespeare's language, structure and imagery, and that aims to enable them 'to sift through and reflect on the printed words, to pause where [they] will or move back and forth making new connections and realising new truths' (Adams 1985: 12). These last two phrases, 'making new connections' and 'realising new truths', especially indicate a way of studying Shakespeare that remains incomplete without the close-reading activities espoused by the literary criticism of the Cambridge school, including that of I.A. Richards and Leavis, and New Critics in the early twentieth-century. For these critics, only such meticulous techniques can truly value Shakespeare (or any other writer) as a craftsman – 'no haphazard worker': what Ben Jonson termed his 'well-turned and true-filed lines' are seen as 'the product of judgement, not luck' (Adams 1985: 13). Richard Adams' discourse here draws strongly on Leavis and Thompson's analogy between the truly great writer/critic and the artisan wheelwright (1985: 56–57). Additionally, Adams' declaration that 'the danger of insufficient attention to textual study is that we may be dazzled into responding quickly to the vitality of the lines, but fail to discover their more *profound secrets*' (1985: 13, original emphasis) strikingly echoes Leavis' emphasis on close reading as a way of resisting the seductive temptations and 'mindless' pleasures of reading. Leavis conceptualised close reading as involving 'the closest and fullest working attention, the most acutely perceptive, the most delicately discriminating responsiveness' (1969: 90). Study of Shakespeare conceived thus is a matter of getting at the buried meaning of words.

Such an approach to Shakespeare is similarly manifest in L.C. Knights' appeal to readers to remind themselves that the plays' 'end is to communicate a rich and controlled experience by means of words – words used in a way to which, without some training, we are no longer accustomed to respond' (in Hudson 1954: 4). Similarly, Wilson Knight refers in his work to the plays as extended metaphors and characters as symbols to be identified through sustained reading. For A.C. Bradley, meaning could be unlocked, at least in Shakespeare's tragedies, by the identification and recognition of a character's tragic flaw. In paraphrasing such writing, Adams' statements are indisputably reflective of the tenacious grip of early-twentieth-century criticism on the teaching profession of the mid-1980s, and, to some extent, beyond. These critical influences have proved enduring in schools. For instance, in the 1980s John Salway writes about his empirical observation of Wilson Knight's continued presence in the *Shakespeare and Schools* magazine, decades after the latter's most influential works were first published (1986: 8). More recently, Joseph Francis, describing his teaching practice at Eton in the twenty-first century, rejects critical theory approaches to Shakespeare in favour of devoting time to close reading (2003: 92). Writing in 2009, John Haddon asserts, in *Teaching Reading Shakespeare,* that studying the plays involves 'a *discovery* of language which simply says more, which suddenly engages with, articulates or brings into existence our sense of something' (2009: 180–181, my emphasis): a statement which, yet again, presents a mystical account of studying Shakespeare as revealing hidden meanings behind the words.

The endurance of literary critical approaches as pedagogies to be deployed with older children (fourteen- to sixteen-year-olds) preparing for coursework or examinations is reinforced in examinations and coursework questions that demand that students respond to questions on character or Shakespeare's use of literary and linguistic techniques, with *close* textual reference (see DCSF 2008: 33). Its influence is also apparent in Curriculum 2000's demand that A-level students should be acquainted with and be able to deploy multiple interpretations of texts by other (implicitly scholarly) readers: 'Candidates should be able to articulate independent opinions and judgments, informed by different interpretations of literary texts by other readers' (Assessment Objective 4, McEvoy 2003: 99).

In more junior classrooms, literary critical approaches have tended to place an emphasis on (what are constructed as) the inherent and intrinsic properties of the plays: especially language, plot and character. Literary critical approaches suggested in *Shakespeare for All Ages and Stages* involve, for instance, drawing up a continuum of Shakespeare villains from the 'complex' and 'flawed' to 'likeable rogues' (DCSF 2008: 34). Such exercises can be considered as practice for later, more extended, writing in the form of answers to traditional literary critical essay questions. They also demonstrate a continued resort to essentialist notions of characters as real individuals with a psychological integrity, prominent in previous decades. This is evident in activities such as 'with your partner, discuss how Macbeth felt when the dagger was tempting him' and 'pick out three lines that Macbeth says during [Act 3 Scene 1]. For each one decide what he is really thinking' (O'Connor 2004: 248, 249). The key supernatural force in this suggested treatment of the play is not the witches or a vengeful victim but A.C. Bradley's ghost.

Literary critical approaches still dominate editions aimed at the school market, that generally include explorations of genre, character and language – rhythm, rhyme and imagery, for instance; and examples of the editor's or other critics' close reading of the play in an introduction or critical essays. This introduction is often broken down into sections dealing with the themes of the play as evidenced by the close reading of key quotations or scenes. Recently (re)issued editions of *Hamlet,* for example, deal with the following topics: 'delay and revenge', 'God and man', 'the individual and the state' (Spencer 2005) as well as 'Hamlet's questions' and 'conscience and revolution' (Bate and Rasmussen 2008). Editions such as T.J.B. Spencer's Penguin *Hamlet,* first published in 1980, contribute to the continuing prevalence of old literary critical pedagogies in schools by reprinting old scholarship reflecting past critical trends (even if they add a revised 'further reading' list). My own year twelve Shakespeare edition, the New Swan Shakespeare Advanced Series *Hamlet*, was first published in 1968 and had reached its thirtieth impression when I bought it in 1999 (Lott 1999). Ironically, given its age, its introduction, by C.S. Lewis, opens with a sub-section entitled 'The significance of Hamlet today' (Lott 1999: ix). It is indicative of the role of school editions in maintaining these textual approaches to the plays that the suggested further reading includes Bradley's *Shakespearean Tragedy* (1904), G. Wilson Knight's *Wheel of Fire* (1930) and W. Raleigh's *Shakespeare* (1907). The most recent work listed is Hilda M. Hulme's 1963 *Explorations in Shakespeare's Language*. Many of these works still appear on the bibliography of the recent RSC *Hamlet* edition: although here they are juxtaposed with recent criticism by Stephen Greenblatt and Fintan O'Toole. Thus the older material in this edition is at least contextualised for readers as 'classic' or historically 'great' literary criticism. These editions' enduring presence in classes exemplifies the longevity of older literary-criticism, which survives after newer books, with newer interpretations and activities, have entered the educational publishing market (Olive 2006).

The use of traditional literary critical pedagogies currently exists alongside alternative methods, largely manifested from the 1950s onwards. Part of forging these newer approaches has involved a critique of their predecessors – especially their underlying values. Teaching Shakespeare through literary criticism has been condemned by some educators as a remnant of philological and linguistic approaches to texts, carried over from classics departments. Writing in the 1950s, Hudson decries the

> attempt to carry over into the study of English literature the methods which were traditionally thought to be appropriate to the study of classical texts. The *Iliad* was held to be great literature and therefore to demand word by word treatment [...] Shakespeare, so the argument ran, is great literature and therefore the method which does justice to the *Iliad* must also be appropriate to a Shakespearean play.
>
> (1954: 11)

In addition to this criticism of close-reading techniques as ignoring the specifically dramatic form of Shakespeare's plays, Hudson also singles out for censure the way in which much literary criticism of his time, and earlier, treats Shakespeare's plays 'as dramatic poems rather than human documents' (1954: 4). This statement displays his own assumptions around the differences of the two genres – for example, that poems are not 'human documents' and, by implication, that drama is a realistic documentation of human experience.

Apart from the tendency to elide the dramatic nature of some texts, a further weakness of literary critical approaches has been identified as the potential for students to succeed in the subject by uncritically receiving and recycling their understanding of the plays from teachers and existing literary criticism. The 'construe method', where a teacher leads a class through a word by word translation, glossing or interpretation of a passage, is criticised for producing 'passive understanding' (Hudson 1954: 10). Similar criticisms of traditional pedagogies have been expressed in recent years by Jon Davison:

> the learner is passive – the individual is neither empowered nor invited to engage in the construction of knowledge, nor to debate it. The individual simply learns to conform to a defined set of rules; to regurgitate a predetermined set of attitudes about a prescribed body of texts; to appreciate rather than to critique; and to acquire rather than to actively generate knowledge.
>
> (2000: 251)

Furthermore, left-wing critics, such as Sinfield, have argued that students' literary critical interpretations are also limited to a 'prescribed range of possibilities': that they are encouraged to arrive at a set of fixed, mystified meanings through the mechanisms of examination and assessment (1985: 139).

If one criticism of literary critical pedagogies is that students' critical thinking on a play is too much filtered through the influence of teachers, examination boards and so on, another is that the approach effaces the very mechanisms or 'learnt procedures' through which it operates. Detractors of literary critical pedagogy posit that the conclusions that it aids students towards are frequently presented as the result of unmediated, 'automatic' and 'objective' interaction between the critic and the text. That is to say, as the critic standing impartially 'outside the text', rather than as a social practice where experience of Shakespeare is filtered through schools, teachers and editions (Kennedy Sauer and Tribble 1999: 35, 44). Again, it is overly simplistic to see this as an inherent flaw of the approach itself – literary criticism has, for the last half-century, been increasingly concerned with reflexivity and the influence of readers' subjectivities. This is manifested, for example, by reader-response theory. Nonetheless, beyond setting questions on female or non-white characters for assessment, little recognition or discussion of the radical possibilities for criticism, offered by revolutions in critical theory from the 1950s onwards, from semiotics to post-colonialism, can be traced in governments' conceptions of pedagogies for Shakespeare at school level.

However, such criticisms can be explained, to some extent, as a limitation of the implementation of the approach in schools rather than as an intrinsic feature of literary criticism, given Leavis' ideal of the fully engaged student and AO4's exhortation that their criticism should be 'independent' (McEvoy 2003: 99). Russ McDonald, Nicholas Nace and Travis Williams' *Shakespeare Up Close* demonstrates a conceptualisation of close reading for undergraduate students that goes beyond the almost-caricatured idea of close reading criticised above. In this collection, close reading is still bound up with the 'mental pleasures' to be derived from returning to and 'scrutinising' passages from *Early Modern Texts* as 'legible objects' in a way that invokes Richards and Leavis (2012: xxvi, xxxiii). Yet, the editors' attempts to define close reading also reveal it to be a more heterogeneous practice than is often acknowledged. They recognise that it is variously figured as an instrument for an author to reach a grand 'analytical conclusion' (McDonald et al. 2012: xxiii) and as an end in itself; limited to the study of letters, sounds, words and patterns (xix) and expanded to encompass an awareness of historical context (xxvii). Close reading, as it is often depicted at school level, therefore arguably represents a rather reductive, inflexible and out-moded reality of a more exciting and malleable ideal.

In terms of the pedagogic literature in teaching journals, the embrace of new theories and practices differs depending on editorial policy and identity. While journals such as *English in Education* (affiliated with NATE) have explored multimodal texts and text-world theory in recent issues (Dymoke 2010), *The Use of English* continues to accept traditional literary critical essays on, for example, Bradley's *Shakespearean Tragedy* (Douglas-Fairhurst 2006: 126–137), or exemplar close readings that are close successors to Leavis. This is in spite of AO4's demand that students' work should demonstrate awareness of a range of external interpretations of the plays – presumably not confined to those emanating from the first half of the twentieth century.

The influence of new historicist and cultural materialist theories can be seen in the expansion of contextual pedagogies for teaching Shakespeare. These are becoming increasingly widespread, even required by statute, as I demonstrate in a later section of this chapter. Many of the above criticisms of literary critical pedagogies originate from the exponents of these critical theories, who place an epistemological emphasis on knowing Shakespeare through his historical context (for example, early modern theatre practice) rather than a direct communion between the author's writing and reader. A different strand of criticism, rooted in progressive education, takes issue with the impact of literary critical approaches on students' capacity to achieve personal growth through the study of Shakespeare. Rex Gibson was most vocal in critiquing the dominance of literary criticism in schools, claiming that it 'is part of a tradition that is deeply suspicious of enjoyment, that it finds it hard to accept that pleasure and learning can go hand in hand. It sees literature as "serious" and "work", and drama as merely "play"' (1998: 7). This criticism prepared the ground for Gibson's own pioneering work on active methods for school Shakespeare that took students' enjoyment of Shakespeare as a prerequisite for successful learning of the plays.

Active Methods

'Active methods' is a pedagogy popularised by Rex Gibson, through his leadership of the Cambridge School Shakespeare project, to describe approaches to Shakespeare that avoid older models of a seated, whole class read-through of the plays. Active-methods pedagogy is distinct from the carefully delimited requirements for drama in the curriculum discussed earlier (which exist in that document as a set of mandated skills foregrounded over any theoretical or philosophical context). However, their techniques do overlap and Cox was inspired to include drama in the curriculum by Gibson's project. As Gibson himself indicates, 'active methods' is an umbrella term under which categories such as 'practical work' and 'dramatic work', with their slightly more specialised denotations, also fall (Stredder 2007: xv). For the sake of simplicity and clarity, I will use Gibson's term, as defined below, throughout this chapter:

> Active methods comprise a wide range of expressive, creative and physical activities. They recognise that Shakespeare wrote his plays for performance, and that his scripts are completed by enactment of some kind. This dramatic context demands classroom practices that are the antithesis of methods in which students sit passively, without intellectual or emotional engagement.
>
> (Stredder 2007: xii)

Immediately, Gibson's definition of active methods establishes it as a critique of, and in tension with, the literary critical pedagogies for Shakespeare discussed above. It places the emphasis on Shakespeare as a process rather than a product – multiple, dynamic and constructed rather than single, unified and received. Performance, active-methods proponents argue, is 'a graphic device for confronting students with moment-to-moment choices, so that students escape the reductive overview mode of interpreting' (Kennedy Sauer and Tribble 1999: 44). The pedagogy figures Shakespeare's work as something that individuals can 'possess' and enjoy, but which is also ideally collaborative (Gibson 1990: 3; 1998: 17; Reynolds 1991: 4). Manifest in active methods publications aimed at teachers, this argument derives strength from the growth of performance criticism in Shakespeare studies by reconceptualising performance as an act of critical interpretation. This was characterised by H.R. Coursen's claim, in 1992, that 'a Shakespearean script exists only in performance. Period' (1992: 15) and further embodied, a few years later, this time beyond the academic monograph, by Al Pacino's 1996 documentary *Looking for Richard*.

Gibson also connects the collective nature of the approach to its purported Shakespearean authenticity. He likens active methods to

> Shakespeare's own working conditions as he and his colleagues at the Globe rehearsed together to produce a performance [...] Like actors in rehearsal, students work together on the script helping each other to understand a scene and to find dramatically effective ways of presenting it.
>
> (1998: 12)

Gibson forms an analogy between active methods and a vision of Shakespeare's working practices – presumably based on his knowledge of early modern theatre practices in general – given the paucity of Shakespeare-specific evidence. For Stredder, active methods also derive value from claims that such collaboration is still current in modern theatre practice: 'working in this way is similar to the way that actors and theatre practitioners work in education' (2007: xii). For Adams, the value of active methods is more generic, offering a much-needed connection to the realm of theatre: he describes one of two main barriers to students' understanding and enjoyment of Shakespeare as 'a lack of familiarity with the medium in which he worked' (1985: 1).

A characteristic of the approach related to its supposed theatrical authenticity is that active methods figures Shakespeare as script rather than text, drama rather than literature, multimodal rather than 'purely verbal icon' (Kennedy Sauer and Tribble 1999: 35). Gibson argues that 'Shakespeare was essentially a man of the theatre who intended his words to be spoken and acted out on stage. It is in that context of dramatic realisation that the plays are most appropriately understood and experienced' (1998: xii). For Gibson, valuing, and correspondingly treating, Shakespeare's plays as scripts is part of his wider aim to reclaim them as a dramatic, rather than literary, form and to 'rescue' them for school students from 'the procedures and apparatus of university scholarship' that he views as inappropriate for younger learners (1998: 8). This attitude was translated under New Labour almost directly into government documents such as *Shakespeare for All Ages and Stages*, which advises teachers 'to understand that the text is a script which is brought to life in performance' (DCSF 2008: 9).

Influenced by the rise in status of school drama and the theatre world, the value of the playwright's work as a series of scripts is also connected, by Gibson, to his value for Shakespeares plural, over Shakespeare singular. He argues that treating Shakespeare as a script suggests an uncertainty, 'provisionality and incompleteness' – rather than the 'authority, reverence and certainty' that accompany treatments of Shakespeare as text – which invites multiple and varied enactments and interpretations (1998: 7). Consequently, for Gibson, valuing Shakespeare in this way enables students to turn away from traditional ideas 'that studying Shakespeare involves the pursuit of a "right answer"' (1998: 7) – exploring instead 'the vast range of possibilities for meaning' (Reynolds 1991: 8).

Gibson was demonstrably aware of developments in literary criticism, from the post-modernist embrace of plurality to critical theory's determination to reveal the social constructedness of 'great' works and 'right' answers, which have produced critical titles such as *Alternative Shakespeares* and *Philosophical Shakespeares*. He featured reviews of key works in the *Shakespeare and Schools* newsletter. That he chose to ignore these developments in writing about the negative effects of literary critical exercises on students' experience of Shakespeare suggests that, to some extent, his criticisms are selective. They are aimed at the prevalent use of older literary critical pedagogies in schools: approaches that he declares 'unsuited' to the school classroom (1998: 8).

In active methods, there is an emphasis on both intellect and emotion, as well as an impetus to render Shakespeare approachable and accessible rather than a remote literary monument. Its exponents argue that active methods are most likely to enable students to 'stake a claim to the text that is personal, and not simply that of their teacher' (Reynolds 1991: 9) or to 'enjoy the sense of power and control that comes from animating words that, on the printed page, had seemed flat and remote' (1991: 7). These quotations from Reynolds illustrate the way in which active methods has harnessed a discourse of empowerment and ownership around its methods and their outcomes. In chapter three I will demonstrate how this has been adopted by the RSC in marketing its education department.

Feelings of enjoyment, which students are said to experience through an active methods approach to Shakespeare, are foregrounded not only as an end in themselves, but also as a means to learning. Rebutting Leavis' belief that to be seduced by a text divorces the body and mind, compromising 'the supremacy of consciousness' (Day 1996: xiv), Gibson argues that enjoyment 'goes hand in hand with insight and understanding' (1990: 1; 1998: 25). The value of Shakespeare as an enjoyable experience was proliferated under New Labour in policy documents such as *Shakespeare for All Ages and Stages*, with its dual focus on the instrumental value of skills and the supposedly intrinsic 'pleasure' of experiencing Shakespeare's work (DCSF 2008: 1, 5). The very existence of such documents, however, seems simultaneously to undercut claims that Shakespeare's work is innately and immediately rewarding: their publication suggests that unmediated experience of the plays (if such a thing is possible) rarely results in enjoyment.

The spread of active methods can be largely attributed to the galvanising efforts of Gibson, who provided formidable impetus to, and became a point of nexus for, the pedagogy. This is not to say that other exponents of similar methods did not precede him, or were not practising at the same time. What makes Gibson worthy of unparalleled attention is his achievement in disseminating his ideas through publications, large and small, monumental monographs and regular magazines – as well as a phenomenal network – all backed by, or emanating from, a Leverhulme-funded research project. This is a model that the RSC has since successfully emulated through its Learning and Performance Network, publishing ventures with Macmillan and research collaborations with the University of Warwick. Indeed, the RSC and organisations such as Shakespeare Schools Festival now received government funding for related projects (see the afterword). Many current advocates of and writers on active methods were teachers trained by Gibson through the summer schools that colleagues on his project ran at the Shakespeare Institute, in Stratford-on-Avon. Others, including Peter Thomas, Jane Coles and Ros King, contributed first publications to the *Shakespeare and Schools* 'newsletter' or edited a play for the Cambridge School Shakespeare series before developing successful academic careers and publication records. Susan Leach wrote about workshops for the Cambridge School Shakespeare project in 1992, the same year that she published *Shakespeare in the Classroom: What's the Matter?* Perry Mills, working at the King Edward VI School in Stratford, has applied Gibson's methods to his teaching of non-Shakespearean early modern drama through performance.

Gibson's work on active methods for teaching Shakespeare is a prime example of action or participant research, in that data were collected through interaction with teachers in order that the research would offer a point of intervention for improvement in their practice. Furthermore, it had an emancipatory research agenda: to empower teachers with the knowledge and skills to tackle Shakespeare in their classes without fear of ignorance or inability. It is also important to note that the research was promoted on local, regional and national levels – at a then unprecedented scale for qualitative, empirical research on Shakespeare in education. This attention to the desires and needs of teachers country-wide, its immediacy in engaging with teachers and encouraging bonding between them, constitutes one of the reasons why active-methods pedagogies have achieved such a pronounced take-up in schools and beyond.

The power of Gibson to mobilise his colleagues and teachers towards a pedagogy en masse resembles his fellow Cantabrian Leavis' successful endeavour to shape the nature and methods of English teaching. Beyond his work with teachers, the expansion of active methods was secured by the way in which Gibson pulled together influential people from theatres, heritage organisations and higher education. The *Shakespeare and Schools* newsletter features lengthy interviews with heads of theatre-education departments as well as senior figures in the International Shakespeare Globe Centre, the Shakespeare Birthplace Trust and Folger Shakespeare Library. Directors, arts practitioners and actors were also interviewed. This network of exponents, many nurtured through and all united at some stage under the Cambridge Shakespeare and Schools project, goes much of the way to explaining the strength, success and endurance of active methods as a pedagogy for teaching Shakespeare. For example, Reynolds writes of the importance of rekindling 'the enthusiasm of teachers for teaching Shakespeare' (1991: 4), while Stredder addresses the issue of maintaining teacher autonomy in the face of a National Curriculum (2007: xvi), and Gilmour insists on the importance of in-service education and training for teachers (INSET) (1997: 2) – all issues important to and addressed by Gibson. Since his death in 2005, his lobbying activities have been continued by such followers as well as organisations such as the RSC.

Thus, teaching Shakespeare through active-methods pedagogy, as defined by Gibson, has become significantly established in pedagogic literature and, as shown earlier, drama methods are a required element of the English curriculum. Indeed, the active methods at the centre of Gibson's project were embraced at the inception of the National Curriculum in the *Cox Report*:

The project has demonstrated that the once traditional method where desk-bound pupils read the text has been advantageously replaced by exciting, enjoyable approaches that are social, imaginative and physical. This can also be achieved by: use of film and video recordings, visits to live theatre performances, participation in songs and dances, dramatic improvisations, activities in which Shakespeare's language is used by pupils interacting with each other. Pupils exposed to this type of participatory, exploratory approach to literature can acquire a firm foundation to proceed to more formal literary responses should they subsequently choose to do so.

(1991: 83)

This paragraph gives some idea of the particular strategies active methods might involve. Additionally, it conveys a sense of the value of Shakespeare as a body of work to enjoy – an element at the centre of Cox's personal vision for the curriculum. However it does also suggest, contrary to most exponents of active methods – including James Stredder, who writes strongly in support of continuing with the use of active-methods pedagogy in higher education settings – that it is a preliminary approach to Shakespeare; and that it is to be superseded, as students mature, with textual approaches. This attitude has been occasionally reflected in the writing of some of the most vocal advocates of active methods. Others figure it as one tool best used alongside others. Peter Reynolds, for example, writes that the practical approach to Shakespeare is not 'intended to be a replacement for more formal "desk-bound" modes of study. It is an additional input' (1991: 5). He exemplifies pedagogues who take a relativist, or at least pluralist, approach to teaching methods for Shakespeare.

Notwithstanding the limitations that Reynolds, Cox and traditionally dominant, literary critical approaches place on drama-based pedagogies, teaching Shakespeare through active methods has become increasingly well established in pedagogic literature and education policy since Gibson's Cambridge School Shakespeare project. The instrumental value of Shakespeare is often highlighted in this pedagogy in terms of its capacity to build students' team work and expressive abilities: 'Drama is skills-based', writes James Stredder (2007: xvi). This element of the pedagogy made it popular with the Labour governments of Blair and Brown (1997–2007 and 2007–2010). These governments simultaneously emphasised tangible, transferable skills as a means of creating employable citizens and a stronger economy while embracing the arts as a way to achieve this end. Recognition of Shakespeare's plays as belonging to the medium of theatre is evident in government documents from the period, such as *Shakespeare for All Ages and Stages*. This National Strategy advises teachers 'to understand that the text is a script which is brought to life in performance' (DCSF 2008: 9), to enable children to work with 'actors and arts educators', to experience 'some learning outside of the classroom' and to see 'a professional production' at key stages two and three (DCSF 2008: 8). It also contains appendices on 'Working with a theatre practitioner in schools' produced by the Globe and 'Preparing pupils for a theatre visit' by the RSC (DCSF 2008: 40–44). The theatre sector has been endorsed, and frequently funded, by recent Labour governments in an attempt to convey the progressive nature of their educational ideals and credentials (although chapter two has suggested that the tangible – if not ideological – difference between the governments' education policies was limited). This contrasts with the hostility experienced by the arts sector during Thatcher's premiership, mentioned in chapter one, although the recommendations above remain non-statutory.

In terms of available resources for teachers, the pedagogy has spread from the occasional monograph in the early twentieth-century (Caldwell Cook's 1917 *The Play Way*, Hudson's 1954 *Shakespeare and the Classroom*) to dominate the output of books and resources on teaching Shakespeare. These include, during the past twenty years, Gibson's *Teaching Shakespeare, Secondary School Shakespeare*, and the Cambridge School Shakespeare editions, Peter Reynolds' *Practical Approaches to Teaching Shakespeare*,

Maurice Gilmour's two *Shakespeare for All* volumes, the *RSC Shakespeare Toolkit for Teachers* and James Stredder's *The North Face of Shakespeare*. Milla Cozart Riggio's *Teaching Shakespeare Through Performance*, a collection of essays aimed more squarely at the higher education sector, was published within a year of Gibson's *Teaching Shakespeare*. In addition there are the twenty-four issues of the *Shakespeare and Schools* magazine, which ran for eight years from the start of his research project. Teaching journals such as *English in Education* continue to publish articles on active-methods approaches to Shakespeare (and other authors) suggesting its enduring impact. Active methods have also impacted on the content and layout of some editions of the plays aimed at school students. The Cambridge School Shakespeare series, which is currently being revised – suggesting a continued demand for it as a resource – incorporates practical classroom activities on a page opposite the play text, as does the New Longman Shakespeare (Gibson 1993; O'Connor 2004). RSC and Globe education programmes for teachers and students also seek to meet the demand for active approaches to the plays that can be adapted to the classroom and that meet curriculum requirements. I will expand on this in chapter three.

Active-methods pedagogy draws strongly on traditions from the theatre and drama as well as progressive educational theory. Less acknowledged by active methods exponents are the ways in which it makes use of the tenets of literary criticism, whose dominance it seeks to challenge – as I will demonstrate below. In championing the contribution of the theatre world to Shakespeare in schools, most writing on active methods invokes a debt to theatre practitioners such as Charles Marowitz, Cicely Berry, Augusto Boal and Keith Johnstone. While drawing on key figures, techniques and language from theatre and drama, proponents of active methods, such as Gibson and Stredder, carefully address teachers' concerns about the objective of theatres being to produce a full-scale production: they stress instead that the techniques can be fruitfully applied to individual scenes, even lines. Further, they acknowledge that most English teachers are not trained theatre practitioners. While foremost emphasising the accessibility of their approach (to teachers and students of all experience levels, abilities and backgrounds), they also urge teachers to participate in training offered by theatre companies, to take their classes to see a live production or to take advantage of Theatre-in-Education visits to schools.

The influence of progressivism is particularly evident in the derision of 'force-feeding', 'teacher-centred' and 'desk-bound' learning, terms which can be found throughout the active methods literature. The authors of active methods favour the language and tenets of 'child-' or 'learner-centred' approaches – with the implied 'shift from school and adult values to those held by pupils' and from 'traditional disciplines [...] to everyday experience' (Adams 1985: 6–7); 'child development', in a sense that treats creativity and emotional intelligence on a par with academic excellence; and shared learning, with the teacher as 'facilitator' (Stredder 2007: xi, xvi, 4, 7). Although Gibson's work has been accused of conservatism – a criticism that I will elucidate in the following section – he also exposes more progressive influences in his critical writing. He frequently quotes the philosopher and educationalist Rudolf Steiner, in addition to more subtly appropriating his discourse. Examples of this include Gibson asking Steiner's 'abiding question', 'How do we know that an education that makes us weep for Cordelia also makes us hear the cry in the street?' (1990: 8) and repeating his pronouncement that 'If the child is left empty of texts, in the fullest sense of that term, he will suffer an early death of the heart and of the imagination' (Steiner 1989: 191, in Gibson 1990: 8). In using these quotations Gibson is asking to be identified with a movement that demands socially just education as well as attention to children's moral, emotional and creative growth on an equal, if not greater level, than the acquisition of skills and knowledge. In doing so, he defines the value of Shakespeare as the value of his works experienced through progressivism.

Several active-methods authors write of the impact literary criticism has had on developing their pedagogies. This suggests the pervasive influence of such theory, even when trying to revolutionise practice. For instance, James Stredder declares that his book 'aims to demonstrate the continuity of practice with theory, its dependency on theory, even' (2007: xiv). Although he rejects the sedentary nature of Richards' and Leavis' *Practical Criticism*, Stredder acknowledges that his practical work shares their ethos of 'highly engaged and alert critical analysis' (2007: xv). Indeed, Stredder argues that before teaching the plays 'one must first read them critically' (2007: xiii). Gibson's writing also explicitly encourages teachers to read some of the corpus of radical critical theory, which 'makes lively reading and yields a host of ideas' (*Shakespeare and Schools* 1994: 5). In accordance with this, the *Shakespeare and Schools* magazine featured excerpts from overwhelmingly left-wing literary criticism by Terry Eagleton, Terry Hawkes, Graham Holderness, Alan Sinfield, Lawrence Levine and Germaine Greer. Put into the service of active methods to provide it with a theoretical underpinning, these authors' critical tenets are perceived by Gibson and Stredder to add value to Shakespeare in education, whereas these same authors criticised its potential to detract from the study of his plays when used alone in teacher-led pedagogy.

Thus writing on active methods is strategically inflected with discourses from other disciplines and institutions, including literary criticism. Moreover, its authors share a common vocabulary, including phrases such as 'rehearsal room technique' and referring to students' 'self-expression'. This shared and spreading discourse, which implodes the boundaries between active methods in schools, other disciplines and institutions, is an indication of the way in which active methods has ceased to be a mere pedagogy. Among its adherents, it has instead become an epistemology for Shakespeare.

Criticisms of active methods have focused largely on the treatment of character by many of its exponents, specifically the accusation that it has been carried over from older literary critical traditions. There is a demonstrable tendency, in suggestions for activities belonging to the pedagogy, to view 'characters as individuals giving expression to all human experience rather than as representatives of particular social groupings or ideologies' (Doyle and Longhurst 1985: 55), or as psychologically coherent 'real people' rather than expressions of a creative writing process (which might draw on type and symbolism). This is evident among the classroom activities in the Cambridge School Shakespeare editions: 'What's Macbeth like? (in pairs) Macbeth has not yet appeared, but already he has been much talked of. From your reading of this scene [1.2], brainstorm a list of the qualities that you think Macbeth possesses' (Gibson 1993: 6). It could be argued that, at its worst, active methods merely replaces early-twentieth-century written character analyses with the equivalent in actions and the spoken word.

In addition, new historicists and cultural materialists have criticised the way in which active methods stress the universality of Shakespeare, including his characters – apparently placing the author and the student 'outside history, society and politics' (Thompson 1990: 142). Yet Gibson, alongside pronouncing Shakespeare's work to be universal, argues strongly for incorporating a contextual angle into active-methods teaching. Displaying no sense of competition or incompatibility between the pedagogies, he writes that 'wherever possible, exploration, discussion and analysis of the history and value underlying or embodied in any interpretation' should be explored (1990: 5). In addition to his emphasis on the social nature of teaching and learning the plays, Gibson encourages teachers to impart the social context of their production: 'Acknowledge social as well as psychological aspects of the plays. Remember the characters inhabit *social* worlds. Encourage your students to discuss the society, history, ideologies of those social worlds – and of their own' (1990: 9). Gibson may then be more securely indicted for his catholic, even contradictory, values than for ignoring advances in critical theory.

The progressive values that active methods draws on were scorned in *The Black Papers* of the 1960–1970s – although, significantly, their co-author, C.B. Cox, later embraced and endorsed progressivism in writing the National Curriculum for English, only to face resistance from the Thatcher government (see chapter one). More than a decade later, such resistance to ideology is echoed in David Hornbrook's chapter in *The Shakespeare Myth* where he argues that progressivism damages working-class children's chances of gaining cultural capital through their schooling. Progressive values and pedagogies continue to be problematised today. For instance, beyond Shakespeare and looking at English education as a whole, Frank Furedi's *Wasted* and Gove's 2009 Conservative party conference speech both attributed 'failures' in the nation's educational achievement to a lack of authority and discipline in schools, which is, in turn, attributed to the (as they see it) misguided influence of progressivism. In the latter, Gove praised as a 'hero' the new headteacher of a once-failing, now thriving, school, for running his school with discipline – including a uniform; for implementing subject streaming by ability; and for emphasising the traditional subject boundedness (Gove 2009). Such constructions – which confuse progressivism with anarchism, management with pedagogy and surface change with reform – constitute one of the key challenges to active methods becoming the dominant Shakespeare pedagogy for students of all ages and stages.

Jane Coles has critiqued active methods from a teacher's perspective, arguing that it unfairly constructs academics and actors as experts on classroom pedagogy over those who work on a daily basis with school students (2009: 34). Yet more problematic for teachers, she contends, is that the impact of these 'experts' on students' learning is mystified as an 'unlocking' of Shakespeare: accounts of their interventions assert *that* their techniques make an impact rather than showing *how* they do so (at a cognitive level, for instance) (2009: 34). From another perspective, she argues that it has been impossible to reconcile active methods for Shakespeare with the written SATs. She demonstrates the way in which teachers may resort to more transmission-style teaching approaches at the end of their period of study on a play, providing students with a sense of discontinuity and disjunction, where higher value is ultimately placed on knowing facts about the play and skills for writing-exam responses. While she usefully exposes a gap between teacher ideology and practice in preparing for SATs, Coles' criticisms are weakened by the slippage in her writing between criticism of the value of examining Shakespeare and the value of active-methods teaching of his plays; between the possible 'bad' practice of active methods by one particular teacher and an inherent flaw in the pedagogy. In spite of these limitations, Coles' article is empirically evidenced and relatively objective. Other pieces on the subject indicate that it is difficult to assemble a body of criticism of active methods that does not sound right-wing or old-fashioned: as does Richard Wilson's labelling of the pedagogy as 'sugar-coated Shakespeare' (1997: 63) and the accusation that 'this is Shakespeare by overkill' (Blocksidge 2003: 15). After all, it is difficult to argue against the practice of making Shakespeare enjoyable, diverse and inclusive.

Some of the criticisms above thus pertain to the fit (or lack thereof) between active methods and the school system, rather than treating the pedagogy as inherently flawed. For example, the boundedness of subjects under the National Curriculum poses potential difficulties for a pedagogy that seeks to utilise the objectives and methods of drama within the subject of English (whose objectives are clearly delineated in the National Curriculum). There is also a widely perceived incompatibility between active methods and the assessment of Shakespeare in the curriculum, for example the emphasis in the curriculum on producing written work. It is a supposed limitation of the method (or for its advocates, of the education system) that has an historic dimension: for Hudson, the struggle between active methods and assessment was to have Shakespeare's plays valued as works of drama. As such, his campaign involved petitioning for a new style of examination question that assessed pupils' 'impression of the whole play as a play, not as a series of texts' and their 'idea of what the dramatist is trying to do' (1954: 10). Gibson, working forty years later, campaigned for assessment to recognise the value of Shakespeare as a dynamic entity, involving social and collaborative interaction. For him active methods could flourish in schools if assessment took note of the student's process of producing a piece of work, rather than merely the end product (using coursework involving continuous assessment, such as journals). He also argues that multiple Shakespeares and the diverse ways in which students possess or 'grasp' Shakespeare could be preserved by offering a choice of assessment tasks and by embracing the aim of 'informed personal response'. Furthermore, he posits that the prevailing examination system could offer further scope to embrace, rather than inhibit, these values by including more 'experimental approaches' (1990: 7). In doing so, Gibson seeks to influence, rather than be influenced by, the values of powerful examination boards. The way in which the RSC education department has continued lobbying the government to change its assessment polices is shown in chapter three. Finally, the abandonment, by the Brown government, of SATs testing at key stage three weakened challenges to active methods based on its incompatibility with assessment practices in schools. Effectively, a potential criticism of active methods has been rearticulated by its exponents as a criticism of the school system. Despite challenging the state on its provision of education, the very fact that active methods strives to achieve endorsement within systems of formal education renders the pedagogy open to criticism from more radically progressive educators. This includes those working in the tradition of A.S. Neill, the founder of the Summerhill school, and Ivan Illich, author of *Deschooling Society*. Neill fought against the notion that pleasure and play should be the means to the end of a great educational project devised by adults and applied homogenously to all children. Writing of Caldwell Cook's *The Play Way*, for example, he criticised the 'notion that unless a child is learning something the child is wasting his time is nothing less than a curse' (1970: 40). He also argued vehemently that 'great' literature and classical music does not interest young students. As such, he unusually contended, it is not a relevant or necessary part of education, nor does it contribute to emotional growth or to life after school (1970: 10). Under Neill's leadership of Summerhill, Shakespeare was only acted in adaptation (1970: 71). Even more radical than Neill, who was prepared to school children who attended lessons voluntarily, Illich rejected the notion that the most valuable learning always occurs in schools and that children need an education system designed by adults to direct their learning. Instead, he posits a system where children identify their interests and are paired up with an 'instructor' who can teach them the requisite skills and knowledges with which to pursue them (1970: 1–24).

For educators such as Neill and Illich, active methods could be seen as cultivating the pretence of progressivism that instead simply masks adult desires for children's acquaintance with Shakespeare. Furthermore, the determination of active-methods proponents to persuade students into appreciating Shakespeare's writing constitutes an intention that is anathemat for those who believe in non-interference in and non-pressure on the growth of a child, including his or her literary tastes. Their influence is clear in Coles' argument, regarding Shakespeare in education, that 'affording "access" to a reified text becomes [active methods'] prime objective'; moreover, that as a consequence the 'playtext, rather than the student, remains central to the enterprise throughout' (2009: 35). For these critics, active methods do not address fundamental questions of what education should be, or what its purpose is, in sufficient depth to merit the labels 'progressive' or 'radical'.

The above criticisms are united in their accusation, overt or otherwise, that active methods needs to reflect more deeply on its complicity in upholding Conservative educational ideas. Going some way to contradicting this indictment, the pedagogy shows some self-reflexivity in its examination of the practical limitations that constrain its take-up in the classroom. For instance, Gibson (1990: 8), Wheale (1991: 10) and Stredder (2007: xiv, xiii) all acknowledge that the pedagogy may demand more space, time and expense than other approaches to Shakespeare. However, they simultaneously vindicate their own reservations by demonstrating the adaptability of the approach to constraining conditions. Furthermore, they use the debate as an opportunity to fight for change within the education system, thereby demonstrating the active and emancipatory nature of their work. It is this unity, in terms of the core values, influences and discourse of its proponents, as well as their correspondence with currently prevailing forces in education more widely, such as progressive educational theories and a vocal arts sector, that renders active methods dominant in pedagogic literature on Shakespeare. The pedagogy continues to attract special and launch issues of teaching journals such as *English in Education* (45.1) and *Teaching English* (spring 2013), which featured the related Open Space Learning model of Shakespeare as used to teach students at the University of Warwick.

Contextual Approaches

Another alternative to traditional literary critical methods for teaching Shakespeare, which gathered strength in schools around the millennium, is offered by a group of closely-related concerns and techniques. These include cultural materialism, new historicism and critical literacy. All three place an emphasis on context. Cultural materialism insists on 'texts as inseparable from the conditions of their production and reception in history; and as involved in the making of cultural meanings which are always, finally, political meanings' (Dollimore and Sinfield 1988: ix). New historicism foregrounds the 'textuality of history and the historicity of texts' (Montrose 1989: 20). Critical literacy is concerned with the relationships between texts, but also with texts' relationships to language, power and society. A core tenet of critical literacy is that no text is neutral, and, therefore, that reading texts necessarily involves an examination of the assumptions that underpin them and their place in a culture. I will consider them together here under the umbrella term 'contextual approaches', since they share a common concern with the relationship of Shakespeare's texts to material culture, early modern or contemporary, and their core tenets appear to be frequently dealt with together at secondary school level.

Literary critical approaches, in schools at least, are primarily concerned to understand the plays by 'discovering' their inherent 'truths'. Active methods aim at understanding texts through enactment (in its broadest sense, not necessarily productions of a whole play). Contextual pedagogies, however, seek comprehension through an awareness of the constructed nature of the plays: by an author, by a set of socio-economic conditions and by theatrical conventions past and present – not to mention the 'players, playgoers, and playhouses that no longer exist' but for which Shakespeare designed his playscripts (Dessen 1999: 63). Shakespeare's plays as taught through contextual approaches are necessarily recognised as contingent (socially, historically and politically), while Shakespeare himself is figured as a complexly constructed cultural icon: humanist and historicist; a source of pleasure and knowledge; intuitive and difficult. Such values can be seen in the writing of a group of Shakespeare educators peaking in the 1980s and early 1990s (Albanese 2010: 1). It is captured in works such as Aers and Wheale's *Shakespeare in the Changing Curriculum*.

The value of Shakespeare as historically contingent is reflected in the significant body of literature that describes classroom practice, that is underpinned by a dialogue between text and context. Sue Gregory, for example, teaches her students about the cultural and political context of Shakespeare. Furthermore, she emphasises Shakespeare's agency in incorporating this into his writing (2003: 9). Sarah Beckwith's and Elaine Hobby's chapters in *Shakespeare in the Changing Curriculum* urge the incorporation of work on the plays' representations of gender and sexual politics as well as on early modern patriarchal assumptions. More recently, Andrew Hiscock posited comparative reading strategies as a means to contextualising Shakespeare's tragedies. The strategy resonates with Alan Dessen's articulation of the 'focus on difference' made possible by contextual pedagogies (1999: 76). These include comparing texts from different linguistic, generic and historic traditions: for instance, studying *Hamlet* alongside non-Shakespearean tragedy such as *The Spanish Tragedy* or *The Malcontent*; historical documents; other plays from the European tradition; or 'with Shakespeare's Tudor antecedents or variant editions' (Dessen 1999: 70–72). Anthologies that thematically juxtapose non-literary with literary works already exist for the university students market, such as Travistsky and Prescott's *Female and Male Voices in Early Modern England*. The influence on these methods of new historicist and cultural materialist theory demonstrates the trickle-down effect of once-radical academic work being now widely received in school policy and practice.

Active methods, as I have demonstrated, had a niche status in the teaching of Shakespeare from the 1950s onwards but was popularised through the work of Gibson and endorsed by curriculum authors in the 1980s. Contextual approaches, deriving from critical theories prevalent in the higher education sector during the 1980s, have similarly required a period of time to penetrate the teaching of literature in schools. They received official government endorsement in the assessment objectives for A-level issued as part of the Curriculum 2000 reforms, implemented by the Qualifications and Curriculum Authority (QCA). One of these objectives stipulates that:

AO5i (AS Level) Candidates should be able to show understanding of the *contexts in which literary texts are written and understood.*

AO5ii (A2 Level) Candidates should be able to evaluate the significance of *cultural, historical and other contextual influences* on literary texts and study.

(McEvoy 2003: 99, my emphasis)

In the wake of the AO's introduction to A-level English literature, government strategies have applied the values that they embody to work on Shakespeare's plays with students at all levels. *Shakespeare for All Ages and Stages*, for example, describes itself as a 'framework of opportunities' for working with the 'historical and theatrical contexts in which [Shakespeare] worked' (DCSF 2008: 5). This is represented across the key stages, in year-on-year learning objectives. These include, in year four 'to be familiar with Shakespeare's life, times and theatre'; in year eight to understand 'the cultural significance of Shakespeare and his place in our literary heritage' and 'to understand how characters' actions reflect the social, historical and cultural contexts of Shakespeare's time' (DCSF 2008: 9). Similar objectives are reiterated for years ten and eleven.

In this document, ways of encouraging students to see Shakespeare as historically situated include having younger students act as Elizabethan theatregoers or identifying 'some of the most significant events of Shakespeare's life, e.g. his childhood at grammar school, member of the Lord Chamberlain's Players, birth and loss of children, building the Globe, acting before the Queen', and subsequently devising short dramas based on these incidents (DCSF 2008: 17). Teaching Shakespeare through the potted life history above simultaneously strengthens the contextual approach to Shakespeare (making nationally available classroom activities informed by a notion of Shakespeare as contingent) and weakens it by basing these activities on under-evidenced, popularised assumptions about Shakespeare's biography, in an effort to engage younger students – a potential criticism of the approach that I shall return to later.

At the same time as effectively undercutting key theoretical tenets in attempting to suit them to children, *Shakespeare for All Ages and Stages* explicitly opposes the infantilising of contextual approaches by implementing the requirement to use them with students to the end of key stage four. This is in keeping with the QCA's decision to legislate for the teaching and assessment of Shakespeare's context at A-level through the AOs. As a consequence, the pedagogy's status is not confined to that of a trivialised tactic for raising younger students' interest in the plays by, for instance, devoting 'a few initial lessons to the historical background of Shakespeare's theatre' (Harris 2003: 47). Text and context are juxtaposed for older students, for instance, by focusing 'on short extracts from plays which present views found in Elizabethan or Jacobean society, for example, by exploring the very real belief in witches and their malign influence as portrayed in *Macbeth*' (DCSF 2008: 28); by examining the different ways Elizabethan and modern audiences would have regarded the character and treatment of Shylock in *The Merchant of Venice* (29); or by exploring 'the positive representation of leadership in plays such as *Henry V* and *Richard II* in the wider historical and political context of the latter years of Elizabeth's reign in order to idealise the Queen and set the standard for kingship' (36).

Again, while inspired by the value of Shakespeare as historically and politically contingent, this last activity assumes certain conscious motivations for writing the plays and attributes them unproblematically to Shakespeare. In doing so, it suggests that while the value of Shakespeare contextualised has translated from academia to policy, and hence the classroom, there are potentially worrying mistranslations in implementing how such values should be presented to students. The over-simplifications shown above expose the existence of a gap between the awareness of critical-theory informing policy regarding literature/Shakespeare and the suggestions for its classroom implementation.

Seemingly regardless of, or unconcerned by, this and with the endorsement of New Labour's education policy, examining boards have embraced this approach more warmly than active methods. The Oxford, Cambridge and Royal Society of Arts' 2001 Shakespeare examination paper required students to discuss the relevance of *Othello's* Venetian setting to the play. Meanwhile, the Northern Examinations and Assessment Board set AS-level coursework tasks which include:

– A study of the performance history/reception of the text/s
– Comparison of different production(s) seen by the candidate
– Detailed study of how the text was established
– Detailed study of the text(s) in relation to audience (16th/17th century and contemporary)

(McEvoy 2003: 101)

Thus the value of Shakespeare as contextually contingent is reproduced through assessing students on a broad range of knowledges: including the plays' geographical settings, their textual production (potentially including the study of early modern print culture, for example), staging and impact on Shakespeare's and contemporary readers/audiences. Contextual approaches may have been embraced more urgently than active methods because they are perceived to lead more seamlessly into the production of written work: the above tasks are all designed to culminate in traditional essay style responses. As such, they are perceived to be more suited to the existing examination system than the exercises that active methods students engage in.

With the value of Shakespeare as historically contingent endorsed by examining boards and government policy, publishing houses and the heritage industry have capitalised on expanding their own, existing adherence to this facet of contextual approaches to Shakespeare in education. A glut of editions and study guides were made available with 'fact sheets' on Shakespeare's theatre, life and times – notably the New Longman (many of which were re-issued around the millennium, coinciding with the Curriculum 2000 orders) whose section 'Background to Shakespeare' includes the sub-sections 'Shakespeare's England', 'Plays and playhouses', 'The Globe theatre' and 'The social background' (O'Connor 2004). In terms of the SBT's education programmes, Catherine Alexander depicts the evolution of their courses in response to the interest from teachers, and beyond, in the context of Shakespeare's life, theatre and plays. She writes that while 'until very recently one could confidently offer, at school level, programmes that focused closely on language, narrative or the exploration of character, and that used practical or active methods of delivery', the Trust's users are now demanding a focus on how, as well as what, Shakespeare wrote (2003: 147–148). Suggesting the power of market forces to profit from a once radical and oppositional critique, this institutional promotion of Shakespeare's contingent value and fostering of contextual approaches to Shakespeare in education exists in spite of a fundamental tension. There is a contradiction in values between cultural materialism (with its anti-capitalist, anti-nationalist rhetoric) and these cultural organisations that have traditionally embraced the

'Shakespeare trade' and promoted Shakespeare's status as an English hero. Chapter three broaches further discontinuities between such organisations' apparent adoption of critical or educational theory and their practice of it with students.

Political, pragmatic and multidisciplinary influences have converged to promote the teaching of Shakespeare in schools through contextual approaches. Ideas of Shakespeare as contingent and culturally constructed are espoused by politically and socially activist authors, originally drawn to left-wing ideology in response to the perceived oppressiveness of the Thatcher regime and committed to achieving social, sexual and racial equality more generally. Seminal publications include Dollimore and Sinfield's *Political Shakespeare* and Hawkes' *That Shakespeherian Rag*. Eagleton's notion of contingent value – 'There is no such thing as a literary work of tradition which is valuable *in itself* [...] "Value" is a transitive term: it means whatever is valued by certain people in specific situations according to particular criteria and in light of given purposes' (1983: 11) – is used in relation to teaching Shakespeare as a cultural construct. Meanwhile the idea of a 'Shakespeare myth', also the title of Graham Holderness' book on the cultural politics of Shakespeare, is taken up in references to the bard's 'mythological status' in monographs and journal articles aimed at teachers (Armstrong and Atkin 1998: 8; Yandell 1997). Such cultural materialist and new historicist works emphasise the sociocultural situation of texts and combat the idea that literary works have a fixed intrinsic value. Both of these notions have been incorporated into literature on the policy and practice of teaching Shakespeare.

Like supporters of active methods, educators who use contextual approaches value agendas for encouraging self-awareness in students; for imbuing them with critical literacy skills, such as the ability to identify and deconstruct ideologies (nationalist, capitalist etc.) at work in a given text; as well as promoting personal growth, for example, through inviting students to take subjective stances on issues. For these writers, fostering the ability to deconstruct operations of power is central to the purpose of education. Indeed, the activist implications of the academic literature may have secured its success with this particular generation of teachers, many of whom agreed with its responses to the Thatcher regime. For these teachers, statements such as Dollimore and Sinfield's assertion that 'cultural materialism registers its commitment to the transformation of a social order that exploits people on grounds of race, gender, sexuality and class' (1985: x) may have been a call to (pedagogic) arms. Gibson offers a synopsis of Sinfield's chapter in *Political Shakespeare* and quotes from Hawkes' *That Shakespeherian Rag* in the very first issue of *Shakespeare and Schools* (autumn 1986). He continued to review theoretically-informed works, such as Nick Peim's *Critical Theory and the English Teacher* (featured in number 23, spring 1994) throughout the publication's history. The revolutionary tone of such theorists, reported in interviews and book reviews in teaching periodicals such as *Shakespeare and Schools*, may have contributed to securing the spread of their influential ideas from the Shakespeare academy into primary and secondary education.

In addition to the influence of critical theory and left-wing politics, other more pragmatic forces have played a role in the success of welcoming contextual approaches to Shakespeare into the English classroom and curricula. These include New Labour's emphasis on cross-curricular learning as a way for teachers to meet multiple objectives simultaneously. The document *Shakespeare for All Ages and Stages* encourages teachers to link pedagogical approaches for Shakespeare to the National Curriculum History programme through an emphasis on context. For example, year four students' suggested study of Shakespeare's life and times 'relates closely to the National Curriculum history programme. Teachers are strongly encouraged to exploit such cross-curricular links in literacy learning and teaching' (DCSF 2008: 17). Many techniques used within a contextual approach, to juxtapose texts from different linguistic, generic and historic traditions, draw such links. In this way, they also resemble some elements of comparative literary studies, which gained status (not least as subjects in university departments) in the late twentieth-century.

The move to incorporate contextual approaches in teaching Shakespeare also reflects a shift in the concerns of the discipline of history. This change is represented by a growing emphasis on social history: a branch of history that takes as its focal point the working classes, the domestic or mundane and challenges the subject's preoccupation with the experience of (predominantly) white, male, ruling elites over that of women and other races. In terms of studying Shakespeare (one of those dead, white males), much criticism still emphasises his eminence – biographies and criticism alike treat him, as a 'genius', an exceptional 'life' and 'mind' (Bate 1997, 2008). However, the shift described above means that critical and popular authors alike now also read his works in relation to Elizabethan sexual practices, including same-sex relationships (Wells 2010); to the works of his contemporaries (Wells 2006); and to his 'world' more generally. Titles that witness the explosion of this latter trend in the past few years include Stephen Greenblatt's *Will in the World: How Shakespeare Became Shakespeare*; Bate's *Soul of the Age: The Life, Mind and World of William Shakespeare* and Bill Bryson's *Shakespeare: The World as a Stage*, all published within the space of four years. Such works testify to the popular impact of new historicist and cultural materialist critical theory.

In spite of the embrace of contextual approaches by government policy, publishers and the heritage industry, criticisms of the pedagogy do exist. Some critics tackle the theoretical tenets on which it is based. Some opponents argue against theorists such as Montrose, espousing the textuality of history and historicity of the text, that 'texts clearly *can* be separated from their production – I can simply sit down and read the *Sonnets*' (Inglis 1991: 64); that it assumes our experience of the text must be mediated, asking where does critical theory 'leave those of us who believe, certainly [...] that poets are indeed men and women, speaking as directly as they can to other men and women'? (1991: 65). Building on this, others have portrayed contextual approaches as a supplement to an implied core pedagogy (Francis 2003: 92) or echoed a criticism made of active methods that it represents a 'sugar-coating', sweetening-up students for later literary critical work (Armstrong and Atkin 1998: 9). Unlike the act of close reading the plays (whether done individually or with the class, in writing or discussion), which these critics naturalise, contextual pedagogies are decried because they 'lead us away from close engagement with the text, towards the phoney citadels of cultural, contextual and critical abstraction' (Francis 2003: 95). Such reactionary criticisms display a tenacity of belief that these approaches are a frivolous distraction from and interference in close communion between reader and text: an ideal that has arguably never been realised in schools, given the mediating forces of the teacher and assessment requirements, and is discredited as presenting a false binary of text and context by the editors of *Shakespeare Up Close*. Other critics have demanded that contextual approaches demonstrate an increased reflexivity towards the historical situation of critical theory as a response to 1970s world politics, 'the Thatcher/Reagan world of the 1970s' (McEvoy 2003: 103). Some authors point to the theory's declining position in university English departments, as an approach that by no means still dominates the teaching and research of university English departments (Stern 2003: 133; Albanese 2010: 2).

Additional criticisms relate to more practical concerns about the teaching of contextual approaches in schools. On the one hand, it is argued, not enough is known about Shakespeare's life (foregrounding Shakespeare's individual biography as an important context over social and theatrical contexts). This is a criticism that might be somewhat assuaged by the recent glut of biographies or by Alexander's descriptions of the SBT's properties and archival documents made available to schools (and the public) (2003: 147, 150). In describing the education department's work, Alexander shows that not only is contextual knowledge of Shakespeare pedagogically and epistemologically appropriate but it is also a realistic aspiration; and that there is a rich range of extant materials and resources with which to feed such enquiry. On the other hand, concern is shown that contextual approaches would demand English teachers to provide a boundless body of knowledge; that is English teachers 'would have to provide all sort of social, cultural, and historical information of an open-ended nature' (McEvoy 2003: 100). These criticisms, however, may have a limited effect in halting or altering the teaching of Shakespeare through contextual approaches, constituting, as they do, a belated reaction to his incorporation into classrooms and government strategies. Hence, contextual approaches to Shakespeare remain, for the time being, a key part of students' school experience of Shakespeare.

Pedagogies for Trainee Teachers

This chapter so far has drawn on pedagogies for teaching Shakespeare in schools represented in monographs and collected essays by and for the experienced teacher of Shakespeare. One type of literature that remains to be explored is manuals on teaching English generally aimed at the trainee teacher. In discussing this body of writing, I want to focus on how the pedagogies for and discourses around teaching Shakespeare relate to the three discussed above: textual, active and contextual. Five books that are currently being actively promoted to university education departments offering postgraduate certificates in education (PGCEs) by prominent publishers in the education market form the basis of this analysis. They include Stephen Clarke, Paul Dickinson and Jo Westbrook's *The Complete Guide to Becoming an English Teacher*; Jon Davison and Jane Dowson's *Learning to Teach English in the Secondary School;* Mike Fleming and David Stevens' *English Teaching in the Secondary School;* Andrew McCallum's *Creativity and Learning in Secondary English: Teaching for a Creative Classroom* and Trevor Wright's *How to be a Brilliant English Teacher.* Three of the books dedicate entire chapters to teaching Shakespeare; the other two (Fleming and Stevens 2010; McCallum 2012) rather shorter sections. In all five of the books, Shakespeare is the only author to be singled out for such attention, although it is clear from the books' indexes that a variety of other writers are discussed in a more fragmented way, reflecting his uniquely privileged place in the curriculum. Most of the books deal with Shakespeare part way through, although 'Starting with Shakespeare' is the first substantive chapter in Wright's manual – possibly indicating his belief in Shakespeare's primacy in the curriculum and his centrality to teachers' work. This structure could also symbolise a choice on Wright's part to engage with Shakespeare early on to avoid his becoming 'an elephant in the room', modelling for his readership's confidence and enthusiasm in tackling this literary giant.

The most notable, if not completely unexpected, finding from comparing the different teaching manuals is that they advise teaching Shakespeare through a blend of approaches. There is little evidence of the authors as ideologues committed to a single pedagogy (with the possible exception of McCallum, whose book is designed to place the spotlight firmly on multimedia and new technology). The possibility, even necessity, of working with multiple approaches is elucidated by Stephen Clarke's argument that 'What is important to grasp is that although most English teachers may favour one model over another, in practice all models can be visible at some point during the term' (2010: 28). He re-states this later in the book in characterising the good Shakespeare teacher as one who expands their 'approaches to class activities' and understands the way in which 'no one element ever ceases to be important [but that diverse] elements of knowledge and understanding enrich [their] teaching style' (2010: 253). His statement that, 'You never cease to enjoy performing the dialogue, prose or verse, yet the more you understand about the language of that dialogue [...] the better able you are to do justice to performing it convincingly' makes a strong case for a cyclical and dialogic model of pedagogy, where real learning – on both the teacher and the students' part – occurs through the intersection of two or more techniques resulting in perpetual forward-motion (253). This unanimity concerning the value of pedagogic pluralism does not mean, however, that no approaches are rejected outright as lacking value. Wright seemingly describes and evaluates the once-dominant method of reading-around-the-class: 'Perhaps the first time you saw Shakespeare it was in an elderly, soft-bound book [...] The teacher handed out the parts to some keen volunteers who read clearly and entirely without understanding for the next six weeks' (2005: 4). His dismissal of the approach as a way of engaging students is unequivocal and is echoed by his fellow authors.

The influence of active methods for teaching Shakespeare is palpable in these teaching manuals. Gibson alone is invoked as the individual associated with the approach, confirming his pre-eminence as discussed earlier in this chapter. His influence is acknowledged by

Wright as rendering 'reading a play anywhere, and especially in a classroom […] an unnatural act' (2005: 4). Meanwhile Clarke and his colleagues echo Gibson through the vocabulary and syntax with which they espouse active methods: 'the chance to speak, to rehearse and to interact with others to create an actual scene is vital […] it is certain that speaking the lines ought to become a kinaesthetic experience as well as an aural one' (2010: 248). Beyond Gibson, the influence of performance theory that inspired his work is discernible in the manuals' discussion of the instability of texts. Clarke explains that 'texts, runs the now familiar argument about the thing to be learned, are scripts, mere representations of a form that can only be created by acting' (2010: 246). Similarly, Yandell and Franks assert that 'The texts themselves are products of editorial choice' emphasising the idea that meaning resides not inherently and fixedly in the plays, but in the interactions readers have with them' (2009: 243). These quotations evidence theories about the contingent and dynamic nature of Shakespeare's texts, on which both active methods and performance theory are predicated.

Even with the withdrawal of SATs testing of Shakespeare, however, there remains a sense among some of the manuals' authors that active methods, including choral speaking, mime, identifying implicit stage directions, are most suitably deployed as an introduction to the play, 'to familiarise pupils with the language of the plays and for them to respond to its rhythms and images prior to any detailed attempt at understanding and analysis of its content' (Fleming and Stevens 2010: 156). Fleming and Stevens also suggest explaining the aims and objectives of active-methods activities to pupils 'so that they do not feel they are just being asked to jump from one rather strange activity to another with little sense of meaning or direction' (2010: 156). Wright warns teachers of the pitfalls involved in assuming that students' participation in active methods will equate to understanding: 'I have stood in the corner of many drama studios where children have been attempting lively activities whose efforts have been limited by that fact that, ultimately, there were still words and phrases there that they didn't understand' (2005: 13). To limit the possibility of this happening he suggests teacher-led activities, such as reading key speeches stressing words that relate to the chosen focus of the session while students physicalise it. While teaching manuals devote considerable space to outlining active methods for Shakespeare; some are also clearly engaged in critiquing them.

In addition to active methods, contextual approaches are also valued throughout the manuals. Clarke urges teachers to have notes on Elizabethan social mores and the New World at hand to deploy throughout when teaching *Romeo and Juliet* or *The Tempest* (plays he chooses because they reflect set texts at the time of writing). By way of explaining his rationale for this, Clarke, as well as Yandell and Franks, cite the marking criteria that require teachers to 'help GCSE [and A-level] people see their play in terms of events in Shakespeare's time as an instrumental incentive to use contextual approaches' (2009: 250, 253–254). However, there is disagreement as to whether they should be used at an introductory or later stage in working on a text. Wright urges against starting with the historical background of the early modern theatre, arguing that it threatens teachers' ability to 'mak[e] connections between the pupils and the material': 'Doing pictures of the Globe Theatre or knowing that Juliet, as well as being four hundred years old, was also a boy in tights will only serve to reinforce the perceived distance and alienness of the text' (2005: 5). In contrast, Yandell and Franks suggest commencing study of the playwright with the context of Shakespeare in modern everyday popular culture, displaying not only the influence of cultural materialist analyses in their general argument but also in the specific examples they choose:

> Your pupils will know things about Shakespeare – and this knowledge will be derived from hugely disparate sources. Streets and pubs bear his name, while motorway signs proclaim the message 'Welcome to Warwickshire: Shakespeare's County'. There's an episode of *The Simpson's* devoted to *Hamlet* – a play which also figures largely in *Star Trek VI* [...]. The first move for you to make, then, is to find out what your pupils already know – so ask them!
>
> (2009: 244)

The examples they cite are widely used in writing informed by cultural materialism from authors including Richard Burt, Adam Hansen and Douglas Lanier. Falling somewhere between these two manuals, Clarke suggests increasing students' exposure to contextual material 'as they mature' 'so as to increase understanding in the learners [...] of the cultural and political elements that compose the plays, and their roots in a time and place' (2010: 244). In a sense, he risks the ire of those critics of contextual approaches, who argue that it demands an inordinate amount of preparation from teachers, with his advice to them to familiarise themselves with 'authoritative and readable books about Shakespeare, his life and times, provide a growing understanding about the man, the people he worked with and the nature of the political and ideological conflicts around and within his work' (244). Whether that sense of pressure would be ameliorated or exacerbated by following his recommendation of 'co-operating with the history teachers', for example, to explore colonialism and the slave-trade in *The Tempest* (252), remains to be seen. While there is no consensus on what context to cover with students, policy requiring its teaching has evidently made it a ubiquitous feature of suggestions for tackling Shakespeare in teaching manuals.

In largely unacknowledged tension with the emphasis on context, a focus on Shakespeare's universality and continuing relevance persists in explanations of how to engage students with his plays. Wright isolates the struggle between father and daughter over her suitors in *A Midsummer Night's Dream* as one example of Shakespeare's abiding concerns:

> A girl wants to marry a boy, but her father objects. In fact he prefers another boy. This is in no sense uninteresting to most fourteen-year-olds. Many of them live with this kid of unwanted parental interference on a daily basis. They have opinions about it.
>
> (2005: 7)

The same situation in the same play is lighted on by Clarke with identical intent:

> Helena and Hermia, whose friendship disintegrates as they both chase the same man, criticise each other's looks. Those who had never encountered a Shakespeare play would know exactly what is going on as they hurl insults at a former friend out of jealousy and so could well play these characters with true tonal conviction.
>
> (2010: 246)

These statements, with their insistence on the timeless quality of the scenarios and emotions, as well as their reliance on an understanding of characters as 'real people' with psychological integrity, have a clear affinity with the literary critical approaches of early-twentieth-century scholars.

While literary critical approaches are given ample coverage in the manuals, they are never espoused as being sufficient on their own to impart all that students need to know of the plays. All the manuals eschew line-by-line explorations of the plays with the teacher glossing difficult words and phrases – the 'construe' method common until the late twentieth-century and referred to at the start of this chapter. Wright is adamant that 'translation has no part to play in the study of Shakespeare', arguing that 'children must become used to working outwards from the bits of text they understand, rather than staring disconsolately at the bits they don't' (2005: 11). Yandell and Franks link a similar exhortation to the benefits of active methods: 'the best answer to the problem of Shakespearean language lies in performance – not in translation activities or long lectures about the complexities of the iambic pentameter' (2005: 245). The majority of manuals suggest activities based around reading particular passages, alerting teachers to be prepared to explain 'where necessary'. In contrast to the general consensus on avoiding line-by-line explanations of the plays, the manuals offer contradictory suggestions about whether to start with a fragment of the text (Clarke) or an activity that will lead to students having a plot synopsis (Yandell and Franks) or to use students' ignorance of the plot to keep them engaged (Wright).

As with textual approaches, the use of multimedia to teach Shakespeare is included to varying degrees within the manuals – although, again, there is little agreement about the appropriate juncture for doing so. Wright advises against 'start[ing] with the video [...] because the biggest ally you have when teaching a text is the story. Children don't want to spend weeks on end ploughing through a story when they already know how it ends' (2005: 5). Clarke makes the opposite case, arguing against the reified convention of starting with text: 'Shakespeare's plays can never reveal all about themselves within or from any one production, and so it does not matter if the young encounter them in something other than their full or most revered forms when the teacher first introduces them' (246). Nonetheless, all the manuals cohere around the idea that students should encounter multiple interpretations of the text for comparison. These include watching two film versions (Clarke), reading play text alongside a graphic novel version (Fleming and Stevens 2010; McCallum 2012) and using print alongside online editions (Fleming and Stevens 2010). There is a widespread emphasis on stimulating students to think about the influence of the genre or medium on its particular interpretation as well as an awareness of terminology and concepts from disciplines such as film and cultural studies. In summary, the manuals demonstrate an awareness of the debates around pedagogies for teaching Shakespeare that have emanated over many decades from academic research, educational theory and practice. On the whole, they opt for a pluralist model of pedagogy – with teachers exhorted to use a range of approaches but left to steer their own course between contrasting advice on the point in students' development at which each pedagogy should be introduced.

Common Influences on Pedagogies

This chapter has shown that, while the National Curriculum for English is not overtly concerned with pedagogy, approaches involving ICT, media, drama, personal response and creative writing are demanded by the document itself. Furthermore, other policy initiatives, such as the National Strategy, *Shakespeare for All Ages and Stages* and Curriculum 2000, variously foster pedagogies including literary critical, active methods and contextual approaches. While much of the emphasis in this chapter has been on elucidating differences between the approaches, I want to consider here some features that unite them. The first element is the liberal-humanist focus, whether explicit or implicit, of these pedagogies on access to great literature. All three effectively place an emphasis on Shakespeare and English (whether defined by the study of a literary canon, mundane texts or language) as central to education. Leavisite literary criticism casts the activities of reading literature and writing criticism as pivotal to a person's development as a human being: morally, socially, and mentally. Active methods are openly motivated by desires to keep the teaching of Shakespeare a high priority in schools and to widen access to his works for all students. While many writers espousing contextual approaches seek to question Shakespeare's uniquely high place in the curriculum and the focus or methods of teaching practices, they rarely argue outright against the teaching of his works. Indeed, even initiating debate around Shakespeare's profile can be interpreted as recognition that he (and other literature) *matters*.

The second striking theme that has cross-cut this chapter is the influence that cultural and educational institutions, such as theatre and academia, have had on pedagogy for teaching Shakespeare in schools. This suggests a flow of inspiration akin to Bruner's notion of the cultural saturation of education that stresses the way in which education is shot through with tenets from and references to everyday culture. The influence of theatre education departments on students and teachers will be demonstrated in the following chapter. Moreover, the way in which school pedagogy is inflected with academic tenets (of varying ages and directions) is unavoidable. Meanwhile, higher education has, and continues to have, an enduring influence on Shakespeare in schools. School Shakespeare is replete with a hotchpotch of academic scholarship from English and education departments past and present, Bradleyean notions of character (now widely reviled in the university sector as 'naïve' HEA/ESC: 7); educational research on children's positive response to active methods; and conceptions of literary readings as contingent and literary icons as culturally constructed from critical theory. Analysis of this using government policy documents and pedagogic literature suggests that there is a significant time lag between the inception of these ideas as radical in academia and their manifestation in school classrooms, meaning that much of what is appropriated as cutting edge in schools is actually held by then as a blunt knife among academics, roundly criticised or neglected altogether. This time lag in the transmission of scholarship is perhaps explained by the need for such notions to permeate that part of academia that offers a bridge between itself and the schoolroom: teacher training. This chapter, however, suggests that once the transition between these educational institutions has been made, the influence of ideas has considerable longevity. Pedagogies seem to endure beyond particular educational vogues, beyond the careers of a generation of teachers, beyond changes of government (and the subsequent changes to policy documents), perhaps aided by the (un)reasonable longevity of published resources – such as editions of the plays – available to students and teachers.

The higher education sector frequently articulates concerns about students moving from school to university, evidenced by perennial complaints about the 'dumbing down' of the curriculum and efforts to improve the transition from governments and individual organisations (Thompson 1934: 3). Although aimed more at policy-makers and exam boards than teachers, a degree of scepticism about the quality of students' school experience of Shakespeare is evident in the 'Teaching Shakespeare' survey of those who teach undergraduates. Eighty-nine per cent of those surveyed regarded students as only adequately, and often poorly, prepared to study Shakespeare at university, despite having encountered him at school (Thew 2006: 6). Qualitative data spoke of 'unpicking bad habits' including 'character-based criticism or flat-footed A2 "context"' or 'a provisional, over-generalised and over-simplified conception of genre' (2006: 7). In spite of this lack of praise from the higher education sector for the study of Shakespeare in schools, the clichéd antagonism of teachers on the frontline of school education towards idealistic academics in their proverbial ivory towers was not apparent in the material that forms the basis of this chapter, with the possible exception of Coles' critique of active methods' assumptions (2009). Far stronger, for example, has been a sense of teachers' resistance to the perceived ever-changing demands of hyperactive government policy suggested in chapter one. This may be because the teachers reflecting on their classroom pedagogies in books or journals are necessarily those interested in connecting academic practice with their everyday teaching experience. Furthermore, current teachers are encouraged (or even required by their schools) to return to academia throughout their careers, undertaking study at masters or doctoral level along with other continuing professional development courses run by organisations such as the Royal Shakespeare Company. They may also be asked to participate in, and lead, school-based research to inform decision-making. Incorporating further study, research projects and academic publications into a teaching career may well blur boundaries between the traditionally distinct camps of 'them' (academics) and 'us' (schoolteachers).

Additionally, there is a growing sense in which the university sector has learnt, and continues to learn, lessons about the teaching of Shakespeare from schools: active methods and multiliteracy approaches (using varied audio-visual resources) are increasingly incorporated into or offered alongside traditional lectures and seminars on Shakespeare. However, this could also represent a lateral influence from other departments, such as drama and media studies, within the universities. A module on 'Teaching Shakespeare' on the University of York's BA English in Education, for instance, sends students into schools to research the needs of teachers and pupils in studying a particular play. The undergraduates then produce a research pack for the school group drawing on up-to-date scholarship, research and pedagogy as part of their assessment. As a final part of the exercise, students collect feedback from the teachers and students on the pack: a very tangible way in which university students can learn about what knowledges and skills concerning Shakespeare are valued in the school sector. Again, the impetus behind this cross-sector interaction may come from the interdisciplinary influence of working on English within the single honours programme of an education department.

Whatever the reason for the evident influence of academia on school Shakespeare, it demands that academics be involved in a dialogue with teachers and government. Such contact would also help ameliorate claims that their theories or research have been misunderstood or misrepresented (see the above discussion of the over-simplification of new historicist theory). However, after the excitement of Gibson and Maurice Gilmour's projects on the teaching of Shakespeare in schools, and support for the idea of Shakespeare for all from such academics and authors of the National Curriculum, from the mid-1990s there was a demonstrable lack of concern in the higher education sector how Shakespeare is taught (Coles 2009: 34–35). Publications on Shakespeare in education that went beyond recommending classroom practice to deal with theoretical or political issues were rarely forthcoming (in comparison to the volume of titles on performance history, literary criticism and the textual study of Shakespeare). Education panels at international Shakespeare conferences were few. Furthermore, when education-specific slots occurred, they were largely preoccupied with individual accounts of teaching practice or with workshops on specific techniques. They were well attended by schoolteachers and drama lecturers but only to a negligible extent by those who drive the direction of Shakespeare studies, establish Shakespeare's texts and contexts, through research. This historical paucity of research activity on Shakespeare in schools could be attributed not only to the concern with macro-educational issues demonstrated in chapter one, but also to the period of relative satisfaction, on the part of teachers and academics, with government intervention concerning the curriculum during Blair's and Brown's premierships. It may be that their time in power provided these two education sectors with less impetus to collaborate on research than the Thatcher government's abrasive policies.

Not entirely coincidentally, I would argue, debate around Shakespeare in education has been reinvigorated since the election of the Coalition government in 2010 and its subsequent announcement of a curriculum review. If the debate around Shakespeare in the

National Curriculum for English in the 1980s and 1990s is anything to go by, the imminent outcome of the Coalition government's revision to the curriculum – if it directly affects the place of Shakespeare – could provide the greatest aegis yet towards the discussion of the value of Shakespeare in education this millennium. Additionally, there has been a flourish of cross-sector research and teaching projects on Shakespeare in education, as well as evidence of interest in the topic at conferences. 2012 saw the start of an AHRC-funded project, Shakespeare's Global Communities, which included a remit to investigate the education elements of that year's World Shakespeare Festival and productions for children and young people alongside the 'mainstream' shows. Publications such as *Extramural Shakespeare* and *Shakespeare for Young People,* written by Denise Albanese and Abigail Rokison respectively, explore British and American students' engagement with Shakespeare inside the classroom and encounters with his work outside it through popular culture. An education seminar at the Shakespeare Association of America congress in 2013 specifically requested papers not on anecdotal instances of teaching Shakespeare, but which look at the historical development of policy, pedagogy and practice. However, with almost every child nationally experiencing Shakespeare in the classroom, in terms of English as a subject in the academy, there is still much work to be done to balance literary critical interests with cultural studies or cultural criticism – interest in Shakespeare's work (and life) with his afterlives. The following chapter will demonstrate that the gap left by lukewarm or limited academic engagement in Shakespeare in schools was readily filled, with much acclaim from teachers, by the education departments of cultural organisations such as the Globe, SBT and RSC.

Pedagogies Globally

This book is centred on Shakespeare in education as experienced in England. However, it is worth noting the global situation in this chapter on pedagogy, particularly because the (somewhat limited) evidence analysed herein suggests that the pluralist model of methods for teaching Shakespeare prevalent in England is anomalous rather than ordinary. The RSC's wiki Shakespeare is a wide-ranging collection of information about Shakespeare in education in sixty-seven countries conducted between 2010 and 2012. The majority of entries are derived from the results of a RSC/British Council survey that sought to ascertain information about what Shakespeare is taught, when, how and why, located in the broader context of each country's education system. Forty-three out of one hundred British Council offices sent surveys responded, indicating some of the issues of validity and reliability that may arise from its use and begging users (as I have done) to triangulate it with other, existing research in the area. To supplement this data, some posts are written by RSC education practitioners who have taught groups visiting from other countries, working from that experience. Some are interviews with RSC employees with experience in arts and education outside England (part of a project called 'personal voices'). Additionally, there are a very few posts by teachers and academics. The overall finding from the survey, which the RSC has made the most use of, particularly during the World Shakespeare Festival in 2012, is that 'approximately 50% of schoolchildren across the world, at least 64 million each year, are studying Shakespeare at school' ('Survey results' 2012). They also assert that '65% of countries have Shakespeare as a named author on their curriculum' – although unlike England, this does not always mean he is compulsory. These statistics are highly problematic – they elide the variation in educational legislation from state to state in countries such as Australia, the United States and India, to name a few. However, they serve an important function for the organisation's education department in establishing that, because Shakespeare is widely taught internationally, there should be revitalised attention to *how* he is taught so that students' early encounters with Shakespeare are positive.

The wiki suggests that, at the moment, the majority of countries where Shakespeare is taught use 'a more traditional, desk-bound approach'. Entries containing vocabulary valuing Shakespeare as a 'literary text', part of a literary or humanist education, a creator of universally vivid stories and characters and painter of 'human nature' (Canada, Denmark, Malta, Peru, Poland, Serbia, Spain, Ukraine), and a skilled craftsman (Canada, China, Finland, Nigeria) prevailed, indicating the prevalence of literary critical pedagogies. Similar rationales for teaching Shakespeare are evident in Daniel Gallimore's account of Shakespeare in Japan that argues that he is valued in their education system for his use of an 'unparalleled range of sources', 'lexical and rhetorical range', ability to 'transcend generic boundaries' (2009: 110). They also appear in Natasha Distiller's descriptions of Shakespeare in South African schools, where he is depicted as a writer of extraordinary 'linguistic aptitude' (2008: 384), 'common humanity' (2008: 386) and 'universally applicable human stories' (2008: 382–383). In fact, Distiller argues, historical context, cultural references, early modern language are actively erased from his texts by 'enterprising teachers' in modernised re-tellings to reduce Shakespeare's problematic nature and enable the 'universal themes' to shine out (2008: 391). André Lemmer, writing of the same nation, explains that studying Shakespeare in South Africa is dominantly textual, involving reading, glossing words and figures of speech, plot summaries, 'line-by-line explanation' and a strong 'story content focus' using outdated editions (2001: 67–68). However, he also offers an insight into small-scale change: instances of acting, approaching plays as performance scripts as well as active methods approaches more generally, as well as examining students on their ability to envisage directing a scene (Lemmer 2001: 69). In spite of this, literary critical approaches continue to dominate the teaching of Shakespeare internationally, regardless of whether he is prescribed on the curriculum or featured more optionally in schooling; whether taught in translation, modern English or original spelling; whether instruction is in English or another language; whether taught predominantly in private or state-funded education; whether the whole play or extracts are offered (the latter is more prevalent).

Performance of Shakespeare, rather than active methods, is offered in these countries predominantly through extra-curricular drama activities or at university level. Student performance and performance history is used in teaching *Twelfth Night* at the National Taiwan Normal University (Lin 2010). Reading aloud around the class, decried as a passive experience by most active methods exponents, was the most common performative element invoked in describing Shakespeare in formal education. However, active methods appear to have growing currency in America, Hungary, Oman, South Africa and the United Kingdom. In terms of contextual approaches, students' experience of Shakespeare in several countries included details of his biography and historical context, 'life and major achievements' (Zhang 1996: 191) but – in that these details did not seem to be taught in relation to the plays – they do not appear to amount to evidence of a historicist approach to interpretation of his works in schools. Rather, Shakespeare as a literary icon and historical personage from early modern England is taught as part of a programme of European history and culture in countries such as China, Kuwait, Mexico and Peru. However, Xiao Yang Zhang's *Shakespeare in China* offers anecdotal evidence that cultural materialist and new historicist approaches are offered at university level (1996: 195). For these English-as-an-Additional-Language students such 'fact'-oriented knowledge of Shakespeare arguably has value as a cultural commodity (Distiller 2008: 382), rather than being seen 'as a means of acquiring the practicalities of the English tongue', as was once the case (Chaudhuri 2008: 83).

Multimedia and ICT resources, including film adaptations of the plays, are documented as being used to teach Shakespeare in Egypt (El-Shayal 2001: 35), Finland, France, Greece, India, Italy, Morocco, Norway, New Zealand and South Africa (Lemmer 2001: 69). Evidence in the wiki of how these elements are used overwhelmingly suggests that they are intended to supplement students' understanding of plot, theme and character in the written text, particularly where their first language is not English, rather than representing a genuine engagement with film or cultural studies epistemologies. The overall impression given by the wiki is that new technologies are more likely to be adapted and fitted to prevailing literary critical methods of studying Shakespeare than active or contextual methods. This is partly because they are perceived to require changes beyond the English classroom, to the wider purpose and theoretical underpinning of education, such as the revoking of teacher-led, instruction-heavy pedagogy. However, performance and historicist methods may be incorporated into lessons as stand-alone activities, rather than wholesale pedagogies where ideology and action cohere. The wiki is far from comprehensive, although it offers a snapshot of Shakespeare in several countries in 2012 as driven by literary critical methods with opportunities for performance rather than more integrated classroom teaching using active or contextual methods.

Chapter 3

Shakespeare in Theatre and Heritage: Three Education Departments

The two preceding chapters have focused on the value of Shakespeare in the classroom, as constructed through government policy and various pedagogies. Beyond formal education, theatres and heritage institutions have long played a role in Shakespearean education, whether hosting visiting school groups, taking their work into classrooms or encouraging families to attend. Evidence of these activities can be found in oral history archives with theatregoers such as the Theatre Archive Project, available on the British Library's website, focusing on post-war Britain. The memories of childhood theatregoing include being taken by parents to see Shakespeare, or, more rarely, asking to be taken; school excursions; and sustained attendance as preparation for examinations, entering university or drama school.

Very occasionally, the archives capture a sense of the post-war flourishing of performances of Shakespeare designed specifically for young people, as well as the Theatre-in-Education movement, whose techniques intersect with those of active methods. A couple of interviewees with careers in acting mentioned touring, often potted, versions of the plays to schools – particularly when other employment was thin on the ground. Julia Jones describes working with a colleague on 'some schools tours when we were out of work one summer and we sort of said, "Well, why don't we do some Shakespeare for schools?". We did a kind of potted version of *Twelfth Night* and took it around all the schools in Lancashire. And then we did *As You Like It* and Joan got wind of what we were doing and she decided that she would direct'. The casually-mentioned 'Joan' is Joan Littlewood, then director of the Theatre Workshop in Stratford East. Renowned in Britain at the time for drawing on, rather than rejecting (as did the mainstream theatre with which she competed), European theory about movement and other techniques for actors, the company was also an early contributor to the Theatre-in-Education movement. Another of the actors she directed, George Collins, recalls Joan's strategy here – motivated by a need to raise funds as well as a pedagogic commitment to drama methods and the value of seeing Shakespeare live – 'they were doing a Shakespeare for schools. Whatever the School Certificate was – what choice of Shakespeare – they would do, so they could tour around and show the kids, you know, what it was like'. Jones and Collins' first-hand accounts of Littlewood's pioneering work in playing (with) Shakespeare for children mirror those available in existing research. Shellard, for instance, describes using improvisation, direct participation and teaching skills in productions for young people (2000: 87). Her commitment to playing Shakespeare in schools and working with young people on Shakespeare through theatre education departments is now commonplace among theatre companies. The latter part of this chapter will demonstrate the ways in which the RSC and SBT, for example, tailor provision according to the National Curriculum. The RSC also offers its actors the opportunity to study towards qualifications, awarded by the University of Warwick, in teaching Shakespeare – arguably designed, in part, to insulate actors against protracted periods of unemployment by skilling them up as educators. However, at the time, companies such as Theatre Workshop were in the minority in actively seeking to reach out to schools through their provision of Shakespeare.

This does not mean that Littlewood was operating alone in her exploration of the relationship between Shakespeare, theatre and schools. In the same period, the directors Brian Way and Margaret Faulkes' work on children's theatre, through the Theatre Centre in London, is recalled by the actor Brian Cook, who, when he first met them, was about to graduate from RADA. He was subsequently employed within their company, which explicitly aimed to keep actors working through periods of unemployment by harnessing their pedagogic potential. Cook's memories trace the striking reconception of how young people could encounter Shakespeare:

[Brian and Margaret] thought that theatre shouldn't be something aside and sort of special – it was all very well to put children on a bus and take them to see Shakespeare in a theatre which requires a whole different sort of 'theatre manners', if you like, really – they thought it should be very much part of the school day and school education. So we used to take plays into schools and we'd play not on the stage but usually on the floor in the school hall with the audience sitting round and always within the play at some point there was a point where we could involve the audience in some way – I mean very daring. One [play] we did had alternative endings and according to how the audience took the play we'd play whichever ending [...].

The revolutionary aspect of their engagement with children, as presented by Cook, lies in their progressive assumption that children were not just miniature adults to be taken to passively view productions conceived with a grown-up audience in mind, but that they deserved and required a more familiar, easily approachable theatregoing atmosphere, tailored to their age group and involving a degree of active participation, such as choosing an ending (something which radically privileges spectator over text). Wider acceptance of the benefits of their work was recognised, in 1966, when they gained Arts Council funding. Others who contributed to the development of Theatre-in-Education post-war include Peter Slade's Pear Tree Players, Tom Clarke's Compass Players, Caryl Jenner's England Children's Theatre (whose touring Mobile Theatre was funded by the Arts Council in 1950, after three years' self-funded work), as well as Buzz Goodbody at The Other Place in Stratford upon Avon. Buzz played a key role in building up the social and educational work of the RSC (Shellard 2000: 87). George Devine's somewhat short-lived Young Vic children's theatre company toured plays performed by young people, primarily for young people, in line with Arts Council's attempts to get companies into 'areas deemed in particular need of access to professional provision' from 1946 to 1948 (Cochrane 2011: 160). Also working with young casts was Michael Croft, described as 'the ultimate influential school master' (Cochrane 2011: 209). His Shakespearean productions at Alleyn's school, Dulwich, between 1950 and 1955, 'laid the foundation for the boys' theatre group, which eventually evolved into the National Youth Theatre of Great Britain' (Cochrane 2011: 209). The group initially took boys up to the age of twenty-one, with girls admitted only in 1960. These practitioners derived strength and influence from one another during the post-war period.

Goodbody's work, for example, owed a particular debt of gratitude to David Holman and Gordon Vallins' work in nearby Coventry (White 2008: 186–195). In 1958, the Belgrade theatre had been publicly funded as part of the post-war regeneration of Coventry, with the proviso that its remit included developing a social centre and outreach to schools, as well as performing space. One of the ways in which this mission was put into practice in the mid-1960s was by recruiting a group of actor-teachers 'to take drama into local schools and utilise drama-teaching methods and performance skills in the overall educational programme' (Shellard 2000: 87). They conducted research prior to their arrival at the schools with teachers and educational advisers, as well as offering follow-up work post-performance. This differed from the generic and 'one-hit' nature of the experience of students being taken to see a play in the theatre, which Vallins saw as a disappointment for students and practitioners alike. He recalled, of a 1964 matinee performance of *Hamlet* at the Belgrade for a schools audience, that:

> There had been no administrative time to say what the play was about; the teachers generally saw it as a day off. The play would start. There'd be mutterings in the auditorium – the play would go quicker. Polo mints would be spun out of the audience onto the stage and the play would go even quicker.
>
> (Vallins in Turner 2011)

Innovative elements of the Belgrade's Theatre-in-Education work designed to counteract such disaffection included devising, reminiscence, youth issues and local history. Shellard describes the Belgrade's educational remit as 'illustrating how the link between drama and schools would become increasingly important for theatres from this moment on' (2000: 87). Indeed, its work was replicated by groups from Leeds, Nottingham, Bolton, Glasgow and Edinburgh, representing a decentralisation of Theatre-in-Education from London and other national theatres, such as the RSC, in terms of geography as well as the content of their provision (Shellard 2000: 88). Such work, however, was often enabled by public funding and was severely hit, in the 1980s, by the Thatcher government's cuts to the arts sector. Nonetheless, as will be demonstrated in later sections of this chapter, collaborations between arts organisations – including theatres – flourished again under the New Labour governments of the late 1990s and early 2000s.

RSC, SBT and Globe Education

Apart from learning the repertoire, the Theatre Archive Project participants recall their early encounters involving learning how to behave as an audience member: there is no sense of explicitly or actively being instructed by the theatre companies about Shakespeare, theatre etiquette, or any other knowledges or skills. In the past few decades, however, the Royal Shakespeare Company (a theatre group), the Shakespeare Birthplace Trust (a heritage organisation) and Shakespeare's Globe (which represents a combination of these two industries) have become internationally recognised providers of education programmes on Shakespeare, each with dedicated education departments. Although I concentrate here on their provision for school-age children and young people, their work extends to higher and adult education, lifelong and leisure learning. These organisations have made it their mission to extend the state education offering of Shakespeare for all: specifically, active, performance – or historically – contextualised Shakespeare for all. The three departments demonstrably share a belief in certain 'inherent' values of Shakespeare. These include Shakespeare as universal, relevant, entertaining, a genius, a keystone of national culture and father of the English language. These values are apparent as clichés, circulating in wider culture. In addition to these intrinsic values, the organisations also manifest common ideas about the instrumental value of education departments in cultural institutions. These values are at least fourfold: they include Shakespeare's accessibility, the inclusivity of their provision of Shakespeare, their accountability as organisations to the public and the high standard of the educational services they provide.

This consensus is partly strategic, in that these values for arts education are a condition of public funding, on which the RSC is reliant. These values have been communicated to the arts sector through the writing and speeches of New Labour's Tessa Jowell (as Secretary of State for Culture from 2001 to 2007) and David Lammy (as Minister for Culture from 2005 to 2007). This government's politicians asserted that such institutions should exist to make 'Teaching, education and scholarship, available to all: the values of the Enlightenment kept alive for each generation' (Jowell 2005: 1). Additionally, they argued that these organisations possess 'the capacity […] to contribute to enjoyment, to inspiration, to learning, to research and scholarship, to understanding, to regeneration, to reflection, to communication and to building dialogue and tolerance between individuals, communities and nations' (Lammy 2005). While the SBT and Globe are not dependent on government subsidy – receiving a significant income from fund-raising activities undertaken with individuals and corporations – such values have become a standard that other donors and funders may also require of them. The potential outcomes listed above, which relate strongly to instrumental values for arts education (including the agendas for skills, standards and social inclusion discussed in chapter one), may also be attractive to these private sponsors – for example, companies looking to boost their corporate social responsibility portfolios. Pressure from government and interest from the private sector explain why such values for arts education have been universally embraced.

The homogenous nature of these three organisations' declarations of Shakespeare's and arts education's value, however, presents each of them with the same difficulty: they are commercial competitors in the Shakespeare education market (or, at least, quasi-commercial depending on the level of government subsidy they receive) and therefore need to differentiate the products and services they offer, partly through 'aggressive branding and marketing' (de Groot 2009: 240). Their commercialism has been encouraged by successive governments, from Thatcher's severe cuts to the arts budget to New Labour's continuation of a Conservative policy of rendering public services more businesslike. As with state education, these policies have led to the widespread uptake of 'demand-driven models' that 'empower the customer and emphasise choice, value and experience' (de Groot 2009: 240). In this 'competitive leisure market', each organisation needs to identify and market its experience of Shakespeare as uniquely valuable (240). This is akin to the unique selling point (USP) required for an advertised product to achieve an advantage over its rivals in the marketplace.

In the process of rendering themselves distinctive, these education departments 'assign [Shakespeare] particular values' and formulate diverse ways of knowing him (Hodgdon 1998: 194). It is these constructions of the exclusive value of Shakespeare with which this chapter is particularly concerned. Using publicity materials and education resources, both in print and on their websites, from the period 2009–2011, as well as my first-hand observation of their activities, I will demonstrate that the SBT locates its unique and authentic experience in the supposedly physical proximity to Shakespeare which it offers. This nearness is constructed through its custodianship of historic Stratford houses and increasingly through activities such as re-enactment. For the Globe, it is achieved through its commitment to a 'Shakespearean' ethos of play and community. For the RSC, it is embodied in their use of the resources of the acting company (both tangible, such as rehearsal spaces, and intangible, such as rehearsal techniques) to overcome the challenges that (it perceives that) Shakespeare presents to students.

These organisations need to differentiate their provision of Shakespeare, not only from that of their competitors but also from their past selves, to keep pace with social and economic changes as well as academic research. Previously, Hodgdon has highlighted such change in relation to the SBT, stating that in the 1980s Shakespeare was presented in accordance with the prevailing values of Western capitalism. For example, she argues that one of the ideal attributes of a successful person at the time was home ownership and that this ideal was retrospectively projected onto Shakespeare's Stratford life. Thus, Shakespeare's town houses come to epitomise his 'bourgeois existence', 'his membership in a rising middle-class of merchant gentry' (1998: 205, 207). Over a decade after Hodgdon, the SBT is having to adjust its provision around its visitors' use of new technologies; their self-conceptions as bloggers, tweeters and virtual tourists (Owen 2010). In 2007, Dr Diana Owen was appointed as director of the organisation. Owen had, in her previous position with the National Trust, contributed to the successful rebranding of that institution: widening participation through increasingly progressive, participatory and hands-on opportunities for the public.

Finally, Shakespeare's value and that of the organisations that deliver experience of him are often conflated. One example of this is the elision of notions of the curative value of Shakespeare for disengaged students with that of education departments' methods. Thus, the chapter closes with a case study of the RSC as a cultural chemist, the value of whose prescriptions for the treatment of Shakespeare is demonstrably confused with that of his works. It suggests that the term 'cultural chemist' offers a means to critique the recently popular conception of Shakespeare as a cultural catalyst, a metaphor that obscures the agency of organisations and individuals in perpetuating the value of Shakespeare and implies that Shakespeare is unchanged by his place in education and culture. Furthermore, it enables a critique of the inconsistencies and tensions in the RSC's construction of its educational mission.

Throughout the following sections, the arguments are evidenced with analysis of ephemera including websites, play programmes, advertising material and observation of events. These are plentiful sources, much used by – and presumably intended to be influential on – visitors to these organisations but rarely incorporated into academic writing on Shakespeare (with the possible exception of performance history). Thus, this chapter also serves to provide a snapshot of these organisations' educational offerings in the first decade of the twenty-first century, something that may prove hard to research or reconstruct in years to come given the low archival status of much of this material. Indeed, the SBT has expanded its online offerings beyond recognition since 2010, engaging with users through multiple social media platforms and websites. Produced to sell these organisations' Shakespeare(s) to students and teachers, these sources are rich in explicit constructions and declarations of Shakespeare's value. However, their commercial imperative notably influences the impartiality of their content: they represent, almost exclusively, positive and ideal experiences of Shakespeare. Any negative and/or real experience cited is the result of my own observation of events and productions targeted at, and often directly involving, school groups.

Physical Proximity at the SBT

The value of the experience of Shakespeare through the education department of the SBT is constructed as one of proximity to Shakespeare's personal history (especially his childhood and retirement). This relates to the nature of its collections: unmissable on the streets of Stratford are the houses (and sites of houses) owned by Shakespeare and his family. A sense of Shakespeare as embodied in the houses is conveyed partly through reference to the 'birthroom' or the wooden settle and infamous (if inauthentically Shakespearean) bed at Anne Hathaway's, both items that offer the possibility of a tangible connection to his body: a chance to reconnect with a physical thing now lost. The birthplace is described as 'the house [...] Shakespeare would have known [...] as a boy' and Mary Arden's as 'the childhood home of Shakespeare's mother' (Shakespeare Birthplace Trust 2010a). These statements emphasise the SBT's holdings as heritage in its most literal meaning: that of an inheritance, a legacy from Shakespeare. Meanwhile the library possesses archival documents relating to the lives, business transactions and public offices of himself and his relatives. Early publications of his works are also represented, offering perhaps a historical connection to his career as a playwright and time spent in London that Stratford might otherwise be lacking:

> Our resources are second to none: the most significant Shakespeare library in Europe (and one of the most important of all world collections), unique documents relating to Shakespeare's life, the archives of the RSC (representing a hundred and thirty years of Shakespeare in performance), and the house where Shakespeare was born, grew up, and in which he began to write.
>
> (Shakespeare Birthplace Trust 2008)

It is evident in this description from the SBT website that two strands – Shakespeare's life and works, and his incarnations as early modern person and author – jostle for supremacy within the organisation. In terms of their educational provision, it seems that the first is targeted primarily at younger students and the latter at those older students completing GCSE exams or advanced-level assessments. For younger students, especially, the proximity to this iconic figure and his historical context is heavily emphasised by the SBT. Shakespeare is made to re-inhabit the houses, resurrected, through a series of pamphlets for key stage two and three students visiting the properties, which 'he' narrates: 'Hi I am Will, that's William Shakespeare to some' (Shakespeare Birthplace Trust 2010a). He guides students around the houses and their histories, pointing out items such as the mulberry tree – which, 'he' tells them, is *like* his favourite mulberry tree, now long since cut down. Shakespeare's presence and absence sit uncomfortably alongside each other throughout these pamphlets and throughout the SBT's offerings more generally. Alongside concrete facts such as Shakespeare's acquisition of New Place in 1597, more tenuous authenticity is suggested through speculative connections to Shakespeare's inhabitation of the houses: of the parlour in the birthplace 'Will' says, 'This stone floor is the oldest in the house. I may once have stood on these very same flagstones' (Shakespeare Birthplace Trust 2010a). Shakespeare in the fabric of this building is thus 'everywhere but is also invisible' since 'none of the objects displayed actually belonged to him' (Hodgdon 1998: 202). Of Anne Hathaway's cottage, he similarly tells us, 'Some of the trees in the orchard here are very old indeed. It is possible that these trees are descendants of ones I plucked apples from as a boy' (Shakespeare Birthplace Trust 2010b). In this way, the collections at each property can be said to 'constitute a cult of fragments, an assemblage of material objects that stand in synedochal, metaphoric, or metonymic relationship to Shakespeare; a context for the subject substitutes for the subject himself, its episteme, resemblance to a lost Elizabethan world' (Hodgdon 1998: 203). Thus the cult of authenticity turns out to be a cult where authenticity is almost irrelevant, or at least, constructed rather than absolute: it is the authentic 'feel and look' of the houses and visitors 'imaginative simulations' which seem to matter most (de Groot 2009: 9).

The two opposites, presence and absence, are also evident, intertwined, in the narrator Will's recognition of his own historicity. He uses the past tense: 'My bed *was* like the one with the red cover on it' (*Who was Shakespeare?* 2010, my emphasis). Moreover he 'talks' about his own death: 'I don't like to discuss it too much, but probably my wife and daughters laid me out […] They then wrapped me in a cloth called a shroud' (Shakespeare Birthplace Trust 2010a). This renders his guiding a series of memories, gesturing towards an authentic cognitive process, yet invented by the pamphlet's author. His narrative voice and some of his knowledges (e.g. of his death and burial) express a consciousness of himself as a visitor to a lost Elizabethan age, to his own life. Shakespeare, rather than today's school students, becomes the time-traveller.

Awkwardly straddling his past and our present times through his narration, Shakespeare in these pamphlets needs to be understood as part of the imagination, re-enactment and willing suspension of disbelief that students (and other visitors) are asked to participate in at the SBT to bridge the gap between past and present, presence and absence. This represents part of a paradigm shift in the museum world itself over the past few decades, from defining its role as conservator and gatekeeper of heritage towards favouring interpretation and living history. An example of the emphasis on interpretation over sheer volume of objects can be seen at the Imperial War Museum North, in Salford, where the symbolic architecture and minimalist display of collections offer a starting point for an interpretative light-and-sound display that visitors experience in the main gallery. This trend has been embraced by the SBT, which, for example, promises to bring 'Tudors Alive!' through an 'all day hands-on workshop' for history students at Mary Arden's house, depicted as 'a real working farm from Shakespeare's time' (Shakespeare Birthplace Trust 2008). Early modern life is physically recreated here, as students actively participate in domestic activities from the period using imitation implements and ancient processes: they will, the website promises, make, bake, churn, tease, spin, use, knit, launder, tend, hurdle and thresh like a Tudor.

Firstly, this transition corresponds to increasingly accepted progressive notions about pedagogy, which favour 'empathetic engagement and interactive learning' as models for success (de Groot 2009: 42). That notions of empathy, interaction and participation have been applied to the classroom teaching of Shakespeare in schools has already been demonstrated through my discussion of active methods in chapter two. Secondly, it coincides with the growth of participatory models of entertainment. In terms of television programming, for example,

> Where Reithian BBC models conceived of the educative power of television as a transmitter of information, contemporary television experience is more fragmented and far more interested in participation. Interactivity is the key word of the digital TV revolution, for instance. A greater sense of choice, interaction and control is fundamental to the way that television channels now present themselves.
>
> (de Groot 2009: 166)

'Viewers' are exhorted to join in by signing up to become the stars of reality television shows; to interact by voting contestants into or out of game shows; to view programmes at their leisure using recording and playback, such as BBC iPlayer or Channel 4 On Demand (C4OD); and to gain further information using the 'red button' on their digital remote controls. Thirdly, this shift relates to the spread of capitalist, consumerist principles (such as consumer sovereignty and choice) and discourses from economics into the realm of public services, including education – as evidenced in chapter one.

The widespread nature of a movement towards participation, interactivity and choice does not, however, mean that it has been readily accepted by education departments such as that of the SBT. While a vast amount of that ethos is visible in the SBT's education resources and on their website – a medium that Kate Rumbold has argued is replete with such discourse (2010: 314) – there is still evidence of more conservative approaches to learning that distance Shakespeare, rather than embrace a sense of his proximity. For instance, the 'Life on a Tudor Farm' half-day visit provides the opportunity for students to 'see', rather than taste, 'the food they ate' and to 'learn all about', rather than experience, 'the lives of the people that lived on the farm' (Shakespeare Birthplace Trust 2008). Students on the 'Rich Man, Poor Man' workshop at the Shakespeare Centre are assured of the opportunity to 'write', 'find out', 'handle', 'examine', 'make' and 'take' – a rather less vigorous group of verbs than those that used to describe learning at Mary Arden's house (Shakespeare Birthplace Trust 2008). Although the SBT offers 'set text workouts', 'exploratory work', 'practical exercises', 'practical sessions' and 'practical engagement', its website emphasises that these potentially lively activities are not an end in themselves, rather a means to 'intellectual reflection' and 'organised discussion' (Shakespeare Birthplace Trust 2008). Thus it reinforces a hierarchy, where action and participation are figured as an introductory rather than integral element of learning. Underlying this hierarchical view, Jerome de Groot explains, is a 'professional distaste' among historians for 'the various popular forms of history': a viewpoint that emerges from 'a critique of the popular and a theoretical model of the cultural industries which encourages a binary of high (History) versus low (heritage or "the historical")' (2009: 4). This critique has its counterpart in early-twentieth-century literary studies. The writings of Leavis and T.S. Eliot, as discussed in chapter one, bemoaned the debasing of literature and culture through then new, mass-produced forms such as cheap paperback fiction and cinema, polarising the academic and the consumer. The emphasis in these sessions for older students is suggestive of the SBT's recent past in which academics have dominated its management and staff and its educational provision has been centred on traditional textual and historicist approaches.

A frequently expressed concern on the part of such ideologues, which is relevant to the SBT's attempts to fall in line with wider cultural trends, is that the value of authenticity is neglected in favour of artifice by heritage institutions. The human geographer David Lowenthal, who has written widely on the relationship between history and cultural heritage, suggests that 'heritage practitioners take pride in creating artifice, the public enjoys consuming it' (de Groot 2009: 4). Similarly, Hewison has written that 'Heritage is gradually effacing History by substituting an image of the past for its reality' (1995: 21). A core problem with this view is that it erroneously supposes that we *can* obtain the reality of the past. It ignores that what we have of the past is limited to some objects, ascertainable facts, contemporary narratives and subsequent interpretations of these – the experience of the past's reality will always, by its very nature, be elusive to us. There is no physical, objective entity called 'history', only clusters of processes and meanings that constitute it. Peim has previously noted that this is also true of English: 'There is no English – no real, essential English – outside of its institutional practice' (1993: 5). Literature is barely more tangible: despite the existence of physical books, not all such books are seen to constitute literature. Traditionally these processes have been cast as education and, even more narrowly, the accumulation of facts (the accession dates of kings and queens) and skills (source study). Long held sacrosanct, their proponents have clashed with newly popular attempts to constitute history as entertainment and experience witnessed by, de Groot argues, a forceful and insatiable appetite among the English public in recent years for 'cultural histories, celebrity historians, historical novels, star-studded historical films, TV drama, documentaries and reality shows, as well as cultural events and historical re-enactments' (2009: i). That is to say, there is a demonstrable public demand for history above and beyond that constituted by academic research.

The implications of this context for the SBT's valuing of its educational experience of Shakespeare as a proximate one, despite residual resistance from an old ideology that values critical distance over empathetic engagement and is wary of consumerism and populism, is that their provision offers a good fit to the newly 'voracious audience for all things historical' (de Groot 2009: i). That is to say, the SBT provision matches the mood of a public that is more interested in early modern history and Shakespeare's life than his works. What, however, are the implications for those visiting the houses as part of a formal educational experience – many of them are English rather than history students? How does this value of Shakespeare as an immediate presence at the SBT – through emphasis on the reconstruction of his historical context and a focus on his domestic life, through methods of guiding that require participation, whether empathetic or physical – sit with the requirements of the National Curriculum? Happily, for the SBT, it correlates well with the values of personal growth, new historicism and active methods witnessed in the National Curriculum for English, the attainment objectives introduced in 2000 and national strategies (such as *Shakespeare for All Ages and Stages*) discussed in chapter two.

Play and Community at the Globe

In Globe education, the value of their proffered experience of Shakespeare is situated in what the organisation claims is an authentically 'Shakespearean' ethos of play and community. This authenticity derives largely from the organisation's rebuilding of a theatre, for which Shakespeare wrote, acted, and in which he held a share, near its original site in Southwark. A prime site described by Sam Wanamaker as having 'national and international significance and value' (Holderness 1988a: 17). The organisation's nature (as a reconstructed theatre) and location are seen to offer a connection to Shakespeare not only through the physical building and site but also through the Globe's ideology, methods and activities. These include original practice stagings; Shakespeare heard in the context of his contemporaries, through the Read not Dead series of staged readings, run at the Globe since 1995; and contrastingly, the encouragement of new works of drama – partly informed by the idea of fostering potential new 'Shakespeares', i.e. new play-writing talent.

'Play', both as a noun and as a verb, centrally contributes to constructing the value of Shakespeare in Globe education. The department's main page opens with a reference, ironically not to Shakespeare, but to the playwright John Marston and his concept of the play in performance as 'the soul of lively action' (Marston 15). This phase recurs throughout the site, connecting the experience of a lively Shakespeare with live performance; linking the value of play and playwright to the process of playing. The importance of playing, in Globe education, amounts not only to productions of play, in the sense of a dramatic work performed by a group of actors, but also to the activities sometimes associated with the leisure activities of children and in modern education theory, regarded as an essential part of development and learning. 'Play', 'playful', 'play-filled' and 'playground' all occur in one paragraph on the website, consciously reinvigorating the sense in which the Globe is a 'playhouse' (Shakespeare's Globe 2008). Thus the language of the organisation connotes both Shakespearean authenticity and important developments in educational theory and pedagogy in modernity. These developments include those outlined by Jean-Jacques Rousseau through to Maria Montessori, whose writings promote experiential and experimental learning through play. Indeed, educational provision at the Globe is described on the website through a discourse of active methods: commonly used phrases include 'active engagement', 'practical exploration' and 'research activities' (as opposed to the more usual 'research interests').

The Globe's emphasis on the play in performance and active methods pedagogies, like the movement towards living history at the SBT, has the effect of reinvesting Shakespeare with life: the Globe proclaims 'Shakespeare Lives!' under the subheading 'Teaching Shakespeare Through Performance' on its website (Shakespeare's Globe 2008). Their use of this phrase connotes resurrections – from that of Christ as described in the Bible, and encapsulated in the phrase 'Jesus Lives!' used in Christian services, to conspiracy theories that suggest that the 'kings' of the music world Elvis Presley and Buddy Holly live on (either figuratively, through their music, or literally, through conspiracy theories surrounding their deaths). Although the Globe cannot resurrect Shakespeare's body natural, it can, and does, make the claim that its summer schools will breathe new life into his works, his body politic. Through their methods, they assure teachers, Shakespeare's stories will '*live* in the classroom' (Shakespeare's Globe 2008). Shakespeare and his works will be reanimated through their exertions: 'words do not lie lifeless on the page in Globe Education workshops' (Shakespeare's Globe 2008). Bringing Shakespeare (back) to life through theatre (both by staging productions and adapting theatre into pedagogy) is at the centre of Globe education, and, as will be demonstrated in the next section, the RSC education department too.

To (re)build a theatre for playing with Shakespeare or, more specifically, experiments in early modern theatre and staging might seem a potentially exclusive thing to do, centred as it is around the needs of academic research. Yet the Globe Trust has always emphasised its other motives. These include, in its founder Sam Wanamaker's words, 'the educationalist's wish to provide a demonstrative model of a Renaissance institution for pedagogic purposes' as well as 'a commercially viable and potentially profitable' tourist enterprise to fund its scholarly endeavours, thereby avoiding dependence on virtually non-existent public funding for the arts during the recession of the late 1980s and early 1990s (Holderness 1988a: 18). Nonetheless, the values of the Globe project were certainly interrogated as elitist and motivated by capitalism in Graham Holderness' 1986 interview with Wanamaker. Commencing with a discussion of the organisation's acquisition of land, which left-wing political campaigners argued should be used for new public housing and open space (16–17), Holderness questions Wanamaker on people's perceptions of the dispute as 'a conflict between "high culture" and housing needs' (17). In answer, Wanamaker points out that a 'community-benefit' contribution was built into the project by the Labour council that initially approved the development (before a new council, opposed to the project, was elected) (Holderness 1988a: 16–17). He adds that further community input was initiated by the Globe through its inclusion of local community organisations and businesses on its advisory board, as well as running a programme of activities for local people (Holderness 1988a: 18). Throughout the interview he refers to two other, non-London-based Globe communities, national and international, making the organisation's apparent inclusivity, geographically, even wider (Holderness 1988a: 18).

Whatever the original need to ameliorate criticism of a possible capitalist, elitist imperative, the Globe continues to invoke a notion of the value of community (and its role in upholding that value), cast as authentically Shakespearean by its location in a London borough where the playwright lived and worked. Its mission for outreach is stated on its website: 'Shakespeare and the Globe should extend beyond our building, beyond schools and into the streets and homes of Southwark' (Shakespeare's Globe 2008). Furthermore, the website highlights the belief of its founder Sam Wanamaker, 'in the power of the arts as a force for change to transform communities' (Shakespeare's Globe 2008). To demonstrate Wanamaker's continuing legacy in proliferating a sense of local community, the website refers to its 'Concert for Winter' led by Southwark school students – an event featuring, not Shakespeare, but the songs and music of the borough's diverse population. This event implicitly draws on Shakespeare's Globe as a site of local entertainment for its authenticity. Much of the organisation's work thus goes beyond running workshops, tours, lectures and talks for visiting tourists and academics. There is a definite attempt to foster a shared consciousness of the theatre as situated within the community of this London borough as well as a wider (more geographically dispersed) community of creative types, theatre practitioners and academics. There is an 'adopt an actor' scheme for schools. Rutgers students 'work with Globe Education Practitioners in schools in the community to discover how actors can share their skills and knowledge with young people in workshops and projects'. Additionally, they explore the 'role and impact of the creative arts across the curriculum' with attention to the work of local (and national) arts organisations, artists, arts practitioners and teachers (Shakespeare's Globe 2008). Collaboration between 'theatre practitioners and academics', traditionally seen as two distinct and polarised communities, is also embraced through events such as the Shakespeare's Globe Theatre History Seminars.

Related to its attempts to be seen as sharing its resources and knowledge with the local community, as well as past governments' values for social inclusion (discussed in chapter one) is the Globe's discourse of accessibility. The language of its website employs metaphors around the physical openness of their sites throughout to convey this point. The Globe declares itself, for instance, 'an open house and is open to all'; it quotes the *Merchant of Venice*, 'You are welcome, take your place' (IV.i.167); and claims that 'The Globe is never dark'. While this is patently untrue in a literal sense – witness the locked gates to the yard and ushers clearing it of patrons between matinée and evening performances – it invokes the idea that light, enlightenment, illumination and learning are available twenty-four hours a day, seven days a week. Furthermore, such statements emphasise the allegedly unconditional nature of this access: it is extended to all regardless of age, merit, race, sex, class and so on. While such assertions seem overly-ambitious and unachievable, they have at least been matched by a concerted effort to realise the Globe's constant openness in a virtual environment. Provided that they have access to a computer, an Internet connection and the skills to utilise them (a not insignificant assumption) any person can use, at any time, the three-hundred-and-sixty degree tour of the building on the Globe's website. They can also 'see' a production through the freely available podcasts of the 2009 production of *Romeo and Juliet*, commissioned by the Department for Children, Schools and Families; or access a range of resources from actors' character notes to articles from the programme, that are disseminated through the online facility Globelink. Thus the Globe offers itself, and its product, Shakespeare, as the focal point for a global Internet community.

One specific aspect of equal access policy and practice aims to alleviate financial constraints on participation for those from socio-economically disadvantaged households. In its 'Education Events Summer 09' pamphlet, the Globe addresses this requirement by advertising 'Sam's Day', a celebration of the birthday of its founder, which involves 'free workshops, demonstrations and platform discussions' on a more narrowly Shakespeare-oriented theme (Shakespeare's Globe 2009). These include twenty-minute versions of *Romeo and Juliet*, a look at unusual film adaptations of Shakespeare, and storytelling inspired by the plays. Interestingly, unlike the RSC's annual open day for which many events can be pre-booked (from backstage tours to costume department talks) and some of which (such as concerts and staged readings) attract a fee, the Globe offers access to these events on a 'first come first serve basis – just turn up on the day to book' (Shakespeare's Globe 2009). A move arguably intended to elide the advantage of those wealthier families with access to computers, broadband and telephones, with the time and opportunity to plan and book ahead. Specifically, the arrangements may have been designed to stop middle-class families from capitalising on and dominating educational opportunities that are aimed at generating wider participation. It may therefore signal a deliberate response to perennial media headlines critiquing the 'sharp-elbowed' middle-class monopolisation of public services and other opportunities. These critiques can be seen, for instance, in early evaluations of the SureStart parenting initiative aimed at the most deprived families, as well as a subsequent appraisal of the service by the Cameron government (Bennett 2006). The Globe's continuing policy of accessibility, especially as regards its local community, satisfied (and perhaps even offered an inspirational model for) the bent towards raising the inclusivity of participation in the arts under New Labour.

Elsewhere, the value of Shakespeare at Globe education as allied to an ethos of play intersects strongly with trends in educational theory and, in recent years, policy towards participatory, child-centred learning. It is particularly interesting that the values of this privately funded organisation have coincided with some of the state's during New Labour's years in office. This cannot be explained simply by understanding the Globe as conforming to government policy – since much of its work began long before New Labour policies took root and it is less obliged to reach a concord with government policy than an equivalent publicly funded organisation, such as the RSC. It is also unfeasible to propose that the Globe alone could influence government uptake of these policies. Yet it is possible that these two flows of influence, along with gradually changing trends in education and for corporate social responsibility – its purposes and pedagogies – have seen the Globe and New Labour's values around Shakespeare cohere.

Ensemble Plus at the RSC

The value of Shakespeare in the RSC education department is constructed as embodied in the techniques and spaces of the acting company that it uses. These techniques and spaces are invoked as authentically Shakespearean in supposedly channelling those theatrical methods and spaces the playwright would himself have used, from co-operating on scripts with fellow company members to playing on a thrust stage. Moreover, the RSC channels the way Shakespeare is done now by actors, including at its own institution: working in ensemble and collaboratively experimenting in the rehearsal room. The company publicises its use of 'ensemble learning' methods; 'creative learning methods adapted from the theatrical process'; and 'active, theatre-based approaches' modelled on the rehearsal process – an approach foregrounded by Gibson, as shown in chapter two (Royal Shakespeare Company 2008b; Gibson 1998: 12). Thus there is a sense of the early modern and the contemporary acting company as dual models for classroom work. Whereas the SBT's educational provision focuses on learning through historic re-enactment, for the RSC the simulacra are theatrical ones (with the Globe incorporating elements of both).

The RSC's representations of its value are staked on its educational practices as solutions to various 'problems' with Shakespeare that it perceives confront students and teachers. These include the restrictiveness of classroom practice and pedagogic ethos presented by government education policy, which I will examine in the following section. I want to concentrate firstly on the RSC's perception of Shakespeare's language as both the source of his difficulty and of his beauty. The former is tackled by their use of 'fun' methods to build students' confidence. Secondly, the problematic themes and length of the plays for young people are addressed through productions targeted at young people: such as the abridged, physical theatre-informed *Comedy of the Errors* (the first RSC Young People's Shakespeare, staged in 2009). In taking these measures, the RSC can also be seen as constructing a new form of disadvantage around Shakespeare: youth. For example, the company writes on its website that students may find 'Shakespeare's work remote or inaccessible' unless they are offered tailored education provision (Royal Shakespeare Company 2008). In doing so, it builds on a long tradition of reworking Shakespeare for children and young adults from the Bowdlers' editing of the plays in the eighteenth century. Detailed accounts of this practice historically are available in the work of Abigail Rokison (2012) and Jennifer Hulbert, Kevin Wetmore and Robert York (2006).

The RSC promises to tackle young people's struggle with Shakespeare's language through immersing them in the spoken word. Indeed, it uses the term 'language' in its programme for the Regional Schools Celebration thirty-three times. In its emphasis, the RSC combines its traditional reputation as supreme and reverent handlers of his words in production with its more recent push towards playfulness in word and action, balancing educational gravitas with the appeal of 'fun'. It maintains a respect for Shakespeare's widely accepted role as father of the English language, while recognising that the historical isolation of his early modern vocabulary and phrasing makes it increasingly difficult for children and non-specialists, who encounter little other writing from the period, to understand. One of the techniques used to introduce students to Shakespeare's language, which the RSC has included in its pedagogical portfolio, is the use of Shakespearean insults. This was also adopted by the SBT in its resources for key stages two and three students that feature an 'insult creator' table, to help you 'mix and match your own Shakespearean sounding insult' (Shakespeare Birthplace Trust 2010b). The following insult exercise was suggested by the RSC as part of the template for a *Romeo and Juliet*-themed assembly entitled What has Shakespeare ever done for us? This formed part of nationwide events publicised across primary and secondary schools for the 'Stand Up for Shakespeare' assembly week in January 2009. Teachers were encouraged to use the table below during the assembly, or to use it beforehand to allocate insults to the students who will represent the warring Montague and Capulet families:

Are you a Montague or a Capulet? Would you really like to annoy your enemies? Use this table to come up with your own insult using genuine Shakespearean words.

Pick one adjective from the first column, a noun from the second, put them together and you've got an insult that can start a duel in seconds:

gorbellied	boar-pig
rump-fed	maggot pie
pribbling	Ratsbane
clapper-clawed	Giglet

(Royal Shakespeare Company 2009d: 3)

The activity resembles an exercise that might be used with actors to get into character; to build emotion; to gain familiarity with archaic vocabulary; or to test their voice projection. Cicely Berry, for example, encourages actors to throw vowels, rather than insults, in a voice-coaching book based on her work at the RSC (1974: 41). Not only can the activity claim theatrical authenticity, it also explicitly claims to have Shakespearean authenticity with its reference to 'genuine Shakespearean words'.

Having demonstrated its theatrical and academic credentials, the activity can be seen as striving for another type of credibility: 'street-cred'. 'Shakespeare insult' badges are widely available at museum and gallery shops nationwide, including those at the three institutions featured here, and for several years there has been a Facebook application dedicated to allowing users to invent and send such insults to their 'friends' (Anon. 2010). Thus the RSC education department, and their counterparts at the SBT, have capitalised on (and possibly further contributed to) a phenomenon from popular culture to convey the value of Shakespeare's language to their young learners, suggesting a two-way flow of influence such as that identified by Bruner (1996: ix).

Another instance of the RSC targeting the disadvantage faced by youth in approaching Shakespeare – involving a specially tailored, theatre-based solution – is the annual Young People's plays, including, in 2009, *The Comedy of Errors*. This seventy-five-minute production of the play was specially adapted by the RSC, in collaboration with the Shakespearean-titled theatre company, Told by an Idiot, to engage school audiences. Rokison, writing *Shakespeare for Young People*, has argued that having only begun to explore cut-down versions for children in 2004, the RSC found itself following, rather than leading, other theatres (2012: 104). This may relate to the 'snobbery' Hulbert discusses around heavily cut Shakespeare. *The Comedy of Errors* adopted much of Told by an Idiot's ethos to generate an 'experience' that would be universally accessible to primary and secondary school children: 'Through collaborative writing, anarchic physicality and a playful but rigorous approach to text, the company is committed to creating a genuinely spontaneous experience for the audience. Using a wealth of imagery and a rich theatrical language, we aim to tell universal stories that are accessible to all' ('Company history and artistic policy'). In this sense, the production represents Shakespeare *for* not *by* young people (unlike the same season's Youth Ensemble *The Winter's Tale*): something about which the title 'Young People's Shakespeare' is ambiguous. Its use of features such as pre-show, (sometimes improvised) direct address and cut-down original language scripts have been noted elsewhere in productions of Shakespeare for young people – such as the National Theatre Primary Classics and Pocket Propeller (Rokison 2012: 104). The production premiered in schools in the West Midlands. This was followed by a tour to Newcastle-upon-Tyne and a small run of seven performances at the RSC Courtyard Theatre in 2009 and a revival for the 2010 summer season. Here, unlike the other venues, members of the general public were able to attend – which extended the age range of the audience upwards, as well as potentially the universal appeal that it can claim.

The production made two noticeable assumptions about what is problematic in staging Shakespeare for students: the adult concerns his plays deal with (their themes) and their length. With regard to *The Comedy of Errors*, its brevity and farcical elements could be seen as appealing to a younger audience, while its handling of emotionally demanding issues, likely to be relevant to some of the audience, such as the separation of siblings (through divorce or adoption perhaps), fit with long-held perceptions of the need for literary education, evidenced in previous chapters, to offer opportunities for personal, emotional and moral growth through vicarious experience. In this way, it might be seen as a good choice for an audience of children. However, much of *The Comedy of Errors* is concerned with adult themes – unhappiness in marriage and adultery, for example. In this production such content was noticeably imbued with value for young people through the physical theatre style that drew attention towards itself and, to an extent, away from the challenging issues raised by Shakespeare's plot. A similar reliance on 'physically expressive' performances is noted by Rokison in her evaluation of the 2009 Regent's Park Theatre *Tempest* aimed at children (2012: 101).

The character of the Courtesan, for example, is difficult to present to school students, given the taboos around prostitution that persist in an education system that still insists on discussions of sex primarily in the context of anatomy-focused biology lessons or as part of personal, social and health education (PSHE). In one, sex tends to be rendered as a scientific process, stripped of social and emotional significance. In the other, sex is overwhelmingly characterised as a part of loving, rather than pecuniary, relationships. In this production, while the Courtesan kept her title – surely bound to raise probing questions from uncomprehending children in the classroom and perhaps sniggers from any 'in the know' – her sexuality was rendered comic. With a long blond wig and eccentric but non-sexual dance moves, she narrated some of the story through a song. This was performed in the style of a 1960s style pop concert (complete with backing singers and a band provided by the other actors). Thus the courtesan became a wannabe starlet – possibly alluding to the notion of a courtesan as an entertainer – rather than a prostitute, that is to say, a woman who sells her body for sex. This treatment of the Courtesan constitutes part of the way in which adult themes were rendered child-friendly through the RSC's processes of adaptation and staging. In addition to the Courtesan, marital turbulence and the physical abuse of the Dromios by their masters were dealt with comically, used to produce laughter and as a vehicle for frenetic physical movement across the stage. Rokison goes further in pointing to a potential conflict between the suitability of certain themes in Shakespeare for children and the RSC's insistence on starting it early (2012: 17).

Action is clearly perceived by the RSC to be something a young people's Shakespeare must not fall short of – '*see* it live, *do* it on your feet, *start* it earlier', was the mantra of the 'Stand Up for Shakespeare' campaign (Royal Shakespeare Company 2008a). As if to compensate for the humorous treatment of these issues in the production, the programme – perhaps also intended to fulfil some of the role of an education pack – flags up the actors' process of exploring feeling in rehearsals and asks the audience (mainly students and teachers) to engage in empathetic analysis or stagecraft: 'How do you feel when Dromio is hit? How do the other actors make sure he doesn't get hurt?' (Royal Shakespeare Company 2009c). The play is made fast-paced and funny, with little time to absorb the seriousness of its themes during the show, while the programme indicates a space for education in anticipation or reflection of its performance. Furthermore, while effectively 'neutralising' the adultness of the play that might render it inaccessible to a younger audience, the production and programme failed to highlight potentially fruitful social issues for class discussion. These include the sale of the Dromio twins into servitude – an example of the exploitation of children for economic gain, which students may encounter in school through contact with the Fairtrade movement or when studying slavery in history – as well as issues of justice surrounding Egeon's imprisonment and trial. Thus the RSC appears enlightened for choosing to stage a play that is not generally deemed attractive to children. Yet it is also old fashioned, if not patronising, in its assumption that the best way to present certain adult themes to children is to render them comical. In summary, the RSC appeals to children's faculty for enjoyment of Shakespeare using models of action and participation derived from actorly or directorial methods, often deployed in the physical environ of the theatre or an imagined theatrical context, to overcome young people's struggle to understand or engage with the plays. I will expand on this further in the following section, proposing the RSC (and specifically its Regional Schools Celebration) as an example of such institutions' agency in shaping experiences of Shakespeare.

The ostensibly unique value of Shakespeare in each education department has been shown to be more a part of each organisation's branding through the discourse of their marketing materials, designed to accentuate (even construct) their USPs. Some difference in what they offer does emanate from their diverse natures as theatres, heritage organisations, libraries or a combination of these. However, their educational products and services are built out of fairly homogenous values. These include Shakespeare as experienced through their education programmes as lively, active, authentic (whether authenticity is attained through place, methods or ethos) and accessible. Whether these values are inherent in Shakespeare or are added-values that these organisations bring to his works needs to be considered further. The following section uses the metaphor of a 'cultural chemist' to propose that the two different loci of value are often conflated by organisations such as the RSC.

The RSC as 'Cultural Chemist'

'Shakespeare as cultural catalyst' was the theme of the 2010 International Shakespeare Association conference. The phrase was widely referenced in many speakers' papers. Others still engaged with definitions of what it is to be a catalyst: literally, in chemistry, a substance that initiates or speeds up a reaction but remains itself chemically unaltered by that process. Jonathan Bate's paper, for instance, proposed Shakespeare to be a 'catalytic converter' (2010). Thus by modifying terms and proposing additional metaphors, some critiques of the limitations of the original phrase began to emerge. The remainder of this chapter expands the critique, problematising the possibility that Shakespeare is a cultural catalyst, since a truly catalytic substance remains unaltered by the reaction. Narratives of Shakespeare as a cultural catalyst involve him unilaterally conferring kudos onto individuals, corporations and other organisations that associate themselves with his person, life and works, or acting as a spur to further creativity and greatness. However, I will demonstrate that Shakespeare *is* altered by the interaction between his works, institutions and audiences. My analysis examines the way in which the phrase, 'Shakespeare as cultural catalyst', fails to acknowledge that not all reactions are naturally occurring, unaided by human intervention. It contends that the phrase attributes Shakespeare with agency while obscuring the power of those who act on him. These agents include editors, directors, conservators, teachers and the institutions to which they belong. Their numbers are further swelled by independent scholars, Shakespeare enthusiasts and bloggers. I argue that these organisations and individuals, like chemists, facilitate reactions, or processes, around Shakespeare by bringing together the necessary ingredients; these might include readers and students with his works, tourists with his Stratford houses and so on.

Furthermore, to describe the author as a cultural catalyst neglects the different subjectivities, contexts, objectives and assumptions of those contributing to the catalytic process. In *Cultural Selection*, Gary Taylor argues that an author such as Shakespeare cannot endure, let alone continue to dominate vast areas such as English education, without the help of what he terms a 'survivor': 'Culture is not what was done but what is passed on. Culture therefore depends not only upon the maker who stimulates but upon the survivor who remembers, preserves and transmits the stimulus' (1996: 89). If it is envisioned at all in Taylor's conception, the catalytic role is shared between the work's author and a survivor or survivors. Like many successful 'makers', Shakespeare has had multiple survivors or carriers (another term that Taylor applies to those who act in ways that secure an artist's legacy) who have promulgated his value – early examples include Heminges and Condell, editors of the First Folio, as well as contributors to the volume, such as Ben Jonson. In turn, they recruited new guardians of Shakespeare's value through their readers, through inspiring other editors, other eulogisers, and so the cycle continues. Policy-makers render him compulsory, while educators debate the value various pedagogies add to or detract from his works. This is necessary, explains Taylor, 'Because the dying of human carriers never ceases, the need to pass on memories to new carriers never ends' (1996: 8).

Given this naturally high turnover of advocates, it could be argued that institutions rather than individuals offer security or stability in ensuring Shakespeare's ongoing influence. Indeed, Terry Eagleton has argued that Shakespeare is brought to life as a construct of institutions rather than as an authorial source (1983: 205). These establishments include libraries like the Folger; places of study, such as the Shakespeare Institute; heritage organisations, for example, the Shakespeare Birthplace Trust; dedicated Shakespeare theatres along the lines of the Royal Shakespeare Company and the Globe; regular Shakespeare festivals, for instance, Ontario; as well as conference committees, like that of the Shakespeare Association of America. These organisations offer a strong degree of continuity, in terms of the size and focus of their operations, even as they evolve from time to time. Shakespeare remains at the core of these organisations whether they vary their purpose from conservation to providing access, from engaging a domestic audience to an international one.

To reinvest the discussion of Shakespeare as a cultural catalyst with a sense of institutional agency, I offer here a case study of the RSC's role as a 'cultural chemist', through its provision for schools. My discussion draws particularly on the second Regional Schools Celebration and the Young People's *Comedy of Errors* staged in 2009, supplementing first-hand observation with analysis of printed material including programmes. It suggests that the RSC can be understood as wittingly combining various elements (play texts, theatrical spaces, people, the company's ethos) to set in action, observe and reflect on processes around a pseudo-catalytic ingredient: Shakespeare. These processes include staging plays or educating teachers and students. As a consequence of these activities, Shakespeare, unlike a true catalyst, is altered. His value is reconstituted as the value of RSC ethos and pedagogy. A similar metaphor for the RSC has been previously deployed in Richard Wilson's article 'NATO's pharmacy: Shakespeare by prescription'. I have been inspired by Wilson's use of pharmaceutical imagery but also, to some extent, by the substance of his argument: for example, his assertion of the hidden prescriptiveness that underlies progressive pedagogies used by the RSC in their teacher training (1997: 62–63).

I have anticipated the criticism that, in doing so, I am setting up yet another metaphor: that I have failed to heed the warning, delivered by the eponymous heroine of *Educating Rita,* that 'any analogy breaks down eventually' (Russell 1981: II.i). The risk of an analogy breaking down is even greater when using terms from outside one's own field of knowledge. Yet, although the idea of institutions as cultural chemists may not endure, I argue that the metaphor helpfully allows me to critique and delimit the use of the term 'cultural catalyst' by highlighting the changes Shakespeare and his value undergoes through contact with such organisations. It also underlines the agency of those involved in what is, after all, a cultural rather than scientific process, 'a process of human development' rather than the 'tending of natural growth' (Williams 1983: 87). Although not my primary concern, I have found it impossible to ignore the potential for critiquing the institution itself that a notion of the RSC as cultural chemist facilitates. Thus throughout this discussion, I pause to show contradictions or gaps in the RSC education department's self-fashioning. The chapter concludes with a consideration of the organisation's interrelation with another institution and agent in shaping Shakespeare: government. In this way it connects with the other chapters in this book to suggest a dual and cyclical flow of influence, in determining the value of Shakespeare, between cultural institutions, such as theatres, and political ones.

That the values of the RSC are made, by the company, to stand in for the value of Shakespeare, in a way that changes what constitutes Shakespeare for students and teachers, is demonstrable through an analysis of events such as the Regional Schools Celebration. I contend that this value shift is represented through the use of the discourse of professional theatre, including an emphasis on ensemble work and the actor's journey; within that, the development and sharing of a discourse for Shakespeare that equates to a shaping of him in collective memory; slippages in discourse concerning terms such as 'text' and 'production'; and the promotion of Shakespeare done actively and outside the classroom as the supreme experience (both in terms of educational and personal development potential). Before addressing these elements directly, I will briefly outline the event itself.

The Regional Schools Celebration, held at the Courtyard Theatre in Stratford-upon-Avon over two days in June 2009, was the culmination of the RSC Learning and Performance Network's interaction with state schools nationwide. The network involves the RSC forming three-year partnerships with schools, many of which are situated in areas of economic and social deprivation. A key feature of the programme is that a smaller group of schools act as 'hub schools', sharing their knowledge and experience with a larger group of local schools to explore 'Shakespeare's work through performance' (Royal Shakespeare Company 2009b: 2). Teaching staff involved are drawn variously from English, drama and the arts more widely. For the Regional Schools Celebration, each of the eleven regions that the schools fell into was assigned a Shakespeare play. Schools within the same locale divided the play between them: each looked at different scenes or themes or characters to produce twenty-minute performances. In addition to teachers' input, each school worked with an RSC practitioner before showcasing their work at a regional festival. I attended the enthusiastic and enjoyable performances on 16 June, when six schools from Cumbria, Yorkshire, Cheshire and Surrey performed their 'responses' to *Much Ado About Nothing*, *The Tempest*, *The Winter's Tale*, *The Comedy of Errors*, *King Lear* and *Macbeth* on stage at the Courtyard. The responses constituted cut-down versions of the plays or specific scenes. Shakespeare's language was variously foregrounded or subdued depending on the age of the students: older students worked with lines directly from the plays while younger ones worked with varying combinations of 'edited Shakespeare text, negotiated adaptation and complete improvisation' as well as re-ordering and modern paraphrase (RSC 2009b: 3). Three of the performing schools were primary (or junior) schools and three of them high schools, so the performers ranged in age from six to sixteen plus. Their audience consisted of the classes' fellow students and teachers, parents, RSC governors and some members of the general public.

While waiting for the performances to begin, images of the school groups and news clippings covering their work were projected onto the stage, provoking cheers from their student members in the audience. There was no interval in the two hours' running time, which included a welcome and a summing up by the writer, broadcaster and comedian Hardeep Singh Kohli, who also presented certificates after the performances. There was also a warm-up for the participants and audience taken from rehearsal room exercises designed to engage the actor's 'three tools' of body, voice and brain. This was run by the Masters of Ceremony Ann Ogbomo (an RSC actor and graduate of the Teaching Shakespeare programme, which is jointly run by the RSC and the University of Warwick) and Steve Marmion (who has worked with the RSC as an Assistant Director). Ogbomo and Marmion's role included interviewing a teacher and group of students from each school on stage before their performance, as well as soliciting and fielding feedback from the audience after each production. Thus, without discussing the performances individually (a task beyond the scope of this chapter), an intertwining of education and entertainment was evident throughout, from the figures of the presenters to the content of the event.

The RSC is, by its very nature, an agent in presenting Shakespeare as theatre over other possibilities, including Shakespeare as poetry, as artefact or as the object of textual study. The RSC determines Shakespeare's value as such and shares this valuation outside the theatre realm through its education programmes in addition to staging his plays. Its naturalisation of Shakespeare as theatre is reinforced by its appropriation of certain strands of academic discourse, particularly the work of Rex Gibson, and establishment of ongoing academic collaborations (with, for instance, the University of Warwick's Teaching Shakespeare centre and, previously, its CAPITAL Centre) to affirm externally the validity of such a value.

That the RSC's ethos of teaching Shakespeare as theatre draws strongly on the work of Rex Gibson was acknowledged at the 2010 International Shakespeare Conference by Jonothan Neelands (Neelands and O'Hanlon 2010). As shown in chapter two, Gibson asserts that 'Shakespeare was essentially a man of the theatre who intended his words to be spoken and acted out on stage. It is in that context of dramatic realisation that the plays are most appropriately understood and experienced' (1998: xii). He also encouraged the use of rehearsal-room techniques in the classroom on the basis that they offer a connection with the way Shakespeare would have worked with his acting company (1998: 12). Divorced from their association with Gibson in the programme for the Regional Schools Celebration, these methods and discourse are implicitly rebranded as those of the RSC. The contributors to the programme, including the teachers and students quoted in it, praise the 'rehearsal room techniques' and 'physical' 'work' involved in the production of this event.

The RSC's agency in constructing the value of Shakespeare as synonymous with theatre was also visible throughout the Regional Schools Celebration in their emphasis on the importance of taking a play from rehearsal to its realisation on the professional stage. This focus was noticeably transmitted to the teachers it collaborated with: 'From understanding and dramatising the Shakespearean language in small groups, to working with the RSC practitioner, to actually performing at the Festival, has been an incredible journey. Now, the Courtyard Theatre!', enthuses teacher Tracey Bennett (Royal Shakespeare Company 2009b: 3). Additionally, the actor's journey – not always attended to in the experience of playing Shakespeare in the context of an English classroom – is praised as a useful part of the process by teachers: RSC methods, writes Steven Little, a head of department, have enabled 'students to fully get "inside" the characters' (Royal Shakespeare Company 2009b: 7). That the students involved, as well as their teachers, have picked up on and see value in RSC professional theatre is evident in their absorption and use of its discourse to describe their experience. They write of 'putting this fantastic play together', of 'going on stage', declare that 'acting is a great way to learn', and that 'the thing I most enjoyed was playing the trust games because they made it easier to act in role as we were thinking about the motivation of our characters' (Royal Shakespeare Company 2009b: 7, 9). This discourse is arguably derived from that of the RSC itself, for example, their exhortation to 'do it on your feet' – a phrase deployed throughout their 'Stand Up for Shakespeare' campaign (Royal Shakespeare Company 2008a). It is their experience of (personal) development through the activities of the RSC that is evidently in their minds, rather than Shakespeare's plays which are notably absent from many of these quotations. This signals the confusion of participants and company of intrinsic value with instrumental value; the inherent value of Shakespeare with that of the methods used to teach him. These absences and confusions are problematic elements of the RSC's determination of Shakespeare's value. As such, they will be traced throughout the following discussion.

The RSC has also been successful in turning ensemble casting into a hallmark, not only of its productions, but of its education programmes – being inspired to do so by the artistic direction of Michael Boyd (Neelands and O'Hanlon 2010). Five out of the ten teachers writing in the programme identified the collaboration of, as teachers including Diana Lucas and Michelle Thresher termed it, their 'ensemble' or 'cast' as particularly valuable:

> Throughout the rehearsal process I have been impressed with the way in which these students have embraced the method of ensemble acting adapted from the Royal Shakespeare Company strategies. This has enabled them to take ownership of their scenes and work collaboratively to explore Shakespeare's language.
>
> (Royal Shakespeare Company 2009b: 8–9)

Here, Thresher explicitly attributes the ensemble and collaborative methods with having positively impacted on her students' understanding and ownership of Shakespeare. Moreover, they become, through her words, branded 'RSC strategies', rather than those of Gibson, or more generically, those belonging to 'active methods', 'practical' or 'dramatic' work.

The transmission of an ethos from the RSC to teachers can be identified in the way that Thresher picks up and deploys the term 'ownership': a term used by the RSC in much of their literature to capture their mission 'to give young people ownership of Shakespeare by unlocking the power of his language and exploring the contemporary relevance of his plays' (*Education News* 2009). Such examples illustrate the way in which a collective re-membering of Shakespeare is being successfully transmitted between 'survivors' through the use of a common discourse (Taylor 1996: 2–6). However, this mission statement also demands that some pressure be put on the sense in which the RSC is 'giving' 'ownership' of Shakespeare to students and teachers. Firstly, it must be remembered that although their website materials are freely accessible, as is some face-to-face contact, elements of the RSC's school education programmes are sold commercially through teacher training, INSET days and class excursions. The 'mixed imperatives' of Shakespeare institutions 'broadcasting a public good and marketing a product' have also been noted by Rumbold (2010: 317). Half-day workshops on a play, for example, cost £180 for thirty students. In 2010, Continuing Professional Development courses for teachers amount to £130 per teacher for a day's training (Royal Shakespeare Company 2010a). Secondly, in claiming to be able to bestow ownership of Shakespeare on these groups, the RSC reinforces its ownership of a certain (in the above quotation, presentist) understanding of his works. It makes a public statement that Shakespeare is theirs to give: that they hold the key with which to 'unlock' his works. Jennifer Clement has further problematised 'ownership' in terms of its capitalist and neoliberal associations as well as for the way in which it suggests an untransformative experience, both for the student and Shakespeare (14). However, the RSC's Tracy Irish responded to this article in a subsequent issue by emphasising the collective and participative nature of ownership as envisaged by the education department (4). This imparting of ownership can also have a limiting effect on *what* Shakespeare is possessed: within the RSC's focus on Shakespeare as theatre, he is constructed, not as a wide range of knowledges and practices on which students will be assessed through coursework or examination, but primarily as performance and rehearsal.

A consequence of the RSC's emphasis on the value of teaching Shakespeare as theatre is that pedagogy and the plays are falsely elided, with the result that the non-Shakespeare-specific, perhaps unconsciously, comes to be valued over the Shakespearean. Physical theatre, ensemble work, the actor's journey and other elements of drama methods, portrayed above as the quintessential experience of Shakespeare, can all be used when studying other playwrights. If taken out of the context of the programme, the quotations cited in support of the RSC's education programmes – such as 'we all learnt to be more confident and join in more' – could be testimonials to the benefits of staging any play, by any playwright (Royal Shakespeare Company 2009b: 4). Furthermore, during the Regional Schools Celebration, the audience's enjoyment was occasionally divorced, if only humorously, from any Shakespeare-specific grounding in the plays at all. Singh Kohli, for example, joked that hosting last year's Regional Schools Celebration offered him 'genuinely new insight into writing that's four-hundred years-old but mainly what I wanted to come back for was the hairstyles'. The down-playing of Shakespeare specificity in this event raises the following question: are teachers and students being given ownership of Shakespeare or of a set of techniques that can be applied equally well to other authors? What both of these examples share, however, are humanist values for the experience of literature as enriching, an addition to a student's intellect, their social capacities and artistic skills.

A second way in which the RSC exercises agency in defining the value of Shakespeare is through promoting his plays done actively and outside the classroom as the ultimate experience of his works, both in terms of the potential for educational and personal development (a key component of C.B. Cox's rationale for English, and one which RSC education has made central to their own operations). This tenet of their education department has its origins in the RSC ethos, discussed above, that first and foremost Shakespeare is theatre and he is 'active'. The RSC's belief that performance is not just a pedagogy, but *the* pedagogy through which to experience, and with which to overcome, barriers to Shakespeare is made evident not only on stage but also in the pages of the Regional Schools Celebration programme. As the then Assistant Director, Michael Boyd, explained, 'Through our manifesto for Shakespeare in schools, *Stand Up for Shakespeare*, we want to see young people doing Shakespeare on their feet, seeing it live and starting it earlier. The schools taking part in our celebration today are the manifesto in action' (Royal Shakespeare Company 2009b: 1). Versions of the verb 'perform' appear seven times in sentences alongside 'Shakespeare'. For example, the Learning and Performance Network is described as giving 'students the opportunity to explore and gain ownership of Shakespeare's work through performance' (Royal Shakespeare Company 2009b: 2). The emphasis on performance in the programme text is further reinforced by the high-quality, colour images from the productions that adorn most pages, many of which capture the movement of the student actors.

Alternative pedagogies are dismissed in testimonials to RSC practice by teachers and students alike: 'My own memory of Shakespeare was in the third year at high school studying *Macbeth*, sat behind a desk with no visual idea of what on earth was happening' writes one teacher, incidentally denying her own capacity for imagination (RSC 2009b: 8). Further anecdotal evidence of the RSC's superior pedagogies is drawn from student participants in their programmes. The following opinions from students, which express a belief in active Shakespeare as fun, represent a unanimous majority in these materials: 'I enjoyed learning practically. It was challenging but it was fun'; 'I liked today because we approached the play through games rather than just reading the text'; 'Shakespeare is so much better on your feet' (Royal Shakespeare Company 2009b: 4, 9, 8). These students certainly rate their RSC experience above other ways of learning Shakespeare, and thus rank RSC constructions of Shakespeare (as practical, on your feet and as games) above others. However, the RSC must be recognised as the agent in putting forward the superior value of Shakespeare experienced in this way: it chooses and uses these anecdotes and sound bites to confirm its narrative of desk-based, literary criticism as the proverbial 'bad old days'. This is despite counter-evidence about students' engagement with these methods historically, for example, those who spoke of their enjoyment of reading around the class in the Theatre Archive Project.

A related problem with the RSC's educational provision – premised as it is on the superiority of active pedagogies – is that prescriptivism is somewhat inevitable in trying to roll out any scheme, belief or pedagogy on a nationwide scale, however inherently liberal it might be. Richard Wilson has previously traced the way in which such unintentional prescriptiveness undermines not only the freedom to choose such pedagogies, but also freedom within the teaching itself. Using pharmaceutical metaphors to explain the dominance of active approaches to Shakespeare, he writes that 'Gibson's "Shakespeare in Schools" project is charismatically anti-intellectual in its exhortation to joy, though his instructions to pupils sound like matron's most muscular instructions to swallow the medicine whole' (Wilson 1997: 63). He also suggests that 'Music and movement in the aisles is the sugar that makes the bitter pill go down in Gibson's regime, which seems a perfect prescription for schools compelled by law to study Shakespeare yet starved of funds for critical or historical support' (1997: 63).

Rather than dismissing the value of active methods outright like Wilson, I want to convey here a sense that the relationship in RSC education between prescription and progressivism remains troubled, over a decade after Wilson identified it as such. At the Regional Schools Celebration, the RSC was unquestionably keen to share the way it values 'doing' Shakespeare with the schools involved in the event (and the long lead up to it). Its eagerness to do so, however, creates a potential contradiction between its ideology and actual practice. A discourse of progressivism is evident, with explicit references to child-centred learning, exploration and 'play' (a word frequently used in proximity to Shakespeare throughout the Regional Schools Celebration programme) as well as overt criticism of traditional approaches, seen above. However, a more dogmatic, transmission-oriented approach was also discernible – in repeating relentlessly the 'Stand Up for Shakespeare' motto (do it on your feet, see it live, start it earlier); having children in the audience chant 'What's happened to the Bard? I don't know'; and correcting children's responses to questions about their experience of Shakespeare. As an audience member, I witnessed one particularly striking incident in which a girl playing Cordelia was asked, on stage, what she had most enjoyed about the putting on of *King Lear*. She answered by saying that she had enjoyed playing a leading role. To this the RSC practitioner responded negatively, criticising her lack of 'ensemble spirit': 'there's no such thing as small parts, only small actors'. The value of Shakespeare for this girl (providing the opportunity to take a lead role) did not match the master of ceremony's idealised value for the company (providing the opportunity for ensemble work, supposed equality among actors). Thus her experience of Shakespeare was effectively invalidated because it did not fit the RSC paradigm. Sharon O'Dair has suggested that much of the online Shakespeare activity instigated, run and censored by institutions (often with input from marketing and publicity departments) represents a faux-democratisation of the bard – as opposed to that started and administrated by Shakespeare enthusiasts without a professional affiliation or salaried position (2010). Similarly, the gap here between acknowledged values for and the implementation of a progressive ethos, combined with blatant prescriptivism, 'Stand Up for Shakespeare!', represents a faux-progressivism.

The third way in which I want to discuss the RSC as an agent in equating the value of Shakespeare with the value of its organisation is through the confusion of elements of the play with elements of the production, including slippages in the company's use of discourse concerning text/production. 'Play' and 'production' are often used interchangeably, making the location of value hard to determine. The Young People's Shakespeare *Comedy of the Errors*, along with the Regional Schools Celebration and the Youth Ensemble's *Winter's Tale*, formed a cluster of RSC activities in 2009 aimed at engaging a school-age audience. This youthful target audience was evident in the programme, where traditional actor biographies were replaced with short, actor interviews covering their 'favourite bit of this play' (not production), first experience of Shakespeare and favourite Shakespeare character. In answer to the first question, only three out of twelve actors named elements from the text of the play. These included Antipholus of Ephesus trying to enter his house when Adriana is inside with Antipholus of Syracuse; Antipholus of Syracuse hiding from Adriana in the priory; and the pursuit of Antipholus of Ephesus for debt. Noticeably, all these examples emphasise the potential for physical theatre afforded by the plot over other elements of the text. The other responses were exclusively concerned with characteristics of this individual production including their participation in a whole-cast song worked up from the Courtesan's lines: 'My favourite bit is playing the double bass with dark glasses on during the Courtesan song because I think it looks funny and I like the music' (James Traherne/Solinus); slapstick violence between Dromio and Antipholus – 'I love doing the scene where I get to dunk Richard in the water' (Dyfan Dwyor/ Dromio) (Royal Shakespeare Company 2009c); a slow motion chase; and a puppet show that summarises the action before the reunions that end the play. What is being valued in the above quotations is not only production over play, but *added*-value, RSC-brand productions.

Other examples of RSC added-value include hallmarked features of their productions, such as the enviable resources in its music and choreography departments with which to create high-production value, song-and-dance routines. In addition, the RSC's style of production is increasingly associated, away from a tradition bent on verse speaking, with the physicality of the actors' bodies, movement and set as determined by the director's concept (in this case, cartoon violence). To paraphrase the British department store Marks and Spencer's now-infamous marketing of their chocolate pudding, 'it's not *just* Shakespeare, it's *RSC* Shakespeare'. Admittedly, an assumption that one is referring to a specific production in talking about a play is natural in the realm of theatre. However, for the purposes of a theatre's education department – working with school students who will face examiners who insist on rigid distinctions between the two – such an elision is a potentially problematic element of their provision.

The need for a clear distinction of key concepts in teaching students, through the RSC's brand of active methods, is further demonstrated in a story related in the programme for the Regional Schools Celebration. The ultimate confusion between author and company, between Shakespeare and the RSC, is jocularly expressed in the anecdote of a year two teacher: 'having got over the shock and initial disappointment that Shakespeare himself was not coming to work with them, the children embraced Gemma [the RSC practitioner] as the next best thing' (Royal Shakespeare Company 2009b: 9). In these, admittedly young, students' minds Shakespeare and an RSC actor had become one and the same.

I have suggested above many implicit ways in which the RSC effects an amalgamation of its values for education with values perceived as inherent to Shakespeare, in ways that alter how students and teachers define him. It is also important to acknowledge the RSC's agency in transforming Shakespeare explicitly and deliberately through campaigns like 'Stand Up for Shakespeare!' targeted at changing both teaching practice and government education policy. In 2009, the RSC could well have claimed some victory in the abolition of the testing of Shakespeare at key stage three. This move, on the part of the government, marked the most radical change to the status of Shakespeare in education since he was rendered the only compulsory author in the 1989 *National Curriculum for English*. At first, the RSC welcomed the decision as allowing more freedom for teachers to embrace RSC-style pedagogies. The consequences of the change they had agitated for, however, were soon perceived as having a negative impact on the RSC education department's finances and on teachers' training. Jacqui O'Hanlon, the RSC's Director of Education, publicly decried the decrease in enrolment by teachers on their courses, with forty to fifty per cent of teachers booked on training courses cancelling (Lipsett 2008). The same *Guardian* article quoted her as saying, 'School managers will not release teachers for a day's training because Shakespeare is no longer seen as a priority'. For school management, at least, she explained, unassessed Shakespeare equated to a devalued Shakespeare. She then linked these attitudes, on the part of schools, to a possible decline in student's 'entitlement' to Shakespeare. This unforeseen consequence of intervention demonstrates that cultural chemists cannot always predict the effects of their agency, or how forces and ingredients will react together.

The RSC not only lobbies to influence government education policy – another (even rival) agency in shaping Shakespeare – it also responds to it. This can be seen in the way the RSC fits its education activities to the requirements for attainment and programmes of study at each key stage, many of them non-Shakespeare specific. A catalogue of available RSC courses states that 'all our activities for young people are devised in line with the relevant curriculum requirements' (*Education News* 2009: 1). More subtly, the company's adherence to the goals of the curriculum is visible in their adoption of its language in their own publications. The *RSC Education News*, for instance, echoes the curriculum's division of skills into reading and writing, speaking and listening (2009: 5). Moreover, the RSC aligns itself with government objectives for National Curriculum English as elucidated initially in the Cox Report and reaffirmed in subsequent publications. For example, in terms of personal growth, RSC courses commit to developing 'social and emotional intelligence' as well as 'confidence and understanding' (*Education News* 2009: 3–4). The Curriculum 2000's attainment orders, AO4 and AO5, are reflected in the RSC's educational focus on awakening students to 'making interpretative choices' for themes, characters and current productions; seeing 'the play from different points of view'; and having them 'relate the plays to their social, cultural and historical context' (*Education News* 2009: 5). These are only a handful of examples of the RSC's fit to government education policy. Rokison has pointed to a similar phenomenon elsewhere in theatre education departments, with the Globe linking its online provision to the National Curriculum (2012: 26).

In terms of arts policy, this massively subsidised organisation is increasingly forced to justify its receipt of government funding in an environment where public value and the value of the arts are being hotly debated. Witness publications such as *Government and the Value of Culture* (Jowell 2004); *Publicly Funded Culture and the Creative Industries* (Holden 2007); and *Call It a Tenner: The Role of Pricing in the Arts* (Arts Council England 2007). Additionally, they are operating in an environment where key public services continue to be privatised and outsourced. Hence their instrumental use by governments to help fulfil education policy objectives. The organisation needs to demonstrate its own worth – meeting criteria for funding, including increasing participation, widening access and improving their accountability for expenditure – as well as that of Shakespeare as a cultural icon. This perhaps explains, in addition to the use of anecdotes and sound bites, the recent surveying of students' attitudes towards Shakespeare, resulting in the production of statistics with which to evidence the success of school groups' Shakespeare experiences of the RSC pedagogies (Neelands and O'Hanlon 2010). Whether related to arts or education policy, the RSC's attempts to respond to government agendas demonstrate the way in which no chemist (cultural or scientific), especially one receiving significant government funding, works in isolation from their political and economic context.

Afterword

That Shakespeare is deemed by policy-makers and educators to be a valuable part of education for all students in England has been continuously apparent for over a century. Shakespeare's value is constructed by education policy primarily in terms of what it does for society and the economy, and by pedagogy in terms of what it does for students. Ideally the two should achieve a good degree of coherence. This is the case to some extent, for instance on a collective level, he promotes social inclusion in England, and on an individual level, he enables students to develop and use empathy, which might arguably lead to greater inclusivity. It is noticeable that Shakespeare's instrumental value has dominated policy-makers and educators' constructions. Shakespeare's inherent value is subdued but surprisingly stable and resilient in the documents examined in this book (as a genius or father of the language, for example) even when, for instance, he is taught in new and apparently conflicting ways.

Where change is more evident, where his value is more obviously dynamic, is in his relative educational value (compared to other works of fiction or texts from popular culture, for example), the expression of rationales for his value, and beliefs in how best to teach him (to secure the most of that value out of students' encounters with him). These elements of Shakespeare's value are characterised by continuous activity and (re)negotiation, involving an ongoing process of the accretion, sedimentation and metamorphosis of policy and pedagogic literature. Looking back at my descriptions of value throughout the preceding chapters, I have variously described it as ascribed, produced, constructed, received, consumed and projected. There has been an emphasis on processes throughout. This suggests an unshakeable concern that the teaching of Shakespeare may not just 'be for all time' in English education, but that governments and educators need actively to refit it in accordance with prevailing movements and discourses in education to ensure the continuance of 'Shakespeare for all'. Much of the discourse around Shakespeare's value in education over the past hundred years has been predicated on the notion that English students should have universal access to him, at least at some point, during their school studies. The parity of that access has been fought over, in terms of debates about the teaching of whole texts versus scenes as well as whether all students should be able to witness a performance. Shakespeare's value in education, currently rooted in boosting skills, standards and social inclusion nationwide, and the concern with best pedagogic practice for Shakespeare, stands to dramatically weaken should the desire for 'Shakespeare for all' be devalued. It may seem unlikely after a hundred years, but this eventuality is looking distinctly possible under the Coalition government's changes to education.

The influence of a few key individuals or individual institutions on defining and proliferating the manifold value of Shakespeare in English education, through accretion and sedimentation more often than revolution, has been inescapable throughout this book. Regarding education policy, the work of Leavis, Cox and the approaches of various Secretaries of State for education has been fundamental to defining the subject of English in schools in a way that enabled the inclusion of Shakespeare at its core. Where pedagogic innovation in the last two decades is concerned, Gibson's influence in promoting active methods pedagogies is unsurpassed. In terms of the influence of individual organisations in shaping Shakespeare's value, the key players featured in this book have been the RSC, Globe and SBT. The pre-eminence of this triumvirate is reflected in and sustained by national media coverage of the former company's engagement with issues of teaching and performing the playwright's works to young people.

What has rendered the influence of these individuals (and individual organisations) on the value of Shakespeare unrivalled? In part, it is their personal energy, passion for their subject, commitment to it and unwavering conviction – sometimes in the face of opposition and derision. These individuals forged for themselves voices that stretched beyond their immediate institution, editing or contributing to journals and magazines, or gaining publishing contracts for monographs and memoirs. These publications have also endowed these figures with a degree of immortality, at least where their words, opinions and arguments are concerned. However, I also want to emphasise here the institutional mechanisms involved in these individual people and organisations shaping the value of Shakespeare. Elements that they have in common are positions in or affiliations with prominent institutions – for Cox, editorship of an influential journal, access to government and the civil service, and prominent posts in higher education (pro-Vice Chancellor at the University of Manchester 1987–1991); for Gibson and Leavis, the University of Cambridge. Their institutional affiliations gave them access to publication, an authoritative voice, access to funding and/or networks of influence with which to shape Shakespeare in education.

I want to conclude with a final example of the construction of the value of Shakespeare by organisations and individuals that foreshadows the greatest change to Shakespeare in education since 1989, and quite possibly 1882: that of Shakespeare in the new National Curriculum for English, overseen by the Coalition's Secretary for Education from 2010 to 2014, Michael Gove.

Shakespeare Under the Coalition: An End to Shakespeare for All?

Entering his third decade in this unique position as the only writer guaranteed to be studied by all English children, Shakespeare has recently been part of a National Curriculum review, instigated by the Conservative-Liberal Democrat Coalition government, that has been in power since May 2010. In this section of the book, I offer what might be termed a 'state of the National Curriculum' for Shakespeare; an appraisal of his condition in it compared to previous incarnations, its continuity and change. I will also consider Michael Gove's rationale for Shakespeare's place in the curriculum, as outlined in speeches and press releases. Although at the time of writing Gove had been replaced as Secretary of State for Education, he remains the key figure in the Coalition's revised National Curriculum implemented after his departure.

One striking continuity between curricula, old and new, is that Shakespeare will be mandated only by the curriculum for subject English. There will be no first-time implementation of a National Curriculum for Drama by the Coalition government. This is in spite of the obvious potential embracing further arts subjects as core subjects would create for studying *yet more* Shakespeare, something implicitly figured as desirable in Gove's speeches. Shakespeare might have appeared across the school curriculum in a far more expansive way, not just as a literary figure but as a source for theatrical, filmic and televisual performance; even balletic and operatic adaptation. The decision not to include such cultural subjects at the heart of the curriculum flew in the face of pressure from arts educators and practitioners. The Henley review of Cultural Education for example, sounded the warning that their continued exclusion from the National Curriculum may lead to drama, theatre studies, design, dance and music being neglected by students, teachers and parents. In a plea appealing to the Coalition's concern with economic growth, Henley argued that the knock-on consequence would be a shrinking of the range and quality of Britain's cultural industries, their products and services. This report glowingly describes the nation's previous 'creative output' as 'disproportionately large for a country of our relatively small size' (Henley 2012: 16). The government, however, has been resolute in ignoring such suggestions.

This refusal may seem at odds with the endorsement given to Shakespeare as theatre (not just literature) by the government's funding of several projects and products. In 2012, the Department for Education donated a hundred-and-forty-thousand pounds to an educational charity, the Shakespeare Schools Festival, which helps schools stage scenes from Shakespeare in theatres nationwide to expand its programme almost threefold, from 700 schools to 2000, to include more primary schools. At the same time, it gave a similar sum to the Royal Shakespeare Company to 'provide all state secondary schools with a free copy of the *RSC Shakespeare Toolkit for Teachers*, which includes lesson plans and active methods exercises for teaching *Macbeth, Romeo and Juliet* and *A Midsummer Night's Dream* (Burns 2012). At a time when discussion of funding cuts dominated the media, at least two organisations – whose educational programmes and resources offer to increase teachers' and students' skills in playing with and performing Shakespeare – received a boost to their funding from the government. In a 2012 speech, Gove also cited the University of Warwick and Royal Shakespeare Company's Teaching Shakespeare centre as an example of innovation and good practice. He focused in particular on the online professional development learning platform's claim to use 'rehearsal room' methods 'to transform the teaching of Shakespeare in schools' (Gove 2012). In further apparent support of teaching Shakespeare as theatre, a New Labour national strategy document, *Shakespeare for All Ages and Stages*, was rescued from the swathes of web material archived after the Coalition victory and reinstated on the Department for Education pages.

Such gestures towards a financial and ideological investment in teaching Shakespeare as theatre and using active methods may be read as a marketing ploy, distancing the Coalition from Conservative governments' scepticism about the efficacy of practical methods. They may be seen as strategic concessions intended to satisfy Henley's, arts educators' and providers' demands for better, more prominent, arts education. Viewed less cynically, they suggest the government's desire to raise standards around students' experience of and achievement with Shakespeare – a meta-agenda, informing the maintenance of Shakespeare's unique position, that I will return to later – by increasing the resources available to teachers and supporting the optional introduction of Shakespeare, a gold standard author, at an early age.

The new National Curriculum also maintains the status quo by refraining from making Shakespeare mandatory for primary school students (key stages one and two). At this level, teachers are asked to choose literature to develop students 'culturally, emotionally, spiritually and socially' and to ensure that 'all pupils [...] appreciate our rich and varied literary heritage' (DfE 2012b: 13). This may or may not include Shakespeare's works. The primary English curriculum devotes most space to matters of spelling, vocabulary, grammar and punctuation, rather than literature. However, the curriculum at this level does emphasise the co-dependence of its linguistic and literary aspects, arguing that pupils' enjoyment and understanding of language is essential to supporting their increasingly challenging reading and in modelling good writing for them (DfE 2012b: 43–44). It is unusual for the curriculum document itself, rather than ministers' speeches and press releases, to engage in such justification of its requirements. In this way, the primary curriculum seeks to negate criticism that an increased attention to punctuation and grammar – among other elements of language learning – will relegate the importance of engaging with literary texts, such as Shakespeare, as part of their English studies.

In any case, the Coalition may argue that the new National Curriculum for English at secondary school (key stages three and four), set for implementation by 2015, affirms, even increases, Shakespeare's continuing centrality to the subject. Drafts of the document were released for consultation in stages, between 2012 and 2013, with the results from consultations and final versions appearing in 2013–2014. I focus overwhelmingly in this discussion on the final versions but will allude to the drafts where particularly significant changes were made. Comparison of Shakespeare in the curriculum between different governments' iterations and relative to other items on the programmes of study for reading at key stages three and four shows that Shakespeare twice takes pride of place. He tops both Labour's 1999 and new key stage 4 lists but not the 1989 or new key stage 3 ones, which open by requiring teaching of 'the richness of contemporary writing' and 'English literature both pre-1914 and contemporary' respectively. By contrast, world literature's appearance at bottom of three documents, and absence from the first and last, arguably evidences its relative lack of priority across parties (although the DfE has argued that it is a case of encouraging teachers' choice rather than neglect, stating that individual teachers will know best which cultures to focus on and will be left to make such decisions).

Shakespeare, as the table comparing iterations makes clear, continues to single-handedly represent not only a period, the early modern, but a vast swathe of English literary history as he has always done: pre-twentieth century (since the other historical authors and texts mentioned were never statutory), pre-1914, and now pre-1789. On one hand, it could be argued that this government has reduced his position relatively, at least at key stage four: he reigns supreme over just two-hundred rather than four-hundred years of writing in English in the latest iteration. On the other hand, it raises his profile: the new curriculum also marks a return to the 1989 iteration's positioning of Shakespeare as the uniquely statutory representative of drama, erasing the need for students to study drama by other major playwrights, recent and contemporary drama and that by 'writers from different cultures and traditions' (DfEE/QCA 1999: 35–6). Other plays may be taught optionally, competing with other literary forms such as poetry and fiction in the first and latest iterations. The new curriculum noticeably prunes back the detail of other periods and genres legislated alongside Shakespeare, including from an earlier KS4 draft shown in grey in Table 3, making him, in this respect, relatively dominant – generic Romantic poets offering only the merest hint of rivalry. Shakespeare is the one author exempted from the DfE's rhetoric that teachers are able to make appropriate choices about what literature should be studied (a position seemingly at odds with Gove's criticism that exam boards and English departments 'tend to focus on the same texts year after year' and condemnation of the fact that ninety per cent of schools are teaching *Of Mice and Men*) (Gove 2011b). The implication is that he is the one author teachers cannot be trusted to choose; the one author too important to be left to chance. This further reinforces his unique status.

There are also some departures for this government's iteration of the curriculum, highlighted by the comparison in Table 3, which seem intended to outdo previous governments' Shakespearean provisions. His plays are, significantly, the only literature to be quantified in this programme of study. Previous curricula consistently put numerical values on nothing (1989) or almost every item (1999). This version also goes above and beyond its predecessors in demarcating and distinguishing his value by stipulating the largest amount of Shakespeare ever seen on the National Curriculum. The number of plays has reliably risen across the iterations from some, to two, and now under the Coalition government 'at least' three plays during key stages three and four (note also the refocusing, since Cox, on the plays over Shakespeare's poetry). Indeed, at one stage, drafts of the new curriculum mooted the idea of students working on four plays at this level. At least on paper, students' exposure to Shakespeare's works is being heightened. From a comparison of the programmes of study for reading, the current government seems to be raising the stakes, promising *more* Shakespeare for all in both real and relative terms.

In terms of the pedagogies for teaching Shakespeare implied, but not stipulated, by the statutes, evidence of the influence of theatre studies and critical theory persists. Performance studies/history survives in statements requiring students to demonstrate the

Table 3: Comparison of requirements for breadth of reading across national curricula.

National Curriculum for English KS3 & 4 1989	National Curriculum for English KS3 & 4 1999	National Curriculum for English KS3 (final)	National Curriculum for English KS4 (draft Feb 2013)	National Curriculum for English KS4 (draft Dec 2013)
Some of the works of Shakespeare	Two plays by Shakespeare	Two plays by Shakespeare	Two plays by Shakespeare	At least one play by Shakespeare
Some of the works that have been most influential in shaping and refining the English language and its literature, e.g. *the Authorised Version of the Bible, Wordsworth's poems, or the novels of Austen, the Brontës or Dickens*	Drama by major playwrights Works of fiction by two major writers published before 1914 selected from the list Two works of fiction by major writers published after 1914	English literature, both pre-1914 and contemporary, including prose, poetry and drama	A nineteenth-century novel	Works from the nineteenth, twentieth and twenty-first centuries
Pre-twentieth-century literature	Poetry by four major poets published before 1914 Poetry by four major poets published after 1914		Representative Romantic poetry Representative poetry of [World War 1]	Poetry since 1789, including representative Romantic poetry
The richness of contemporary writing	Recent and contemporary drama, fiction and poetry written for young people and adults		British fiction, poetry or drama since [World War 1]	
	Drama, fiction and poetry by major writers from different cultures and traditions	Seminal world literature	Seminal world literature, written in English	
(DES 30) n.b. order of components here is reversed from original	(DfEE/QCA 1999: 35–6)	(DfE 2013a: 4)	(DfE 2013b: 4)	(Crown 2013: 1)

ability to analyse 'the ways that great dramatists make their works effective on stage' (DfE 2013b: 5). New historicism underpins requirements to 'read for understanding through [...] drawing on the wider personal, social and historical contexts of texts and authors and using this information to support comprehension' (DfE 2013b: 4). As shown above, evidence of some support for active-methods pedagogies is apparent within the primary curriculum, although it is not explicitly connected with Shakespearean works therein. The document states, for example, that 'role play and other drama techniques can help pupils to identify with and explore characters. In these ways, they extend their understanding of what they read and have opportunities to try out the language they have listened to' (DfE 2012b: 27). At this level, there is some stipulation of the need for students to script and perform their own compositions too (DfE 2012b: 41, 47). However, by key stage four creative or dramatic performance (embraced by the funding mentioned earlier) has largely been succeeded by formal presentations, speeches and debates, with an emphasis on rhetoric and logic (DfE 2013b: 7). This indicates the persistence of the belief, largely unchallenged by previous governments, that practical drama activities in the English classroom are suitable for and useful to younger students but less relevant to those facing high-stakes examinations.

Even before the curriculum consultations gathered momentum, Shakespeare was constantly name-checked in speeches by Gove and other ministers, establishing their agenda in terms of his centrality to the curriculum and the educational experience it will deliver. Gove's speeches offer an insight into the government's rationale behind Shakespeare's apparently raised profile in the curriculum, not available in the statutes themselves; particularly in relation to macro-educational agendas. Shakespeare is repeatedly figured by Gove as an inherently transformative force and a magical 'moment' or 'gift' that teachers can provide that reflects glory on both students and teachers and represents a pinnacle among students' learning. In his speech at the Conservative party conference in 2010, Gove asked his audience to imagine 'the moment a pupil who says she's never seen the point of books – or, for that matter, school – sits enraptured by a performance of *Hamlet*' (Gove 2010). Ostensibly, this incident, recalled from Gove's own conversations with teachers and school visits, demonstrates the power of good teaching. The role that Shakespeare's unmatched writing skills implicitly play in the student's absorption, in crafting a play whose enactment intrigues her, beyond that of any other text or educational experience – a reason for his inclusion in the curriculum – is also alluded to. It also offers further testimony to the government's championing of experiences of Shakespeare as theatre, at least with younger students.

Speaking to the National College for School Leadership, held in Birmingham during June 2011, Gove put Shakespeare's works at the top of his list of great achievements with which all children should be familiar. He declared that, 'Shakespeare's dramas, Milton's verse, Newton's breakthroughs, Curie's discoveries, Leibniz's genius, Turing's innovation, Beethoven's music, Turner's painting, Macmillan's choreography, Zuckerberg's brilliance – all the rich achievements of human ingenuity belong to every child – and it should be our enduring mission to spread that inheritance as widely as possible' (Gove 2011c). Shakespeare's unique place in the National Curriculum, established in 1989, is reinforced here in his being prioritised ahead of other significant artistic, musical and scientific prodigies.

Since esteeming Shakespeare within the curriculum is a point of similarity across parties rather than of contention, Gove has predictably worked to characterise previous incarnations of the playwright in policy as inferior. For example, there is no explicit acknowledgement from Coalition ministers that New Labour had maintained Shakespeare's place in the curriculum. Instead, there is an upbraiding of the Blair and Brown leaderships for allowing standards around the teaching of his works to slip. Gove is adamant that, under New Labour, Shakespeare was taught to the test and students' engagement with the plays dumbed down. Speaking to *The Spectator* conference in June 2012, Gove argued that under New Labour 'exam boards competed for custom on the basis that their exams were easier to pass than others. They got round the demand for rigour – for example, the requirement to include questions on Shakespeare's dramas – by letting schools know which act and which lines would be examined, whole terms in advance of the papers being sat' (Gove 2012b). Any suggestion that Brown's government might have identified flaws in the key stage three SATs themselves and acted to address this, leading to the discontinuation of SATs at this level in 2008, is ignored. That 'teaching to the test' was a criticism of the consequences of SATs during Major's leadership also goes unmentioned. Gove also berated previous governments' English curriculum and their weak grip on examining bodies over the quality of breadth of reading: 'there is very little requirement to study writers from any period or genre' and 'as many students only read one novel for GCSE, the curriculum's impression of wide-ranging study is misleading' (Gove 2011b). In this way, Gove has been able to create a narrative of sliding educational standards and warped values under New Labour, in readiness for the sequel of Coalition as saviour. He has appropriated as unique to the current situation a myth of decline in education in the United Kingdom that has existed at least since the end of post-war consensus for political gain.

The Coalition, as pictured by Gove, will rescue education not by abandoning testing but by improving the quality of assessment. While there is currently no overtly discernible drive to reinstate the compulsory key stage three Shakespeare SATs removed by Labour, Shakespeare was included in documents for the optional testing of students in year nine posted on the DfE website in September 2012. These involve students working on a passage from *Romeo and Juliet* or *As You Like It* in a way that addresses areas of assessment such as text in performance; character and motivation; language of the text; as well as ideas, themes and issues. In the GCSE subject criteria for English literature, arguably a sop to the abandoned EBacc and Gove's plan to have awarding bodies compete to provide the examination for a subject, the texts for detailed study demand 'at least one play by Shakespeare'. This requirement heads a list that also contains a selection of representative Romantic poetry, poetry since 1850 and British fiction or drama since the First World War (DfE 2013: 4). This means that Shakespeare is not only the sole compulsory author in the National Curriculum, but also the only author that awarding bodies must examine at GCSE – although this has, in fact, been common practice for years. Gove and his colleagues, unsurprisingly, spin their reforms to education as offering an experience of Shakespeare to all students as part of a reformed system of assessment, equated largely with increased examination over coursework across the school system and superior to that of the recent past.

Educational standards are figured as being raised through the teaching of Shakespeare in these speeches not just to the benefit of individual English students, but also for the nation's gain in international comparisons of standards and a shared literary heritage. In the DfE's appraisal of the teaching of national language and literature in high-performing jurisdictions globally, England's requirement that all students study Shakespeare was shown to be unique and yet comparable with Denmark's prescription regarding the teaching of its literary heritage of fifteen Danish authors that all students must encounter at school (DfE 2011b: 46). This is just one example in which English schools have been encouraged to be as good as, if not better than, their Scandinavian counterparts who are reified by the minister, and those conducting the curriculum review, as examples of excellence. Furthermore, on several occasions, teachers of English have been reminded that Poland, whose education system is but 'fast improving' 'has high expectations in their [sic] recommended reading including Homer, Chekov and Shakespeare alongside great works of Polish literature' (DfE 2011a: 52). The message that Gove desires schools to extrapolate from these snapshots of exemplary international competitors is that if *they* privilege *their* national authors, or indeed 'our' national author, in their teaching, so must the English education system.

In such speeches, the Coalition has enthusiastically embraced the tradition (evident in chapter one) of contextualising Shakespeare within, even as a pathway to achieving, its meta-education policy objectives, such as standards and social inclusion. Shakespeare for social inclusion was arguably a problematic notion for Labour, given its unwillingness to be seen to promote a dominant white, British, middle-class mono-culture. In contrast, access for all to an improved experience of Shakespeare promised by the Coalition has been depicted in successive speeches as representing a high point of social inclusion, a meta-educational agenda for successive governments during recent decades. It involves 'giving every child an equal share in the inheritance of achievement which great minds have passed on to us' as part of 'a great progressive cause' (Gove 2011c). This is constructed particularly as an achievement of academy schools, an initiative introduced by New Labour in 2000 but which the Coalition government has come to 'own' through rapid and large-scale expansion of the scheme. In a speech to Cambridge University on liberal education, Gove talked of his experience at one academy, Denbigh High, where 'the students, overwhelming Asian, second and third generation immigrant families, competed to tell me why they preferred Shakespeare to Dickens' (Gove 2011a). Similarly, the Schools Minister Nick Gibb told his audience, at an event used to outline the government's determination to raise expectations of children's reading, that at Thomas Jones Primary School in Ladbroke Grove 'despite the fact almost two-thirds of the pupils do not have English as a first language, and more than half are on free school meals, the children are reading and enjoying Shakespeare's sonnets' (Gibb 2012). The policy message is clear: Shakespeare is in the curriculum for all, to promote social inclusion, and successful schools, exemplified by those that have reformed as academies, teach Shakespeare to all students regardless of racial, social or linguistic background, and their students enjoy it.

The texts that feature in Gove's speeches demonstrate his unashamedly conservative definition of inclusivity as assimilation into great English (at a pinch, British) authors rather than a celebration of diverse cultures and elements of society. He has pronounced that all pupils should 'appreciate *our* rich and varied literary heritage'. However, not only is this rich and varied, great English literature apparently literally that coming out of England, but it is overwhelmingly dead, white, male-authored. Not just Shakespeare but 'Dryden, Pope, Swift, Byron, Keats, Shelley, Austen, Dickens and Hardy should be at the heart of school life' (Gove 2010). This is a list that makes Leavis' great tradition, with its two female authors (Jane Austen and George Eliot), one immigrant to Britain (Joseph Conrad, born Józef Teodor Konrad Nałęcz Korzeniowski in Poland) and one American (Henry James) look progressive. Leavis' favoured novelists in his canon, purveyors of a then increasingly popular form, where Gove has placed a large emphasis on poets, whose work a diminishing number of students and teachers engage with of their own volition (Xerri). It should also be noted that two of Leavis' chosen authors wrote into the twentieth century, only a few decades before his publication seized on them as exemplars of literary art. Gove's relished authors have, on average, been dead for 206 years. If Thatcherite policy represented a new Victorianism, Gove's vision for literary education idealises the long eighteenth-century; equating education with (the) enlightenment and demonstrating his preoccupation, even reification, of hegemonic histories. Gove seems to have (wilfully?) misunderstood Leavis' attack on popular fiction as an attack on contemporary literature, hence a curriculum that singles out Shakespeare and Romantic poetry and lumps together literature from all other periods. The Henley review's insistence that 'any rounded Cultural Education should have space to include newer art-forms, which have yet to pass the test of time, alongside the very best creativity from times gone by' (Henley 2012: 19) is recognised in the curriculum only to the extent that students should be taught some nineteenth-, twentieth- and twenty-first-century literature; 'contemporary' literature is, by implication, anything post-1914. Social inclusion as figured in these speeches, and the consequent curriculum document, is the induction of the masses into an exclusive canon of a few ancient authors, with a broader literature – including that from other cultures – gestured at more weakly.

In terms of a third meta-agenda for education policy, skills, the speeches and other documents boast Shakespeare's potential to develop students' reading, listening and appreciation as well as analytic skills as applied to character, themes, language and performance. A case is made in the Henley review for the importance of historical literature, or 'literary classics' such as Shakespeare, in stretching students' empathetic and imaginative abilities. It argues that, 'Some of these books might be about subjects that are directly relevant to the readers' lives today, but young people should also be reading books that expand horizons and show them the possibilities in the world beyond their own direct experiences' (Henley 2012: 26). This latter phrase is particularly redolent of arguments for the extension of literacy to the working classes from the late eighteenth-century: that reading literature represents the extension of vicarious experiences to this masses, experiences from which they are currently excluded but to which they should aspire to attain and which they may even achieve through self-education (Mulhern 1979). The catalogue of skills that Shakespeare might foster seems rather muted in comparison with the wealth of material under the above discussion of inclusion and standards but eschews previous governments' sometimes over-enthusiastic attempts to champion his value to vocational education and transferable skills. The lesser emphasis on skills in these speeches may also be explained in terms of social inclusion and standards being easier to proselytise about, while particular skills (especially where their existence for or uniqueness to study of a particular author is contentious) may be more easily identified in programmes of study.

Shakespeare may well have been given a real and relative boost in the new National Curriculum. However, it is arguably the overall circularity in meta- and English education policy that has resulted in the continued pre-eminent position of Shakespeare in and beyond schools – rather than any special affection for him demonstrated by ministers such as Gove (who, after all, appears particularly interested in increasingly culturally-obscure eighteenth-century poetry). The circularity in policy identified by education policy experts, such as Geoff Whitty, between the Conservative governments of the 1980s and 1990s and New Labour has similarly typified the transition to the Coalition government, especially in terms of standards, skills and – albeit with distinct definitions – social inclusion (Pring 2005; Whitty 2008). This continuity persists in spite of the Coalition theoretically breaking the two-party politics mould; Gove's publicising his department's hyperactivism – his promises to go 'further, faster' and to set a 'radical' 'pace' for school reform (Gove 2011b); and the amount of surface 'change' being remarked on by some educators: 'the current pace of change in education is so rapid that comments on proposed reforms run the risk of being out of date very quickly' (Anstey: 2013 43). There is, however, one substantial area of meta-policy, related to the agenda for improving standards, enthusiastically embraced by the Coalition, which may, in practice, undermine compulsory Shakespeare for all school children: the continued proliferation of a multi-partite school system.

The Coalition have been vociferous in identifying the burgeoning number of academies, free schools, studio schools and university technical colleges as one of their success stories in improving education nationally. Academies are designed to enable low-performing schools to rebrand, to break entrenched failure through autonomy from local authorities and freedom to seek personal or corporate sponsorship. Free schools operate similarly but are newly established schools with the express aim of filling an identified gap in educational provision in a community. Studio schools offer part-academic, part-vocational education in collaboration with local and national employers, with the intention of closing the gap between knowledge and skills. Meanwhile university technical colleges each specialise in a technical area such as engineering, manufacturing or biomedical science, requiring highly specialised equipment. Access to this is enabled through sponsorship from a university and partnerships with industry. What unites all four is that, while they teach the National Curriculum to varying extents, there are circumstances in which they may depart from it (beyond the disapplication available for individual pupils available to most schools). While, as a bare minimum core, GCSEs such as English and maths are currently taught in university technical colleges alongside technical qualifications, further differentiation of educational pathways could result in the disapplication of the requirement for all children to study Shakespeare. Such a scenario allows the government to maintain the promise of a liberal education, including literature and culture, for all students while extending to some a utilitarian education designed to boost economic productivity. It would enable them to maintain the ideal of 'Shakespeare for all' in policy, while allowing for a rather different reality in practice. It is evidence of the way in which Shakespeare's cultural and political cachet is useful in an abstract, symbolic way for the Coalition, particularly in trying to garner popular support for their proposed reforms. However, when it comes to implementing the study of Shakespeare within the education system as a whole, they are less sure – or forgetful of their pronounced conviction – that the knowledge, skills and experience of Shakespeare really are necessary for all children.

Works Cited

Abbs, Peter. *Living Powers: The Arts in Education*. London: The Falmer Press, 1987.

Adams, Richard, Ed. *Teaching Shakespeare: Essays on Approaches to Shakespeare in Schools and Colleges*. London: Robert Royce, 1985.

Aers, Lesley. 'Shakespeare in the National Curriculum'. *Shakespeare in the Changing Curriculum*. Eds Lesley Aers and Nigel Wheale. London: Routledge, 1991. 30–39.

Aers, Lesley and Nigel Wheale, Eds. *Shakespeare in the Changing Curriculum*. London: Routledge, 1991.

Albanese, Denise. *Extramural Shakespeare*. New York: Palgrave Macmillan, 2010.

Alexander, Catherine M.S. 'Shakespeare at the Centre: The educational work of the Shakespeare birthplace trust'. *Shakespeare in Education*. Ed. Martin Blocksidge. London: Continuum, 2003. 141–161.

Althusser, Louis. *Lenin and Philosophy and Other Essays*. Trans. Ben Brewster. New York: Monthly Review Press, 1971.

Andrews, John F. 'From the editor'. *Shakespeare Quarterly*. 35.5 (1984): 515–516.

Anon. *Shakespearean Insult Generator*. Facebook. 30 December 2010. http://www.facebook.com/apps/application.php?id=2453208254

Anstey, Sandra. 'All change: Proposed reforms at key stage 4 in England and Wales'. *The Use of English*. 64.2 (2013): 43–50.

Armstrong, Isobel. 'Thatcher's Shakespeare?' *Textual Practice*. 3 (1989): 1–14.

Armstrong, Katherine and Graham Atkin. *Studying Shakespeare*. Hemel Hempstead: Prentice Hall Europe, 1998.

Arnold, Matthew. *Culture and Anarchy*. 1869. Ed. John Dover Wilson. Cambridge: Cambridge University Press, 1960.

Arts Council England. *Call It a Tenner: The Role of Pricing in the Arts*. London: Arts Council England, 2007.

Arts Council England. *Children, Young People and the Arts*. London: Arts Council England, 2005.

Baker, Mike. 'Anger grows as diploma support wanes'. *BBC News*. 25 September 2010. 1 November 2012. http://www.bbc.co.uk/news/education-11407563

Baldick, Chris. *The Social Mission of English Criticism: 1848–1932*. Oxford: Clarendon Press, 1983.

Ball, Stephen J. *The Education Debate*. Bristol: Policy Press, 2008.

Balls, Ed. 'Ed Ball's Speech to Labour Conference'. *Labour*. The Labour Party. 2009. 1 December 2010. http://www.labour.org.uk/ed-balls-speech-conference,2009 0930

Barton, Geoff and Geoff Dean. 'The future of English: One subject, many voices'. *English Drama Media*. 20 (June 2011): 15–43.

Bate, Jonathan. 'Catalytic converter?' Shakespeare as a Cultural Catalyst. International Shakespeare Conference. The Shakespeare Institute, Stratford-upon-Avon. 13 August 2010.

Bate, Jonathan. *The Genius of Shakespeare*. London: Picador, 1997.

Bate, Jonathan. *Soul of the Age: The Life, Mind and World of William Shakespeare*. London: Viking, 2008.

Bate, Jonathan and Eric Rasmussen. *RSC Complete Works*. Basingstoke: Macmillan, 2008.

Bauman, Zigmunt. *Liquid Modernity*. Cambridge: Polity Press, 2000.

Bauman, Zigmunt. *Modernity and Ambivalence*. Oxford: Polity Press, 1991.

Becker, Gary. *Human Capital: A Theoretical and Empirical Analysis*. New York: Columbia, 1964.

Beckwith, Sarah. 'The power of devils and the hearts of men: Notes towards a drama of witchcraft'. *Shakespeare in the Changing Curriculum*. Eds Lesley Aers and Nigel Wheale. London: Routledge, 1991. 143–161.

Beehler, Sharon A. '"That's a certain text": Problematizing Shakespeare instruction in American schools and colleges'. *Shakespeare Quarterly*. 41.2 (1990): 195–205.

Bennett, Rosie. 'Poor turned off sure start by middle-class mothers: Families in deprived areas losing out'. *Times Online*. 6 October 2006. 13 September 2010. http://www.timesonline.co.uk/tol/news/uk/article663212.ece

Berry, Cicely. *Voice and the Actor*. London: Harrap, 1974.

Bissell, Chris. 'Putting the accent on dialects'. *Independent. Nexis*. 11 January 1990. 1 December 2010. http://www.lexisnexis.com/uk/nexis/auth/checkbrowser.do?t=1292866057312

Blocksidge, Martin, Ed. *Shakespeare in Education*. London: Continuum, 2003.

Bloom, Harold. *The Anxiety of Influence: A Theory of Poetry*. New York: Oxford University Press, 1973.

Bourdieu, Pierre. *Distinction: A Social Critique of the Judgment of Taste*. Trans. Richard Nice. Cambridge: Harvard University Press, 1984.

Bowles, Samuel and Herbert Gintis. *Schooling in Capitalist America: Educational Reform and the Contradictions of Economic Life*. London: Routledge and Kegan Paul, 1977.

Bradley, A.C. *Shakespearean Tragedy*. London: Macmillan, 1904.

Bristol, Michael. *Big-Time Shakespeare*. New York: Routledge, 1996.

Brocklehurst, Liz. 'Marking SATs has always been a total fiasco'. *Guardian*. 23 July 2008. 24 December 2010. http://www.spectator.co.uk/essays/all/852326/marking-sats-hasalways-been-a-total-fiasco.thtml

Bruner, Jerome. *The Culture of Education*. Cambridge: Harvard University Press, 1996.

Bryson, Bill. *Shakespeare: The World as a Stage*. London: HarperPress, 2007.

Bunting, Catherine. *Public Value and the Arts in England: Discussion and Conclusions of the Arts Debate*. London: Arts Council England, 2006.

Burns, Judith. 'Shakespeare schools cash'. *BBC News*. 5 November 2012. 12 November 2012. http://www.bbc.co.uk/news/education-20206307

Burt, Richard, Ed. *Shakespeares after Shakespeare: An Encyclopedia of the Bard in Mass Media and Popular Culture*. Vol. 2. Westport: Greenwood, 2007.

Caldwell Cook, Henry. *The Play Way: An Essay in Educational Method*. London: Heinemann, 1917.

Carey, John. *The Intellectuals and the Masses: Pride and Prejudice among the Literary Intelligentsia, 1880–1939*. London: Faber & Faber, 1992.

Chaudhuri, Supriya. 'The Absence of Caliban: Shakespeare and colonial modernity'. *Shakespeare's World/World Shakespeare's*. Eds Richard Fotherigham, Cristian Jansohn and R.S. White. Newark: University of Delaware Press, 2008. 223–236.

Clarke, Stephen, Paul Dickinson and Jo Westbrook. *The Complete Guide to Becoming an English Teacher*. London: Sage, 2010.

Cochrane, Claire. *Twentieth-Century British Theatre*. Cambridge: Cambridge University Press, 2011.

Coles, Jane. 'Alas, Poor Shakespeare: Teaching and Testing at Key Stage 3'. *English in Education*. 37.3 (1993): 3–12.

Coles, Jane. 'Testing Shakespeare to the limit: Teaching *Macbeth* in a year 9 classroom'. *English in Education*. 43.1 (2009): 32–41.

The Comedy of Errors. By William Shakespeare. Dir. Paul Hunter. Perf. Jonjo O'Neill, Dharmesh Patel. Courtyard Theatre, Stratford-upon-Avon. 2 July 2009.

'Company history and artistic policy'. *Told By An Idiot*. 12 May 2010. http://www.toldbyanidiot. org/about/history/

Coursen, H.R. *Shakespearean Performance as Interpretation*. Newark: University of Delaware Press, 1992.

Cox, C.B. *Cox on Cox: An English Curriculum for the 1990s*. London: Hodder & Stoughton, 1991.

Cox, C.B. *Cox on the Battle for the English Curriculum*. London: Hodder & Stoughton, 1995.

Cox, C.B. *The Great Betrayal: Memoirs of a Life in Education*. London: Chapmans, 1992.

Cox, C.B. and A.C. Dyson, Eds. *The Black Papers on Education*. London: Davis-Poynter, 1971.

Cunningham, Peter. 'Cook, Henry Caldwell (1886–1939)'. *Oxford Dictionary of National Biography*, online edn, Ed. Lawrence Goldman. Oxford: Oxford University Press. 12 September 2011. http://www.oxforddnb.com/view/article/63805

Davison, Jon. 'Literacy and social class'. *Issues in English Teaching*. Eds Jon Davison and John Moss. London: Routledge, 2000. 243–259.

Davison, Jon and Jane Dowson. *Learning to Teach English in the Secondary School*. Abingdon: Routledge, 2009.

Day, Gary. *Re-reading Leavis: Culture and Literary Criticism*. Basingstoke: Macmillan, 1996.

DCSF. *Shakespeare for All Ages and Stages*. Nottingham: DCSF Publications, 2008.

DfE/Welsh Office. *English in the National Curriculum*. London: HMSO, 1995.

DfE. 'Advisory committee terms of reference'. 26 April 2012. 30 April 2012. http://www. education.gov.uk/schools/teachingandlearning/curriculum/nationalcurriculum2014/ nationalcurriculum/a0073046/advisory-committee-terms-of-reference

DfE. *English Key Stage 4: Subject Content*. London: Crown, 2013.

DfE. *English Literature: GCSE Subject Content and Assessment Objectives*. London: DfE, June 2013.

DfE. *English: Programmes of Study for Key Stage 3*. London: DfE, 2013a.

DfE. *English: Programme of Study for Key Stage 4*. London: DfE, 2013b.

DfE. 'The importance of teaching: The schools white paper 2010'. London: TSO, 2010.

DfE. *National Curriculum for English, Key Stages 1–2 – draft*. London: Crown, 2012b.

DfE. *The National Curriculum in England: Key Stages 1 and 2 Framework Document*. London: DfE, September 2013.

DfE. 'Summary report of the call for evidence'. London: DfE, 2011.

DfE. 'What can we learn from the English, mathematics and science curricula of high performing jurisdictions?' London: DfE, 2011.

DfEE. *Circular 7/98: School Prospectuses in Primary Schools*. Sudbury, Suffolk: DfEE, 1998.

DfEE. *Circular 8/98: School Prospectuses in Primary Schools*. Sudbury, Suffolk: DfEE, 1998a.

DfEE. *Excellence for All Children: Meeting Special Educational Needs*. London: HMSO, 1997.

DfEE. *A Fresh Start: Improving literacy and numeracy. The report of the Working Group chaired by Sir Claus Moser*. London: DfEE, 1999.

DfEE. *The Implementation of the National Literacy Strategy: A Summary for Primary Schools*. London: DfEE, 1997.

DfEE. *The Learning Age: A Renaissance for a New Britain*. Sudbury, Suffolk: DfEE, 1998b.

DfEE. *Learning to Succeed: A New Framework for Post-16 Learning*. Sudbury, Suffolk: DfEE, 1999.

DfEE/QCA. *English: The National Curriculum for England, Key Stages 1–4*. London: TSO, 1999.

DfES. *14–19: Extending Opportunities, Raising Standards*. Green Paper. London: HMSO, 2002.

DfES. *14–19: Opportunity and Excellence*. London: DfES, 2003.

Dessen, Alan C. 'Shakespeare's theatrical vocabulary and today's classroom'. *Teaching Shakespeare Through Performance*. Ed. Milla Cozart Riggio. New York: MLA, 1999. 63–77.

Distiller, Natasha. 'Through Shakespeare's Africa: "terror and murder?"' *Shakespeare's World/ World Shakespeare's*. Eds Richard Fotherigham, Cristian Jansohn and R.S. White. Newark: University of Delaware Press, 2008. 382–393.

Dixon, John. *Growth Through English*. Reading: National Association for the Teaching of English, 1967.

Dollimore, John and Alan Sinfield, Eds. *Political Shakespeare: New Essays in Cultural Materialism*. Manchester: Manchester University Press, 1985.

Dollimore, John and Alan Sinfield. 'Series editors' foreword'. *The Shakespeare Myth*. Ed. Graham Holderness. Manchester: Manchester University Press, 1988. ix–x.

Douglas-Fairhurst, Robert. 'A.C. Bradley's Shakespearean tragedy'. *Use of English*. 57.2 (2006): 126–137.

Doyle, Brian and Derek Longhurst. 'The cultural production of Shakespeare in education'. *Australian Cultural Studies*. 3 (1985): 40–61.

Duggan, Timothy. 'Wrong Shakespeare' seminar. Shakespeare Association of America annual congress, Toronto. 28 March 2013.

Durkheim, Emile. *Sociology and Education*. New York: The Free Press, 1956.

Dymoke, Sue, Ed. *English in Education*. 44.3 (2010).

Eagleton, Terry. *Literary Theory*. 1983. Oxford: Blackwell, 1996.

Education and Employment Committee. *Disaffected Children*. London: HMSO, 1998.

El-Shayal, Dalya. 'A "sea of troubles": Teaching Shakespeare to Egyptian students'. *Shakespeare and Higher Education: A Global Perspective*. Eds Sharon A. Beehler and Holger Klein. Lewiston: Edwin Mellen, 2001. 26–45.

Ellis, Alec. *Educating Our Masters: Influences on the Growth of Literacy in Victorian Working Class Children*. Aldershot: Gower, 1985.

Fleming, Mike and David Stevens. *English Teaching in the Secondary School: Linking Theory and Practice*. London: Routledge, 2010.

Francis, Joseph. 'Shakespeare at Eton College'. *Shakespeare in Education*. Ed. Martin Blocksidge. London: Continuum, 2003. 69–96.

Freedman, Barbara. 'Pedagogy, psychoanalysis, theatre: Interrogating the scene of learning'. *Shakespeare Quarterly*. 41.2 (1990): 174–186.

Furedi, Frank. *Wasted: Why Education Isn't Educating*. London: Continuum, 2009.

Gallimore, Daniel. 'Shakespeare in contemporary Japan'. *Shakespeare in Hollywood, Asia and Cyberspace*. Eds Alexander C.Y. Huang and Charles S. Ross. Indiana: Purdue University Press, 2009.

Gibb, Nick. 'Greater expectations'. *Speeches*. 7 February 2012. 20 November 2012. http://www.education.gov.uk/inthenews/speeches/a00203219/greatexpectations

Gibson, Rex, Ed. *Macbeth*. By William Shakespeare. Cambridge: Cambridge University Press, 1993.

Gibson, Rex, Ed. *Secondary School Shakespeare: Classroom Practice*. Cambridge: Cambridge Institute of Education, 1990.

Gibson, Rex, Ed. *Shakespeare and Schools Newsletter*. 1. 1986.

Gibson, Rex, Ed. *Shakespeare and Schools Newsletter*. 9. 1989.

Gibson, Rex, Ed. *Shakespeare and Schools Newsletter*. 23. 1994.

Gibson, Rex. *Teaching Shakespeare*. Cambridge: Cambridge University Press, 1998.

Gilmour, Maurice, Ed. *Shakespeare for All in Secondary Schools*. London: Cassell, 1997.

Gove, Michael. 'How are the children?' *Speeches*. 26 June 2012b. 20 November 2012. http://www.education.gov.uk/inthenews/speeches/a00210738/govespect

Gove, Michael. 'Michael Gove: All pupils will learn our island story'. *Speeches*. 5 October 2010. 1 November 2012. http://www.conservatives.com/News/Speeches/2012/10/Michael_Gove_All_pupilwill_learn_our_island_story.aspx

Gove, Michael. 'Michael Gove: Failing schools need new leadership'. *Conservatives*. 7 October 2009. 19 September 2010. http://www.conservatives.com/News/Speeches/2009/10/Michael_Gove_Failing_shools_need_new_leadership.aspx

Gove, Michael. 'Michael Gove to Cambridge University'. *Speeches*. 24 November 2011a. 20 November 2012. http://www.education.gov.uk/inthenews/speeches/a00200373/michael-goveto-cambridge-university

Gove, Michael. 'Michael Gove to Twyford Church of England High School'. *Speeches*. 23 November 2011b. 1 November 2012. http://www.education.gov.uk/inthenews/speeches/a0073212/michael-gove-twyford

Gove, Michael. 'Michael Gove speech at the BETT show'. *Speeches*. 11 January 2012a. 20 November 2012. http://www.education.gov.uk/inthenews/speeches/a00201868/michael-gove-speech-at-the-bett-show-2012

Gove, Michael. 'Michael Gove speech to teachers and headteachers at the National College for Teaching and Leadership'. *Speeches*. 25 April 2013. 20 November 2012. https://www.gov.uk/government/speeches/michael-gove-speech-to-teachers-and-headteachers-at-the-national-college-for-teaching-and-leadership

Gove, Michael. 'The moral purpose of school reform'. *Speeches*. 16 June 2011c. 1 November 2012. http://www.education.gov.uk/inthenews/speeches/a0077859/the-moral-purpose of-school-reform

Great Britain. Education Act. London: HMSO, 1996.

Great Britain. Education Reform Act. London: HMSO, 1988.

Great Britain. Education (Schools) Act. London: HMSO, 1992.

Greenblatt, Stephen. *Will in the World: How Shakespeare Became Shakespeare*. London: Pimlico, 2005.

Greer, Germaine. *Shakespeare's Wife*. London: Bloomsbury, 2007.

Gregory, Sue. 'Making Shakespeare our contemporary'. *Shakespeare in Education*. Ed. Martin Blocksidge. London: Continuum, 2003. 20–39.

Groot, Jerome de. *Consuming Histories*. Oxford: Routledge, 2009.

Haddon, John. *Teaching Reading Shakespeare*. London: Routledge, 2009.

Halpern, Richard. *Shakespeare Among the Moderns*. New York: Cornell University Press, 1997.

Hamlet. By William Shakespeare. Dir. Greg Doran. Perf. David Tennant. Courtyard Theatre, Stratford-upon-Avon. 14 August 2008.

Hansen, Adam. *Shakespeare and Popular Music*. London: Continuum, 2010.

Harris, Elaine. 'New Town Shakespeare: A comprehensive school approach at key stages three and four'. *Shakespeare in Education*. Ed. Martin Blocksidge. London: Continuum, 2003. 40–68.

Hawkes, Terence. Ed. *Alternative Shakespeares: Volume 2*. London: Routledge, 1996.

Hawkes, Terence. *That Shakespeherian Rag: Essays on a Critical Process*. London: Methuen, 1986.

Henley, Darren. *Cultural Education in England*. London: DCMS, 2012.

Hewison, Robert. *Culture and Consensus: England, Arts and Politics Since 1940*. London: Methuen, 1995.

Higgs, Lauren. 'Royal Shakespeare Company helps develop humanities diploma'. *Children and Young People Now*. 12 (January 2009). 19 November 2012. http://www.cypnow.co.uk/cyp/news/1046169/royal-shakespeare-company-helps-develop-humanitiesdiploma

Hirsch, James. 'Teaching paradoxes: Shakespeare and the enhancement of audience skills'. *Shakespeare Quarterly*. 41.2 (1990): 222–210.

Hiscock, Andrew and Lisa Hopkins. *Teaching Shakespeare and Early Modern Dramatists*. Basingstoke, Hampshire: Palgrave Macmillan, 2007.

HM Government. *Youth Crime Action Plan*. London: HMSO, 2008.

Hobby, Elaine. '"My affection hath and unknown bottom": Homosexuality and the teaching of *As You Like It*'. *Shakespeare in the Changing Curriculum*. Eds Lesley Aers and Nigel Wheale. London: Routledge, 1991. 125–142.

Hodgdon, Barbara. *The Shakespeare Trade*. Pennsylvania: University of Pennsylvania Press, 1998.

Holden, John. *Capturing Cultural Value*. London: DEMOS, 2004.

Holden, John. *Cultural Value and the Crisis of Legitimacy*. London: DEMOS, 2006.

Holden, John. *Publicly Funded Culture and the Creative Industries*. London: Arts Council England, 2007.

Holderness, Graham. 'Radical potentiality and institutional closure'. *Political Shakespeare*. Manchester: Manchester University Press, 1985. 182–201.

Holderness, Graham. 'Sam Wanamaker'. *The Shakespeare Myth*. Ed. Graham Holderness. Manchester: Manchester University Press, 1988a. 16–23.

Holderness, Graham, Ed. *The Shakespeare Myth*. Manchester: Manchester University Press, 1988b.

Hornbrook, David. 'Go play, boy, play'. *The Shakespeare Myth*. Ed. Graham Holderness. Manchester: Manchester University Press, 1988.

Hudson, A.K. *Shakespeare and the Classroom*. London: Heinemann, 1954.

Hulbert, Jennifer, Kevin Wetmore and Robert York. *Shakespeare and Youth Culture*. New York: Palgrave Macmillan, 2006.

Hulme, Hilda M. *Explorations in Shakespeare's Language*. New York: Barnes and Noble, 1963.

'Ideology, n.'. *OED Online*. June 2014. 25 July 2014. http://www.oed.com/view/Entry/91016?red irectedFrom=ideology.4

Illich, Ivan. *Deschooling Society*. New York: Penguin, 1970.

Inglis, Fred. 'Recovering Shakespeare: Innocence and materialism'. *Shakespeare in the Changing Curriculum*. Eds Lesley Aers and Nigel Wheale. London: Routledge, 1991. 58–73.

Jackson, Peter, Sarah Olive and Graham Smith. 'Myths of the family meal: Re-reading Edwardian life histories'. *Changing Families, Changing Food*. Ed. Peter Jackson. London: Palgrave Macmillan, 2009. 131–145.

Jackson, Peter, Graham Smith and Sarah Olive. 'Families remembering food: Reusing secondary data'. Working paper, 2007. 14 January 2010. http://www.shef.ac.uk/familiesandfood/ resources.html

Jamie's Dream School. C4. 2 March–13 April 2011.

Joughin, John J. *Shakespeare and National Culture*. Manchester: Manchester University Press, 1997.

Jowell, Tessa. Foreword. *Understanding the Future: Museums and 21st Century Life*. DCMS. London: HMSO, 2005. 1.

Jowell, Tessa. *Government and the Value of Culture*. London: DCMS, 2004.

Kennedy Sauer, Dennis and Evelyn Tribble. 'Shakespeare in performance: Theory in practice and practice in theory'. *Teaching Shakespeare Through Performance*. Ed. Milla Cozart Riggio. New York: MLA, 1999. 33–47.

King, Neil. 'Starting Shakespeare'. *Teaching Shakespeare*. Ed. Richard Adams. London: Robert Royce, 1985. 57–76.

Kingman, J.F.C., comp. *Report of the Committee of Inquiry into the Teaching of English Language*. London: HMSO, 1988.

Lammy, David. 'David Lammy, Minister for Culture, keynote address to Museums Association Conference'. 26 October 2005. 13 September 2010. http://webarchive.nationalarchives. gov.uk/+/http://www.culture.gov.uk/global/pressnotices/archive_2005/lammy_ma _speech.htm

Lanier, Douglas. *Shakespeare and Popular Modern Culture*. Oxford: Oxford University Press, 2010.

Leach, Susan. *Shakespeare in the Classroom: What's the Matter?* Bucks: Open University Press, 1992.

Leach, Susan. 'Student teachers and the experience of English: How do secondary student teachers view English and its possibilities'? *Issues in English Teaching*. Eds Jon Davison and John Moss. London: Routledge, 2000. 148–163.

Leavis, F.R. 'Eliot's "Axe to Grind" and the Nature of Great Criticism'. *English Literature in Our Time and the University*. Ed. F.R. Leavis. London: Chatto and Windus, 1969. 85–108.

Leavis, F.R. *Mass Civilization and Minority Culture*. Cambridge: Minority Press, 1930.

Leavis, F.R. *The Great Tradition: George Eliot, Henry James, Joseph Conrad*. 1948. London: Penguin, 1993.

Leavis, F.R. 'Valuation in criticism'. *Valuation in Criticism and Other Essays*. Ed. G. Singh. Cambridge: Cambridge University Press, 1986. 276–284.

Leavis, F.R. and Denys Thompson. *Culture and Environment: The Training of Critical Awareness*. London: Chatto & Windus, 1960.

Lemmer, André. 'Shakespeare among South African schoolchildren'. *Shakespeare and Higher Education: A Global Perspective*. Eds Sharon A. Beehler and Holger Klein. Lewiston: Edwin Mellen, 2001. 66–76.

Lin, Alan Ying-Nan. 'The Uses of Multimedia Resources and Performance History in Teaching and Producing Shakespeare's Twelfth Night at NTNU'. *Shakespeare and Asia*. Eds Lingui Yang, Douglas A. Brooks and Ashley Brinkman, Lewiston: Edwin Mellen, 2010.

Linnemann, Emily. *The Cultural Value of Publicly Funded Theatre*. Diss. Birmingham: University of Birmingham, 2010.

Lipsett, Angela. 'Shakespeare suffers slings and arrows of SATs fortune'. *Guardian*. 26 November 2008. 10 September 2010. http://www.guardian.co.uk/education/2008/nov/26/rsc-education-shakespeareenglish-sats

Longhurst, Derek. '"You base football-player": Shakespeare in contemporary popular culture'. *The Shakespeare Myth*. Ed. Graham Holderness. Manchester: Manchester University Press, 1988. 59–73.

Looking for Richard. Dir. Al Pacino. Perf. Al Pacino. Twentieth Century Fox. 1996.

Lott, Bernard. *Hamlet*. By William Shakespeare. 1968. Harlow: Longman, 1999.

Lowenthal, David. 'Fabricating heritage'. *History & Memory*. 10.1 (1998): 5–24.

Mansell, Warwick. 'Was the government to blame for the SATs marking fiasco?' *Guardian*. 15 September 2009. 24 December 2010. http://www.guardian.co.uk/education/2009/sep/15/sats-marking-fiasco government-blame

Marston, John. *The Malcontent*. Ed. George K. Hunter. Manchester: Manchester University Press, 2000.

McCallum, Andrew. *Creativity and Learning in Secondary English: Teaching for a Creative Classroom*. London: Routledge, 2012.

McDonald, Russ, Nicholas D. Nace and Travis D. Williams. *Shakespeare Up Close: Reading Early Modern Texts*. London: Bloomsbury, 2012.

McEvoy, Sean. 'Shakespeare at 16-19'. *Shakespeare in Education*. Ed. Martin Blocksidge. London: Continuum, 2003. 97–119.

McLuskie, Kathleen and Kate Rumbold. *Cultural Value in Twenty-First-Century England: The Case of Shakespeare*. Manchester: Manchester University Press, 2014.

Monaghan, Frank and Barbara Mayor. 'English in the curriculum'. *Learning English*. Eds Neil Mercer, Joan Swann and Barbara Meyer. Abingdon: Routledge, 2007. 151–176.

Montessori, Maria. *The Montessori Method*. Trans. Anne E. George. Rev. edn. London: Heinemann, 1919.

Montrose, Louis. 'Professing the Renaissance: The poetics and politics of culture'. *The New Historicism*. Ed. H. Aram Veeser. London: Routledge, 1989. 15–36.

Mulhern, Francis. *The Moment of Scrutiny*. London: NLB, 1979.

Murphy, Andrew D. 'Shakespeare and the cultural trajectories of Victorian Ireland: W.B. Yeats vs Edward Dowden'. Shakespeare as a Cultural Catalyst. International Shakespeare Conference. The Shakespeare Institute, Stratford-upon-Avon. 11 August 2010.

Murphy, Andrew D. *Shakespeare for the People: Working-Class Readers, 1800–1900.* Cambridge: Cambridge University Press, 2008.

Murray, Braham. 'On your imaginary forces work'. *Teaching Shakespeare.* Ed. Richard Adams. London: Robert Royce, 1985. 41–56.

National Treasures. BBC Radio 4. 8 August–5 September 2007.

National Treasures Live: Dig Shakespeare Stratford. BBC 1. 24 August 2011.

Neelands, Jonothan. *Learning through Imagined Experience.* London: Hodder & Stoughton, 1992.

Neelands, Jonothan and Jacqui O'Hanlon. 'Stand up for Shakespeare'. Shakespeare as a Cultural Catalyst. International Shakespeare Conference. The Shakespeare Institute, Stratford-upon-Avon. 9 August 2010.

Neill, A.S. *Summerhill.* London: Pelican, 1970.

Newbolt, Henry. *The Teaching of English in England.* London: HMSO, 1921.

O'Connor, John. *Macbeth.* By William Shakespeare. Harlow, Essex: Pearson, 2004.

O'Dair, Sharon. 'Against internet triumphalism'. Shakespeare as a Cultural Catalyst. International Shakespeare Conference. The Shakespeare Institute, Stratford-upon Avon. 9 August 2010.

Olive, Sarah. '"Read on this book": The impact of the National Curriculum on Shakespeare in key stage 3–4 classrooms'. *Use of English.* 57.2 (2006): 138–145.

Olive, Sarah. 'Representations of Shakespeare's humanity and iconicity: "Incidental appropriations" in four British television broadcasts'. *Borrowers and Lenders.* 8.1 (2013).

Olive, Sarah. 'The Royal Shakespeare Company as "cultural chemist"'. *Shakespeare Survey.* 64 (2011): 251–259.

Owen, Diana. 'Putting our arms around Shakespeare: The Shakespeare birthplace trust in the 21st century'. Shakespeare as a Cultural Catalyst. International Shakespeare Conference. The Shakespeare Institute, Stratford-upon-Avon. 10 August 2010.

Ozark Holmer, Joan. '"O, what learning is!": Some pedagogical practices for *Romeo and Juliet'. Shakespeare Quarterly.* 41.2 (1990): 187–194.

Peim, Nick. *Critical Theory and the English Teacher: Transforming the Subject.* London: Routledge, 1993.

Pring, Richard. 'Labour government policy 14–19'. *Oxford Review of Education.* 31.1 (2005): 71–85.

QCA and Arts Council England. *From Policy to Partnership: Developing the Arts in Schools.* London: Directory of Social Change Books, 2000.

Raleigh, Walter. *Shakespeare.* London: Macmillan, 1907.

Restoration. BBC2. 8 August 2003–9 May 2005.

Reynolds, Peter. 'Active reading: Shakespeare's stagecraft'. *Teaching Shakespeare.* Ed. Richard Adams. London: Robert Royce, 1985. 118–132.

Reynolds, Peter. *Practical Approaches to Teaching Shakespeare.* Oxford: Oxford University Press, 1991.

Richards, I.A. *Practical Criticism.* 1929. London: Routledge & Kegan Paul, 1973.

Rocklin, Edward L. "'An incarnational art': Teaching Shakespeare'. *Shakespeare Quarterly*. 41.2 (1990): 147–159.

Rokison, Abigail. *Shakespeare for Young People: Productions, Versions and Adaptations*. London: Bloomsbury/Arden, 2012.

Romeo + Juliet. Dir. Baz Luhrmann. Perf. Leonardo Di Caprio, Claire Danes. Twentieth Century Fox. 1996.

Rousseau, Jean-Jacques. *Emile*. 1762. Teddington, Middlesex: Echo, 2007.

Royal Shakespeare Company. *The Comedy of Errors* [programme]. Stratford-upon-Avon: RSC, 2009c.

Royal Shakespeare Company. *Education*. RSC. 30 December 2010a. http://www.rsc.org.uk/education/

Royal Shakespeare Company. *Education*. *Royal Shakespeare Company*. 30 May 2013. http://www.rsc.org.uk/education/

Royal Shakespeare Company. *Education News: Activities for Students and INSET for Teachers*. Stratford-upon-Avon: RSC, 2009a.

Royal Shakespeare Company. 'Key facts and figures'. *Royal Shakespeare Company*. 14 August 2011. http://www.rsc.org.uk/about-us/our-work/facts-and-figures.aspx

Royal Shakespeare Company. *Manifesto for Shakespeare in Schools*. RSC. 1 September 2008a. http://www.rsc.org.uk/standupforshakespeare/content/manifesto_online.aspx

Royal Shakespeare Company. *Regional Schools Celebration* [programme]. Stratford-upon-Avon: RSC, 2009b.

Royal Shakespeare Company. *Royal Shakespeare Company: Education*. RSC. 21 May 2008b. http://www.rsc.org.uk/learning/Learning.aspx

Royal Shakespeare Company. *The RSC Shakespeare Toolkit for Teachers*. London: Methuen, 2010b.

Royal Shakespeare Company. *What has Shakespeare ever done for us?: A Primary School Assembly*. Stratford-upon-Avon: RSC, 2009d.

Rumbold, Kate. 'From "access" to "creativity": Shakespeare institutions, new media, and the language of cultural value'. *Shakespeare Quarterly*. 61.3 (2010): 313–336.

Russell, Willy. *Educating Rita*. London: Samuel French, 1981.

Salway, John. 'Will the real Shakespeare stand up?' *Shakespeare and Schools Newsletter*. 1. Autumn (1986): 8.

Sampson, George. *English for the English*. Cambridge: Cambridge University Press, 1921.

Saunders, John. 'Circe and cyclops: A Shakespearean adventure'. *Teaching Shakespeare*. Ed. Richard Adams. London: Robert Royce, 1985. 97–117.

Semler, Liam. *Teaching Shakespeare and Marlowe: Learning vs. the System*. London: Bloomsbury, 2013.

Shakespeare's Globe. *Shakespeare's Globe Annual Review 2011*. 15 August 2012. http://www.shakespearesglobe.com/about-us/todays-globe/annual-review

Shakespeare, William. *The Merchant of Venice*. Ed. Jay L. Halio. Oxford: Oxford University Press, 1993.

Shakespeare Birthplace Trust. *Shakespeare's Houses and Gardens: Discovery Pack*. Stratford-upon-Avon: SBT, 2010a.

Shakespeare Birthplace Trust. *Shakespeare's Houses and Gardens: Who was Shakespeare?* Stratford-upon-Avon: SBT, 2010b.

Shakespeare Birthplace Trust. *The Education Department*. SBT. 25 November 2008. http://www.shakespeare.org.uk/content/view/425/436/

Shakespeare's Globe. *Globe Education*. Shakespeare Globe Trust. 25 November 2008. http://www.shakespearesglobe.org/globeeducation/

Shakespeare's Globe. *Globe Education Events Summer 09*. London: Shakespeare's Globe, 2009.

Shellard, Dominic. *British Theatre Since the War*. New Haven, CT: Yale University Press, 2000.

Shepherd, Jessica. 'A-level results: Top universities secretly list "banned" subjects'. 20 August 2010. 23 August 2010. http://www.guardian.co.uk/education/2010/aug/20/a-level subjects-blacklist-claim

Sinfield, Alan. 'Shakespeare and education'. *Political Shakespeare*. Eds Jonathan Dollimore and Alan Sinfield. Manchester: Manchester University Press, 1985. 134–154.

Spencer, T.J.B. *Hamlet*. By William Shakespeare. London: Penguin, 2005.

St. Clair, William. *The Reading Nation in the Romantic Period*. Cambridge: Cambridge University Press, 2004.

Standards and Testing Agency. *Year 9 Optional Tests: English Shakespeare Paper: As You Like It*. London: STA, 2012.

Steiner, George. *Real Presences: Is There Anything in What We Say?* London: Faber, 1989.

Stern, Tiffany. 'Teaching Shakespeare in Higher Education'. *Shakespeare in Education*. Ed. Martin Blocksidge. London: Continuum, 2003. 120–40.

Stredder, James. *The North Face of Shakespeare*. Stratford-upon-Avon: Wincot Press, 2007.

Storer, Richard. *F.R. Leavis*. Abingdon, Oxon: Routledge, 2009.

'Survey results'. *World Shakespeare Festival*. 6 December 2012. http://www.worldshakespeare festival.org.uk/wiki/Survey-results.ashx

Taylor, Gary. 'Afterword: The incredible shrinking bard'. *Shakespeare and Appropriation*. Eds Christie Desmet and Robert Sawyer. London: Routledge, 1999. 197–206.

Taylor, Gary. *Cultural Selection*. New York: Basic Books, 1996.

Taylor, Gary. *Reinventing Shakespeare: A Cultural History from the Restoration to the Present*. New York: Oxford University Press, 1989.

Thew, Neill. *Teaching Shakespeare: A Survey of the Undergraduate Level in Higher Education*. London: HEA/ESC, 2006.

Thomas, Peter. 'Shakespeare page to stage: An active approach to Othello'. *English in Education*. 28.1 (1994): 45–52.

Thompson, Ann. '*King Lear* and the politics of teaching Shakespeare'. *Shakespeare Quarterly*. 41.2 (1990): 139–146.

Thompson, Denys. 'What shall we teach?' *Scrutiny*. 2.4 (March 1934): 379–386.

Times. 'English standards'. *Times. Nexis*. 6 January 1989a. 1 December 2010. http://www.lexisnexis.com/uk/nexis/auth/checkbrowser.do?t=1292866057312

Times. 'Reluctant grammarians'. *Times. Nexis*. 24 June 1989b. 1 December 2010. http://www.lexisnexis.com/uk/nexis/auth/checkbrowser.do?t=1292866057312.

Travitsky, Betty S. and Anne Lake Prescott, Eds. *Female and Male Voices in Early Modern England*. New York: Columbia University Press, 2000.

Turner, Oliver. 'A history of theatre in education at the Belgrade Theatre Coventry'. Belgrade Theatre Coventry. 12 September 2011. http://www.belgrade.co.uk/aboutus/history/

Tytler, David. 'Importance of grammar restored to curriculum'. *Times. Nexis.* 23 June 1989. 1 December 2010. http://www.lexisnexis.com/uk/nexis/auth/checkbrowser.do?t= 1292866057312

Wells, Stanley. *Shakespeare and Co.* London: Allen Lane, 2006.

Wells, Stanley. *Shakespeare, Sex and Love.* Oxford: Oxford University Press, 2010.

Wells, Stanley and Gary Taylor, Eds. *William Shakespeare: The Complete Works.* By William Shakespeare. Oxford: Clarendon, 1986.

Wheale, Nigel. Introduction. *Shakespeare in the Changing Curriculum.* Eds Lesley Aers and Nigel Wheale. London: Routledge, 1991. 1–29.

White, Laura. 'Smashing open the French windows: The acting profession in the 1960s and 1970s'. *The Golden Generation: New light on post-war British theatre.* Ed. Dominic Shellard. London: British Library, 2008. 181–196.

Whitty, Geoff. 'Education, economy and national culture'. *Social and Cultural Forms of Modernity.* Eds Robert Bocock and Kenneth Thompson. Cambridge: Polity Press, 1992. 267–320.

Whitty, Geoff. 'Twenty years of progress? English education policy 1988 to the present'. *Educational Management Administration & Leadership.* 36.2 (2008): 165–184.

Widdowson, Peter, Ed. *Re-reading English.* London: Methuen, 1982.

Wilby, Peter. 'Baker's worst of all worlds'. *Independent. Nexis.* July 6 1989. 1 December 2010. http://www.lexisnexis.com/uk/nexis/auth/checkbrowser.do?t=1292866057312

Williams, Raymond. *Keywords: A Vocabulary of Culture and Society.* London: Fontana, 1983.

Wilson Knight, G. *Wheel of Fire: Interpretation of Shakespeare's Tragedy.* Cleveland: Meridian, 1930.

Wilson, Richard. 'NATO's pharmacy: Shakespeare by prescription'. *Shakespeare and National Culture.* Ed. John J. Joughin. Manchester: Manchester University Press, 1997. 58–82.

Wright, Trevor. *How to be a Brilliant English Teacher.* Abingdon: Routledge, 2005.

Yandell, John. 'Reading Shakespeare, or ways with will'. *Changing English.* 4.2 (1997): 277–294.

Yandell, John and Anton Franks. 'Approaching Shakespeare'. *Learning to Teach English in the Secondary School.* Eds Jon Davison and Jane Dowson. Abingdon: Routledge, 2009. 242–259.

Xerri, Daniel. '"Dissecting butterflies": Literary theory and poetry teaching in post-16 education'. *International Journal of Adolescence and Youth.* 18.4 (2013): 205–214.

Zhang, Xiao Yang. *Shakespeare in China: A Comparative Study of Two Traditions and Cultures.* Newark: University of Delaware Press, 1996.

Index